AF559943

# The Climate Crossroads

Also By Rajat Chaudhuri

*The Butterfly Effect*
*Spellcasters*
*Wonder Tales for a Warming Planet*
*Hotel Calcutta*
*Amber Dusk*
*Calculus (in Bangla)*
*Calcutta Nights (tr)*
*The Great Bengali Poetry Underground (tr)*
*The Best Asian Speculative Fiction (ed)*
*Multispecies Cities: Solarpunk Urban Futures (co-edited)*
*Solarpunk Creatures (co-edited)*

The New Steam Carriage, 1828, by Henry Pyall after G. Morton. Published by Thomas McLean. *c.*1828. Courtesy Teylers Museum, Haarlem, the Netherlands.

# The Climate Crossroads

## *Literature's Encounter with a Planet on Fire*

Rajat Chaudhuri

B L O O M S B U R Y
NEW DELHI • LONDON • OXFORD • NEW YORK • SYDNEY

BLOOMSBURY INDIA
Bloomsbury Publishing India Pvt. Ltd
Second Floor, LSC Building no. 4, DDA Complex, Pocket C – 6 & 7,
Vasant Kunj, New Delhi, 110070

BLOOMSBURY, BLOOMSBURY ACADEMIC INDIA and the
Diana logo are trademarks of Bloomsbury Publishing Plc

First published in India 2026
This edition published 2026



Bloomsbury Academic India
An Imprint of Bloomsbury Publishing Plc



ISBN: 978-93-69520-30-5; eBook: 978-93-69525-07-2
2 4 6 8 10 9 7 5 3 1

Typeset by Integra Software Services Pvt. Ltd.
Printed and bound in India by Replika Press Pvt. Ltd.

*For Anuradha*

# Contents

# Figures

# Acknowledgements

When I published my first climate novel, I had still not considered an extensive academic engagement with stories of the Anthropocene. My interest in the subject deepened through my interactions with a few people and a variety of personal and collective experiences of the climate emergency. I am grateful to renowned translator and academic Arunava Sinha for being one of the first to ask me to write longer essays on climate and literature which I did for *Scroll* magazine. My conversations with bestselling climate fiction author Liz Jensen and her support for my fiction, individually and also through the Writers' Rebel collective of Extinction Rebellion UK, have been a gift for which I am deeply indebted. Also, the evermore powerful cyclonic storms that rise from the Bay of Bengal and batter my city, the expanding reach and severity of the dengue virus that took away near ones, and the rising heat index of summers that seem endless, have been, in their own ways, instrumental in the writing of this book. I acknowledge their powerful, instructive and often uncanny presence in shaping my thoughts.

I am deeply grateful to Amitav Ghosh for his interest in my work and for the conversations, email exchanges and interviews about climate change and literature we have had over the years. His writing about the subject has been a major inspiration for this book. A number of academics have written about or otherwise engaged with my climate writing, both fiction and non-fiction, and I thank them all for their interest. Among them, I must name Sami Ahmad Khan, Bodhisattwa Chattopadhyay, Damini Ray, Md. Alamgir Hossain and especially Christoph Rupprecht for creating several opportunities to delve deeper into the literature of climate change. Their comments, insights and scholarly interventions have enriched my thoughts. Also, my activist colleague Jeffrey Barber has helped me with useful information about new critical work on climate literature, and I am grateful for his insights as well as his hospitality during my stay in Washington DC for a lecture on speculative fiction.

Fellow authors are always a source of strength, support and valuable advice. Among those who have been important in this journey, I must mention Sam Beckbessinger, Sarena Ulibarri, Lopa Ghosh, Shweta Taneja, Priya Sarukkai Chabria, Anu Kumar, Tashan Mehta and especially Samit Basu for his valuable insights about publishing. Also, I would like to thank my writer friend Lijia Zhang for helping me with some Chinese sources for this book and past colleagues Pradeep Mehta and Nabinananda Sen for my first lessons in activism.

Colleges, universities and other institutions who have invited me to speak about climate and literature have helped this book in tangible and intangible ways. I am especially grateful to Professor Ben Grant of the University of Oxford for asking me to speak about climate and literature to his students. Others like Swati Guha, Soujanya Pudi, organizers of the Green Litfest, literary clubs of colleges like St Stephen's and Miranda House, the Science Fiction Museum at Washington DC, Sahitya Akademi (National Academy of Letters), Indian National Library, among several others, have through their invitations and speaking opportunities helped to clarify my thoughts about literature's encounter with climate change. I also owe a special word of thanks to Mary Woodbury of Dragonfly.eco and Mark Goldthorpe of Climate Cultures for their deep engagement with Anthropocene fiction and their valuable resources on climate writing, just as I do to the Climate Fiction Writers League.

Conversations with students and scholars of allied genres have often yielded valuable insights, and for this I must thank two brilliant researchers, Sayantani Sengupta and Debapriti Sengupta, who are both working on solarpunk literature. I also owe a word of gratitude to editors and journalists like Uddalak Mukherjee, Medha-Dutta Yadav, Shrisha Bhardwaj, Sonam Joshi, Antara Baruah and Prasun Chaudhuri for allowing me to share my thoughts on their pages.

The anonymous reviewers who read and commented on the manuscript for Bloomsbury made important and useful suggestions. This book has been enriched by their valuable inputs as it also has been by the insightful suggestions of my editor Chandra Sekhar. I am also grateful to friends like Arpan Chakraborty, Somnath Baidya Roy, Pranab Narzary, Sudeshna Dutta, Priyadarshi Basu, Anupam Pachauri, Suvasree Karanjai and Niharul Islam for their enriching conversations and also to Tanweer Hassan for his large-heartedness. Finally, and as always, this book would not have been possible without the support of my partner Anuradha, my first reader, and the blessings of my parents, whose reassuring presence made this effort worthwhile.

Kolkata
7 August 2025

# Part One

# Maps

# 1

# A rainy night in the North

## *Reading, writing and looking for clues*

It begins with shoes. Rain shoes to be precise. The icy showers of northern latitudes call for high-quality gear which is not something we from the tropics usually prepare for while travelling. Such as a fifteen-thousand-rupee pair of waterproof shoes, with the label of a multinational, stitched in a South Asian sweatshop – beyond my means then, beyond my means now.

So I had to bear the frigid rains in my sodden Khadim sneakers while imagining the radiator warmth of my cosy little cabin which made strange creepy noises all through the night, like those in that old house from Poe's memorable tale. After all, how much does a young activist from a developing nation like ours make? Not enough. Not enough at all to beat the frigid northern weather which, like a ruthless torturer, seemed to be getting worse over the days.

Those days at the turn of the century, climate change was still new, confined mainly to research labs and conference rooms of international organizations and NGOs like ours. The *aam admi* had not heard about it. Global warming was still niche, largely a matter of academic curiosity or denialist manoeuvres in the form of novels like Michael Crichton's famous potboiler.[1] The oil industry, of course, knew[2] that the planet was slowly catching fire but, in keeping with the exacting standards of corporate social responsibility, had chosen to keep quiet.[3]

I had arrived in Stockholm in the early part of that year to research consumption habits of that rich Nordic country and compare them with what we have been doing back home. The Swedes had kindly put me up in this cosy little houseboat which was moored on the shore of Lake Malaren, which is like the placid soul of Sweden's bustling capital. Not far from there was the old town of Gamla Stan, with its medieval buildings and roaring nightlife, the sounds of its beats often floating up to me over the waters of the lake. It was an ideal setting for work or for getting completely wasted.

My days were filled with interviews and meetings supplemented by reading reports about sustainability, climate and the environment. I looked for clues, searched for patterns and gathered as much information as I could about consumption habits and spent the evenings sipping Finnish vodkas in a lonely barge restaurant while lamenting about not finishing my novel as another year slowly slipped by.

So on this particular evening, I was still out working, trying to track down the office of a global refrigeration company, when it had begun to rain. This multinational, like many others, was using harmful coolant gases in their products which were puncturing the ozone layer, besides causing global warming. The ultraviolet rays that were reaching the earth through this ozone hole were causing skin cancer, and the impact of some of these coolants on global warming and the greenhouse effect was just beginning to get noticed.

I had had a very late lunch that day with a weirdly flavoured tandoori chicken (the other option was reindeer meat) at a small restaurant near my office and had taken a train to my destination. But I had gotten off at the wrong station and didn't realize it. By the time I walked out of the station, the sky was overcast, and soon ice-cold drops had begun to fall, chilling me to the bone.

There was not a soul out on the street in this part of the town. It was abnormally quiet with shrouds of rain blocking my view in the bleak dusk light, and the feeling was quite akin to what Snowman would have felt as he woke up in the opening scenes of *Oryx and Crake*, Margaret Atwood's end-of-the-world dystopia. Walking up and down deserted roads for almost an hour, my sneakers soaking wet, my paper map soggy and falling apart, I had finally arrived at the office shivering in my dripping raincoat.

All through that meeting, I tried to impress upon this official from the multinational that companies like theirs were purveying environment-damaging products in my country while supplying environment-friendly versions of the same in their domestic market. Condescending and slightly supercilious, he kept brushing off the issue, drowning me in figures and technology-conversion statistics, till I mentioned that we are planning to work closely with a large activist network which has a strong presence in their country.

A coin seemed to drop, and immediately there was a perceptible shift in mood and tone. The gentleman was suddenly all attention, almost empathetic. The meeting extended a little beyond schedule. We spoke about leapfrogging to new technologies, climate change, ozone depletion and the Montreal protocol for phasing out ozone-depleting substances.[4] I took my notes, thanked him and left. The rain had let up by then, but the temperature had dropped further still.

On the train back to my boat, while bothering about catching a cold, I couldn't decide whether I was satisfied with this particular encounter. However, buttressed by this and many other similar experiences, I slowly began to arrive at the conclusion that there is a real need to expose double standards, the lurking injustices, the glaring inequalities that underpin, perpetuate and aggravate planetary crises like ozone depletion or climate change. And to do this, I kept telling myself, activism could be just one of the instruments in a toolbox which has to include other sorts of engagement, other mantras and other ways of seeing and communicating environmental emergencies. And being a fledgling writer, I had almost immediately caught on to the importance of stories and their possible role in influencing the imagination.

The worldwide activism around ozone depletion did have a happy ending. Over the years, facilitated by the Montreal Protocol, many industries switched from ozone-depleting substances, which were also climate-damaging gases, to better alternatives with the resultant repair of the ozone layer. So much so that we can now expect the Antarctic ozone hole to close by the 2060s, while other regions will fare even better.

But a bigger battle had already been joined. In the first two decades of this century, the world would be swamped by an unprecedented crisis, manifested through forest fires, dangerous heat waves, cyclones, floods, crop failures, disease, forced migration and much more. Anthropogenic climate change was upon us, the biggest existential threat to life on the planet for a long time.

As I pushed ahead with my climate activism and awareness efforts, interacting with people from different walks of life, I was increasingly realizing the importance of new kinds of stories to connect with the public imagination about the looming crisis. With climate change impinging on our day-to-day living, literature had also arrived at a crossroads where it needed to seek new directions. But what are the stories we should read, write and tell to engage with the climate crisis? Should these be dystopian accounts of a climate-ravaged planet or solution-focused tales of hope? How can one write engaging fiction about a phenomenon and a crisis that has its roots in science and meteorology but deals with our exploitative relation with the planet and its less privileged inhabitants? Do poetic language and aesthetic qualities of the text have a role to play in communicating the messages of climate change? Who will be the heroes of such stories, or should we have no heroes at all? As an activist and a writer, how could one bring these two practices together to communicate these urgent messages?

In the course of examining such questions, I had, quite by accident, arrived at this genre of writing that we call climate fiction[5] or cli-fi. I discovered that already in the industrialized West and then gradually in developing countries too, writers had begun to imagine and represent climate change in their fiction. This was hopeful news no doubt.

While my activist work gave me a useful perspective spanning grassroots to policy advocacy at the national and international levels,

I had by then started reading climate fiction extensively while writing my own stories. In this, I was impelled by the need to communicate possible futures as well as the violent climate-changed present to my reader. My hope and belief in this was to be able to prepare readers for drastically changed circumstances, while also inspiring them to debate, discuss and perhaps take action to transform the status quo.

But this is more than enough about my own journey of climate writing. As I became convinced about the importance of this rising genre of writing, I discovered a whole new community of fellow writers across the globe, engaging with the climate crisis. I was introduced to Herzog's *Heat*, one of the earliest climate fiction novels; I enjoyed the comic and the dark in Ian McEwan's *Solar*; I was intrigued by the plot in Liz Jensen's *The Rapture*; and I was inspired by the vision of Octavia E. Butler's *Parable of the Sower*. Then there were more, and more still.

But my intent here is not to present a history or reading list of cli-fi and its worthy practitioners. While I enjoyed and still enjoy reading these books, I was always more interested in the storyworlds and the creative machinery employed by writers, who, like early explorers, were charting out a strange new land. My curiosity was spurred by the palette of techniques, themes, tropes, creative choices and approaches employed by these path-breaking creators and how and if these help us better comprehend climate change and perhaps move us to take action. Do these choices and techniques together constitute a significant departure from the ways stories had been told for a long time? Is it the peculiarity of the material presented by climate change, beginning from the way we produce and consume, leading to emissions and the resulting socio-political and environmental manifestations of a warming planet that has been influencing the ways we tell stories? If climate change has indeed changed our stories, what are some of those significant departures?

Late in 2021, when the second wave of the Covid-19 pandemic had just about receded, I was invited by the University of Oxford to deliver an online lecture on climate change and literature as part of a series involving academics and practitioners, some of whose work I have mentioned in the pages that follow. Already, for some years, I had begun to speak in a variety of academic and popular venues about the climate-literature interface while weaving in readings from my first climate novel, and this Oxford lecture provided the opportunity to refine and structure my views while further enriching my understanding. Much of the first part of this book is developed and consolidated from my lecture notes for the University of Oxford event and other speaking assignments, besides my articles and columns for newspapers and magazines.

At one level, this book is a celebration of the genre of climate fiction and my reading and practice of it as a writer who also happens to be a climate activist. I will start by introducing climate fiction, followed by an examination of the contours and possibilities of this new genre. This will be done over the next three chapters.

I begin the next chapter with brief introductions to climate history and climate science, followed by discussions about the scope, purpose and possible contours of cli-fi. Next, I introduce a simple three-point framework for approaching cli-fi consisting of organizing principles, creative-thematic features and transformative potential. Following this, I discuss the organizing principles in detail by presenting various ways of placing cli-fi into categories like dystopia, utopia and science fiction, among others. In the chapter that follows it, I will discuss the peculiar creative-thematic challenges which bestow certain distinctive features to climate writing.[6] The transformative potential of these stories will be examined in the fourth chapter, where I ask how and if these stories can influence our minds and lead to positive change. That chapter ends with a discussion of postcolonial and ecocritical approaches, exploring their relevance in the analysis of climate fiction.

While laying this groundwork, and to prepare ourselves for the closer engagement with climate novels that we take up in the second part of this book, I will concurrently draw attention to three of the distinctive features of climate writing. Two of these features are closely allied (but not exclusive) to cli-fi and certain kinds of environmental writing, while the third is a more general characteristic or value, commonly associated with 'literary fiction', which nevertheless can be present in other genres.

These first two features are planetarity[7] and justice. Planetarity examines whether the story demonstrates a sense of planetary connections which is pertinent for climate representations in literature because the global manifestations of climate change bind together the natural and the human world of politics, culture, economics and technology through global networks and interlinkages. On the other hand, justice examines how issues of equity underpin climate change and our ability to mitigate and adapt to its impacts.

The third feature that I attempt to examine in climate novels is 'aesthetics' which I try to capture primarily through 'literariness'[8] of the text. In focusing on aesthetics, I am trying to examine whether, despite being a so-called genre and therefore stamped by the common prejudice that genre is not literary, climate stories can also present certain literary values that provide an aesthetic experience akin to what we expect from 'serious' literary fiction or even poetry.

In the course of that discussion, I will argue that these three features, between them, constitute a useful set of analytical lenses for reading climate fiction from various perspectives, including those of an activist-minded reader or a literary aesthete. As a writer-activist who perpetually struggles between the political (closely allied to justice) and the aesthetic impulse while crafting stories, these three points of salience stood out for me as touchstones for a literature where planetary forces and connections translate to impacts on society and culture. Between them, as we shall see, these three features provide shorthand for comprehending, aesthetically representing and engaging with the unequal burden of climate change shared by people across the world.

The reader will note that two of these salient features, planetarity and justice, are thematic choices that authors make while telling their climate stories. Aesthetics, on the other hand, which will be captured through the literariness of the text, dwells in the use of language which is revealed through close reading and communicated as an experience.

It is my expectation that planetarity and justice, by unravelling certain complexities of climate change and its unequal impacts on people, not only help in comprehension but can also allow the reader of climate fiction to engage and possibly take well-reasoned steps towards climate action. By adopting these two features, the author empowers the reader with facts, contexts and understanding which will prepare them to meaningfully advocate for equitable and sustainable transformations to a better future. The third feature of aesthetics, as we will see later, can also provide representational depth to the story in the context of climate change.

Besides these three features, which I focus upon in my analysis, I will also discuss a number of other features including non-human agency, nature-culture entanglements, role of collectives, derangements of scale and the uncanny which are often encountered in climate fiction. By exploring these other features, I will be trying to arrive at a more comprehensive understanding of this evolving genre while also sharpening my examination of some climate novels.

Later in this book, I will further refine the three distinctive features (or major lenses) using relevant theoretical and activist approaches. This will then allow me to apply them as lenses to examine three climate novels, for each of which one of these three features is salient. This exercise will enrich our understanding of how the mechanics of these features and the associated creative choices give impetus to the representational and political goals of climate novels.

The novels studied here are Amitav Ghosh's *Gun Island*, Emmi Itäranta's *Memory of Water* and Anita Agnihotri's *The Sickle*. Through my analysis of these three works, I will demonstrate how and in what ways Ghosh's climate novel is distinctive for its planetariness, Itäranta's for its aesthetics and Agnihotri's for its focus on justice. Going a step further, I will also examine how planetariness is woven into Ghosh's book and its dynamics within the story. Similarly, I will examine how the theme of justice is intrinsic in Agnihotri's climate novel and how this theme operates and informs the text. For Itäranta's novel, I will review the role of the aesthetic impulse, captured primarily by 'literariness', through close readings of sections of the story.

By adopting this approach, I am not suggesting that the three features are necessarily mutually exclusive. A planetary climate novel set in the present, which connects far-flung geographies and peoples, can also be telling a story where justice issues are important. Amitav Ghosh's *Gun Island* is a case in point. Similarly, a cli-fi work strong on justice and politics can still be of planetary scope. What I am suggesting then is that, even on my first reading as a reviewer, I found planetariness, or more specifically the 'sense of planet',[9] stands out as a distinctive feature pervading the plot of Ghosh's novel and likewise for the other two books.

A broader objective of this work is to present ways of reading, enjoying and analysing climate fiction and its possible role in addressing the climate crisis. To this end, the primary approach using the three lenses to examine the three novels, one for each, is followed by shorter analytical readings of each book using the other creative-thematic features of climate fiction, which, for the sake of simplicity, I call minor lenses.

Each of the three chapters in the second part of this book is dedicated to the reading of a climate novel and follows a similar architecture. Divided into sub-sections, they begin with personal stories followed by a detailed summary of the novel's narrative. Next, the relevant major lens is further developed and refined using concepts from the existing literature and activist insights. This is followed by a detailed examination of the novel using the major lens.

Next, in the same chapter, I seek answers to questions like – is this novel science fiction or a realist work? Is it dystopian or a cautionary tale? What is its vision about the future? This is done with the help of the categories of cli-fi discussed in the next chapter. Following this, we ask a different set of questions which have to do with climate-related creative-thematic strategies adopted by the author. How does the work represent the agency of non-humans? Does the text show awareness of nature-culture entanglements? What about the role of collectives in the story? Here we are essentially employing the minor lenses and the two remaining major lenses for a snapshot reading of the novel. Finally, the transformative potential of the story is analysed using a number of activist tools like the United Nations Sustainable Development Goals and findings of empirical ecocritical studies, among others. In the case of the two novels by Indian authors, there is another sub-section analysing the novel from the postcolonial perspective before gathering it all into a few concluding paragraphs.

A few more words about this transformative potential of these climate novels are in order. As mentioned above, and in a nod to my activist self, I will examine how and if these three novels employ characterization, storytelling and other devices that can leave an impression on the reader vis-à-vis the book's climate and allied themes. Therein, I will also try to find if these novels employ storylines or convey information and ideas that are pertinent from the perspective of internationally agreed sustainability goals and whether they have the potential to raise awareness about the causes of climate change. I will also demonstrate with the example of one of the three novels how a climate story represents changes in beliefs, behaviour and worldviews at individual and societal levels, thereby planting the seeds for climate action and policy interventions.

While the three major lenses will mostly focus on the dynamics of planetarity, justice and aesthetics within the story, the above analysis of transformative potential will sharpen our understanding of the possibilities of these novels beyond their pages, indicating their probable influence on beliefs, ideas and climate action. Further research can use some of these findings as starting points, and the observations from such studies can later facilitate decision-making about the adoption of these texts in various contexts of climate education. This focus on the transformative potential of the works is, however, not to rule out the obvious – that the three distinctive features (especially justice) under study and their dynamics within the text will have a bearing on the potential of the novel beyond its pages.

This multi-probe analysis of the novels, incorporating major and minor lenses, categories and transformative potential, will help us arrive at a more comprehensive understanding of the forms, features, creative impetuses and challenges that define climate fiction while informing its representational and transformative possibilities. This in-depth reading will finally allow us, in the last chapter, to compare and dwell upon the reasons for the similarities and differences of these novels as climate texts, where we will also point towards new directions of this genre.

The choice of *Gun Island* for this study hinges on its planetary scope, buttressed by the fact of its postcoloniality. Being a postcolonial Indian writer myself, the climate writing of Amitav Ghosh assumes special significance for the depth of insights and creative imagination connecting his climate fiction and non-fiction. The reading of his work will definitely enrich this book.

The focus on Emmi Itäranta's novel is guided by the fact that, while being a dystopian work of climate fiction, it goes beyond genre expectations from the average dystopian narrative and can easily stand up to the demands of a dyed-in-wool literary aesthete or the average literary fiction reader. *Memory of Water*, as we shall see, is one of those rare cli-fi novels which demonstrates certain features of literary fiction in general as well as some special characteristics of literary writing, which can be approximated in the term 'literariness' found in the work of Russian formalist critics.

Itäranta's novel is also notable in the use of certain techniques of literariness to evoke a specific form of 'the uncanny' which is a distinctive feature of climate novels. It goes without saying that literariness (and certain features of the literary), besides providing aesthetic pleasure, also breaches the imaginary barrier between the cli-fi 'genre' and 'serious' literary fiction, thereby extending the book's appeal to a new group of readers.

Finally, even a surface reading of Anita Agnihotri's novel made it obvious that the author has squarely engaged issues of justice, inequality and political action. The critical community is slowly coming to the realization that the issue of justice is central to climate action, and this was reason enough for me to choose this book. How this engagement with justice is accomplished, what nodes and structures of injustice the book manages to reveal and explore, and what it can tell us about the ways and means climate literature can be another tool for broader political engagement are all questions that will be addressed in the chapter dedicated to Agnihotri's novel. Originally written in Bangla, this novel also presented us with the unique opportunity to examine a translated work of postcolonial climate fiction, of which there are only a few examples.

A few more words about the two postcolonial novels are in order. Amitav Ghosh's postcolonial cli-fi demonstrated features of postmodernity in its cosmopolitan and transnational settings and characters and in the way it excavates forgotten myths and narratives of climate strife, intertwining it with the current crisis, while also engaging both the mythical past and the present in a critique of humanity's problematic relation with nature. Anita Agnihotri's postcolonial novel, on the other hand, in its focus on inequalities and economic exploitation, presents opportunities for a Marxist reading of the exploitative structures, perpetuated and aggravated by the effects of climate change in the storyworld. While we won't attempt a thorough Marxist or postmodernist reading of the two books, this difference between the two novels and the ways this can reflect and refract through our climate-focused lenses was an added justification for the inclusion of these two works.

It has been my conscious decision to attempt this multifaceted analysis of the three texts mapped primarily to three lenses, instead of seeking patterns in a large number of works, which cultural critics have very often done. In fact, it is their work that has yielded some of the categories and perspectives which I employ to enrich my analysis of these three novels. However, as a writer and activist, my primary focus here is to dive deeper into the stories, to examine how, while providing aesthetic satisfaction, climate writers also inform, represent and unravel the twisted yarns of science, ecologies, economies, culture and power that manifest as the climate crisis.

My objective throughout this book will be to tone down the complexities of theory and present simple analysis, while also maintaining a balance of approach between my writerly and activist selves. To these two, I might now add a third one, that of an independent researcher, but that has not been my primary motivation.

First and foremost, my attempt within these pages has been to demystify the complexities of the climate imagination with a simple compass of concepts and features. Beyond that, I have attempted to blend the craft of a book reviewer and critic with the curiosity of a researcher and the experience of a writer-activist to crack the codes of cli-fi and bring it to a wider audience of academics, activists, scholars, writers, as well as the uninitiated reader. While it is unlikely that this work will play a role in pulling down the price of branded rain shoes, I will consider my labours fulfilled if this book is equally at home in academic departments and the activist-reader's ragged backpack.

Over the next three chapters, I explore climate fiction in greater detail and from various perspectives by drawing on a variety of critical work before focusing on the three important features that will be used as lenses to study the three climate novels. But, before we do that, we will take a short interlude, beginning with the story of a fourteenth-century Chinese calligrapher.

2

# Poets, volcanoes and a Chinese calligrapher

## *Climate, history and literature*

On the first day of January 1309, the famous Chinese calligrapher Bi Guo, travelling by boat along the Jiangnan canal back to his home in Zhenjiang on the southern bank of the Yangtze, noticed the weather change. He had been to Wuxi on some business and must have been looking forward to his return. But the artist soon realized that the journey may not go as smoothly as expected.

Guo wrote in his diary, 'A northeast wind broke out, and it was extremely cold.'[1] By the second of January, the cold had gotten worse, and on the next day, 'Ice had closed in from all directions.' The weather didn't improve, and on the following day, the ice had to be broken and piled on the canal bank. 'Piles of ice, two or three *chi* tall, were accumulated on the canal bank', he noted. By the fourth day, the canal froze completely, making sailing impossible. Finally, he had to abandon the boat and return home on horseback.[2]

Why is this Chinese calligrapher's account important for us? This is because Guo's meticulous records of the weather from that period, preserved in the Yunshan diary, have been employed[3] alongside other data sources to study the transition to the Little Ice Age, an extended period of cold weather, lasting almost five centuries, which left a deep impact on planetary history.

Climate, ways of life, human culture and history are inextricably linked, often interacting with each other through complex processes that can aggravate or ameliorate the impact of change. Confucian norms, for example, have been found[4] to reduce the impact of crop failures on peasant rebellion in Qing China, just as education levels in particular Chinese counties during the Ming period[5] had cushioned the adverse effects of climate change. On the other hand, human intervention in nature and ecologies has been observed to be inextricably linked to the histories of imperialism and colonialism.[6] This intervention also lies at the heart of a continuum of processes, beliefs, values, attitudes and more specifically a 'reason-centred culture'[7] that has precipitated the ecological crisis and has begotten existential threats like climate change.

Just as the transition to the Little Ice Age inspired Guo's notings, the changed climate and accompanying weather events may have inspired lines in the most famous of love poems in English literature, Andrew Marvell's, 'To His Coy Mistress'. Around the middle of the seventeenth century (1646–7), Marvell wrote:

Thou by the Indian Ganges' side
Shouldst rubies find; I by the tide
Of Humber would complain. I would
Love you ten years before the flood

Researchers comparing poetry from that period to climate records have argued[8] that the flood mentioned by Marvell, while having Biblical connotations, can also be connected to the frequent flooding and storm surges of the Humber estuary due to the changed weather patterns of the Little Ice Age.

Almost one and a half centuries after Marvell, another climatic event, the volcanic eruption (1815) of Mount Tambora in Indonesia, would further exacerbate global cooling in the final decades of the Little Ice Age. The eruption of Tambora had far-reaching impacts. It triggered droughts, upset the Indian monsoon system and perhaps led to the emergence of a deadly strain of cholera. This most powerful of natural disasters in recorded history, only matched by the Chicxulub asteroid impact 66 million years ago, also led to the 'Year without a Summer', a time of unnatural weather across the globe, which also birthed the first great work of science fiction, Mary Shelley's *Frankenstein, or The Modern Prometheus*. Critics have noted how this work, alongside a poem by Lord Byron and a fantasy story by his doctor John Polidori, written at the same time while living on the shores of Lake Geneva, 'reflect the disorientation and desperation that even a few weeks of abrupt climate change can cause'.[9]

The Little Ice Age, which could have stemmed from a variety of connected or unconnected causes like solar cycles, volcanic activity, changes in ocean currents, the European colonization of the Americas or even Genghis Khan's massacres[10] and the attendant reduction of carbon emissions, had far-reaching impacts on human culture and practices. In China, the adverse climate effects of this period have been implicated as a factor in the complex of reasons leading to the collapse of the powerful Ming dynasty in 1644. Historian Timothy Brook, who has used centuries-old price data to argue for these connections, found that 'The scale on which the climate deteriorated made the fall of the dynasty as irreversible as any morality tale could imagine. Chen Qide credited Heaven with the disaster; we credit climate change.'[11]

From the fall of dynasties to 'frost fairs' with taverns and brothels on the frozen Thames in London, this period of global cooling, with its peaks and troughs, has had far-ranging impacts on human history and culture. The import of this climatic change can be comprehended from Philipp Blom,[12] who has argued that the period of intense cooling in the later part of the Little Ice Age (1570s onwards), via a long-term agricultural crisis, finally broke down the feudal order in Europe, creating conditions for the emergence of the modern world.

Such connections between climatic change and human history have been investigated for periods that are even further back in time. Paleoclimatic studies have discovered droughts to be a factor for the decline of the Mayan civilization[13] while the Late Antique Little Ice Age of the sixth and seventh centuries have been implicated as an environmental factor that weakened the Eastern Roman Empire, led to the collapse of the powerful Sassanians of Persia[14] and could have contributed to the rise of the Islamic empire.[15] Suggesting a direct correlation between climate and nomadic conquests, researcher Qiang Chen has recently shown how the likelihood of nomadic conquests in China increased with reduced rainfall.[16]

Links between the climate, major historical events and the sphere of culture are easily visible in our present era of global warming and climate change. The strife of climate migrants, the displacement of Indigenous peoples and the resultant impact on their culture, the mass mobilizations for climate action, the poetry and the literature about climate, the ongoing efforts to change consumption habits, the work of the Intergovernmental Panel on Climate Change (IPCC)[17] and Conference of the Parties (COP),[18] the transformative politics of climate justice and the growing importance of the green movement, recently noticed in the election of a climate scientist as the president-elect of Mexico, all of these constitute the human response and experience of climate change, as we look ahead to unprecedented times.

Whenever there has been an existential crisis that threatened life on the planet, literature, art and activism have engaged with it through creative representation and action. This we have noticed during the years of the nuclear threat of the Cold War, and also recently during the coronavirus pandemic, which not only led to a groundswell of fellow-feeling and benevolent action but also gave rise to a genre of pandemic literature whose numbers continue to swell.

For the current climate crisis too, this has generally been the case, where we see growing partnerships between scientists, activists and conscientious citizens demystifying and pushing back against the systems, processes, beliefs and worldviews that perpetuate high levels of greenhouse gas emissions.

In all of this, and increasingly over the years, writers and creative artists have had an important role to play. However, their effort is complicated by the complexities of climate science, the unique nature and experience of the climate crisis and the planetary scope of climate change, all of which can resist widely prevalent modes of literary representation. In the next section, we dwell briefly on scientific facts and figures pertaining to climate change. The section that follows discusses the scope, characteristics, purpose and certain proposed guidelines for climate-aware literature. After that, in a new section, we present a broad framework for approaching cli-fi. The last two sections of this chapter present typologies of the climate novel and its evolution. The chapter that follows will take up the creative challenges alluded to before. While we will be focusing mostly on the nature and dynamics of literature's encounter with climate change through an examination of novels, this engagement can be extended to include climate poetry, climate drama and other forms of performative and visual arts.

This, of course, reminds us of the Chinese calligrapher Guo, who we met a little while back. Besides maintaining a meticulous diary that has helped us reconstruct the story of climate from another time, his fine paintings, like that of a withered tree (Figure 2.1) or of a snow-laden bamboo bending over a desolate riverbank, are testaments to this abiding quest for recording and representing the environment, which surrounds us, in which we are embedded, and with which we are forever entangled in life and death.

**Figure 2.1** Withered Tree by Guo Bi, *c.*fourteenth century. Handscroll; ink on silk. Courtesy Kyoto National Museum.

## Climate facts, risks and possibilities

In the summer of 2024, when more than a hundred perished from the heat waves in India, I noticed something strange in my city. The ubiquitous *paan-biri* shops which dot the streets of Kolkata, catering to nicotine addiction and malignancy in pouches, packets, rolled tobacco and biris, had begun to stock a new item. Almost all of them, or at least those that I see on my way to my writing den, had lined their shelves with packs of oral rehydration solution (ORS), the tried and tested antidote to dehydration and electrolyte loss.

The summer had indeed been brutal. Those who were out on the streets all day had been suffering from heat exhaustion, and every day we would hear about someone we know having a heat stroke. In these trying circumstances, it was natural that life-saving ORS would slip out of pharmacy shelves and land up in the humble paan-wallah's shack, thereby perhaps easing his complicated karma a bit.

But humanity's collective karma manifested through such punishing weather is far from being redeemed. Let us take a look at the facts put out by scientific bodies: According to the World Meteorological Organization, 2024 was the warmest year in the 174-year observational record,[19] and terms like global-boiling are now the staple of newspaper reports. NASA figures from their authoritative 'Vital Signs' records show that the planet was about 1.47°C warmer in 2024 than the preindustrial average.[20] Also, the ten most recent years were the warmest since records are being kept. Moreover, these records point out that the recent rates of global sea level rise are unprecedented over the past 2,500 years. In our times, summer Arctic sea ice has been found to be shrinking at a rate of 12.2 per cent every decade because of warmer temperatures, while the ice in Antarctica has been melting away at an annual rate of 136 billion tonnes.

There is no room for doubt that the current climate crisis is anthropogenic, that is, caused by humans. There is solid scientific consensus about this anthropogenic origin, as evinced by statements of major scientific associations.[21] According to NASA, 'scientific evidence continues to show that human activities (primarily the human burning of fossil fuels) have warmed Earth's surface and its ocean basins, which in turn have continued to impact Earth's climate. This is based on over a century of scientific evidence.'[22]

The United Nations-mandated IPCC which monitors and assesses all scientific evidence around climate change and publishes the authoritative IPCC reports has clearly articulated the need for urgent response to the climate emergency. According to them, 'the magnitude and rate of climate change and associated risks depend strongly on near-term mitigation and adaptation actions, and projected adverse impacts and related losses and damages escalate with every increment of global warming'.[23]

To address this existential threat of climate change, nations of the world meet annually under the auspices of the COP to the United Nations Framework Convention on Climate Change (UNFCCC) to negotiate agreements, review progress, raise awareness and build cooperation around climate change. However, progress is slow and far from what is required to deal with the seriousness of the crisis, with issues like lack of adequate funding for loss and damage, implementation, lack of ambitious targets and powerful fossil fuel lobbies standing in the way.

The Paris Climate Agreement, which is the most ambitious endeavour to deal with the crisis, set a goal to hold 'the increase in the global average temperature to well below 2 degrees Celsius above pre-industrial levels' and pursue efforts 'to limit the temperature increase to 1.5°C above pre-industrial levels, recognizing that this would significantly reduce the risks and impacts of climate change'.[24] These temperature thresholds are significant because beyond these, global warming will have increasingly severe effects which will be hard to manage. However, the alarming fact is that the more ambitious target of 1.5°C above pre-industrial average has already been breached for a year-long period.[25] Meanwhile, the US withdrawal from the Paris Agreement during the second term of President Donald Trump has further reduced its effectiveness. What is required right now are urgent and drastic emission cuts alongside all-out efforts for adaptation through equitable and just measures, but this sounds like wishful thinking.

As the planet heats up, we will continue to experience stronger hurricanes, more droughts and heat waves, freezing winters, changing precipitation patterns, intense and repeated storms with flooding, melting glaciers and polar ice caps, longer wildfire seasons, sea level rise, ocean acidification with its impact on marine life, decreasing agricultural yields and loss of livelihoods, among a wide and worrying variety of effects. Besides these, climate change is also implicated in the resurgence and changing geographical range of certain vector-borne diseases like dengue,[26] forced migration and conflict, as well as lesser-understood facts like the increased incidence of airline turbulence and even lightning strikes.

Then there are the ever-growing numbers of more complex outcomes that often lead to further worsening of the crisis. For example, the climate change-induced outbreaks of the mountain pine beetle in North American forests result in increased tree mortality, which in turn reduces the carbon dioxide-absorbing capacity of these same forests, leading to further increase in warming. At a planetary scale, the melting of polar ice caps, resulting in a reduced reflective surface of the earth, is also causing increased warming. Such reinforcing mechanisms of climate change, called positive feedback loops, are many, and till date researchers have identified twenty-six such accelerators of global warming.[27]

Again, some of the effects of climate-related disasters tend to worsen the outcomes of other disasters. The longer forest fire seasons in different parts of the world decrease the water-absorbing capacity of the soil, causing flash floods. In Kolkata, where I live, the loss of tree cover from powerful cyclones has worsened the heat-islanding effect, making summers more unbearable. Even more intriguing is how our efforts to mitigate climate change can impact the local climate, as had been found by an observational evidence-based study of the effect of wind farms on near-surface temperatures.[28] Depending on where and how we live and what we do for a livelihood, some or many of these effects are already impacting our lives in a great many ways.

## Climate literature: Scope, purpose and a prescription

So we have an indication of the complicated scientific and geophysical material that the literature of climate change has to grapple with while fashioning stories out of 'natural' phenomena, projecting backwards or forwards in time or dwelling in the lived present. Not to disregard the human culpability and our entanglement in all these phenomena. Is it up to the task? What are the characteristics, function and role of climate fiction besides the obvious mimetic role of representation? What are the tools and techniques at its command, and what are the obstacles and challenges it has to overcome in trying to achieve its representational and political goals? While literary critics, reviewers, authors and other experts are well aware of the need for literature and other creative arts to engage with the issue of climate change, this awareness always does not translate into increased production of climate fiction, a fact famously highlighted by Amitav Ghosh in his book *The Great Derangement*.

Since the writing of Ghosh's book, literature's engagement with climate change has grown, also in postcolonial developing nations like India, where a dearth has been replaced by a steady trickle. Still, the numbers are not comparable to the output of cli-fi written in English from the West. Besides the novels by the two Indian writers we discuss in this book, some of these recent works published in English by Indians include Janice Pariat's *Everything the Light Touches*, Shubhangi Swarup's *Latitudes of Longing*, Nilanjana S. Roy's *Black River*, Prayaag Akbar's *Leila*, Priya Sarukkai Chabria's *Earthrise Stories*, Rimi B. Chatterjee's *Ashquabad: City of Stories* and Sheela Tomy's *Valli* (translated by Jayasree Kalathil), among others. These books, between themselves, engage with climate, environmental and interconnected justice issues and range across past, present and future storyworlds which are hopeful, dystopian or quite similar to our own.

Later on we will address postcolonial fiction's encounter with climate change and some unique aspects of this engagement. But let us return to our broader exploration of the scope, characteristics, purpose and proposals for climate fiction, or cli-fi,[29] while also examining how authors fashion these stories.

On the temporal scale, climate stories, as we shall see, can and do engage with present transformations, real or imagined, including but not limited to the impact of disasters as well as the mitigative, adaptive and activist strategies that are being negotiated and applied to counter the effects of global warming. Such stories can be as simple as the adventure-laced visual narrative of characters caught up in a real cyclone like Aila or be more complex and politically engaged with equity and justice in their spotlight.

The Hindi drama film *Kadvi Hawa* (Bitter Wind), directed by Nila Madhav Panda, is one such work depicting true stories of droughts and cyclones in the Indian state of Odisha, Bundelkhand and other parts of India. It shows how the lives of a loan recovery agent and a poor farmer get entwined through climate impacts, providing a telling commentary about ethics and justice in the face of disaster.

There are also stories which have explored the links between past climatic change, not necessarily anthropogenic, with the climate crisis of the present, as we shall see in Amitav Ghosh's *Gun Island* while other book-length imaginative essays like Naomi Oreskes and Erik M. Conway's *The Collapse of Western Civilization* have fashioned future histories where a historian in the future looks back and examines the collapse.

Climate stories also tend to have a wide geographical scope. This is perhaps symptomatic of the transterritorial and planetary scale of climate change and the global interconnectivities that explicitly or implicitly come into play when telling these tales. Doris Lessing's *Mara and Dann* ranges across an imaginary continent of the future named after Africa, Amitav Ghosh's *Gun Island*'s narrative unfolds across three continents, while Kim Stanley Robinson's *The Ministry for the Future*, with a similar global scope, also involves international organizations. Later we shall explore whether the planetary scope of climate novels is better suited to examine the geographically scattered manifestations of the crisis besides, in some cases, helping to foreground the global technological, ecological, social, economic, cultural and political connections and networks that are intertwined with it.

On the other hand, there are also more localized climate stories. Paolo Bacigalupi's *The Windup Girl* is mostly set in a partially drowned future Thailand, Anita Agnihotri's *The Sickle* doesn't venture much beyond the drought-affected regions of the Indian state of Maharashtra and Kim Stanley Robinson's *New York 2140* is a story about an inundated Manhattan. But even in their more localized imaginings, these climate novels implicitly acknowledge transterritorial connections and impacts of climate change, as in sea-level rise, while representing 'place' as a crucible for the interaction of planetary forces, human and non-human. This makes 'place' more fluid and contingent in climate fiction which, as Amitav Ghosh points out, is unlike the role played by 'place' in the modern realist novel, where place, bereft of continuities and connections, is important for the telling of the story.[30]

There are still other works which, because of similarities of their settings to climate-affected worlds, have been dubbed cli-fi. Thus J. G. Ballard's *The Drowned World*, published in 1962, which had dealt with climate change *avant la lettre*, attributing it to somewhat different causes, has been labelled 'proto climate-change fiction'.[31] Similarly, Cormac McCarthy's *The Road*, which doesn't mention climate change at all but depicts a father and son walking for days through a dystopian United States ravaged by an unnamed disaster, keeps reappearing in cli-fi lists. Clearly, the variety as well as the temporal and geographical scope of climate stories seems endless.

With this brief background about the spatio-temporal scope of cli-fi, and certain quirks of the genre, we can now direct our attention to the work of critics and activists who have attempted to clarify the purpose and meaning of these works and how they engage with their material.

Many of these novels portray the impact of anthropogenic global warming on individuals and collectives, human and non-human, by creating 'imaginaries' which depict possible consequences, individual and collective responses and the transformations of the relationship between people and the planet. According to my activist colleague Jeffrey Barber, these stories, while portraying concerns around and impacts of climate change, also 'highlight the transitions' and note the 'struggle of individuals to survive and reflect on their identity, lifestyle and livelihoods'.[32] A number of critics have dwelt upon these aspects of reflecting and making sense of the complexities of the climate emergency while representing it through stories.

In *Anthropocene Fictions*, Adam Trexler, acknowledging how climate change breaks down genre conventions, hinges his arguments on the representational advantages of the novel in its task of depicting climate-changed scenarios and their interplay with human (and non-human) lives. Stef Craps and Rick Crownshaw, in their introduction to a series of scholarly essays on cli-fi, similarly convey a sense of hope about the 'capacities of the novel' while noting how the definition of Anthropocene is 'as much cultural as it is geological'.[33] Trexler, while elaborating on his point about the advantages of the novel, explains how the multivocal structure and complexity of the novel allow it to better engage with human responses to climate-changed scenarios besides serving other associated functions. This, he explains, is because climate change is itself a complex network. 'By its nature', Trexler writes:

> the novel assembles heterogeneous characters and things into a narrative sequence ... This complexity allows the novel to explore diverse, human responses to peak oil, alternative energy, carbon sequestration, carbon trading, consumption and air travel, in ways

> that are difficult for non-fiction or other art forms to portray. The novel can also think about climate change's intermingling with cultural narratives … Moreover, the climate change novel can explore the aesthetics of wilderness, gastronomy, domesticity, species, urban life, fast cars and international life. Climate change is itself a complex network of things and effects.[34]

Here Trexler is indicating that the functions of the climate novel include representing human response to climate change in its varied manifestations and aspects, engaging cultural narratives, besides aesthetically exploring both human and non-human life and living in their multifarious forms and experiences. Elsewhere, climate scholar Sophia David stresses on how these stories make meaning and the communicative role of climate fiction. The potential critical functions of these stories, David writes, is 'communicating climate change, engaging readers with the issue and making climate change meaningful and relevant to non-scientific people'.[35]

While Trexler comments on the representational role and David writes about conveying meaning, cultural critic Gregers Andersen of Stockholm University articulates why such representation matters and the 'reflective space' that climate fiction provides. Andersen quotes French philosopher Paul Ricoeur to explain the need for representation: 'The first way human beings attempt to understand and to master the "manifold" of the practical field is to give themselves a fictive representation of it.'[36] 'Understanding', 'mastery' and 'reflection' are key here as Andersen argues how fictive representations of climate-altered worlds through literature can allow insights about feeling and comprehending these worlds, thus having a bearing on our affective and cognitive relations with these.[37]

Stephanie LeMenager, who teaches at the University of Oregon, in an insightful essay on cli-fi and the struggle for genre, has described climate fiction as the 'symptom of a social need' which essentially is a need for genre or 'new patterns of expectation' and 'new means of living with an unprecedented set of limiting conditions'.[38] Delving into the structure of cli-fi, LeMenager describes it as a 'novelistic mode', which responds to the 'intimate and collective questioning of what it means to be human' in the context of climate-affected lived experiences.[39] Advancing from Veronica Hollinger's argument, in the science fiction context, about 'mode' being 'a method, a way of getting something done', LeMenager has argued that cli-fi 'marks another way of living in the world – a world remade profoundly by climate change'.[40]

Thus far, we have gathered some insights about the purpose and meaning of climate fiction which include representation, communication, quest for meaning and providing a reflective space which allows for understanding and feeling climate-affected worlds and our role therein. But how do these stories, this new 'novelistic mode', differ from earlier forms of storytelling, and how are writers supposed to craft stories out of the varied phenomena and cultural manifestations of the climate crisis? How can climate fiction perform its functions of what Trexler calls 'assembling heterogeneous characters and things in a narrative sequence'? What are the means by which climate stories could help us feel and comprehend climate-affected worlds? How can these narratives make the climate crisis meaningful, and what are the challenges that thwart these literary depictions? These are questions with many nuances, which we shall attempt to address throughout this book.

Before moving ahead, let us take a look at an insightful essay by Nick Admussen which provides some answers. In his 'Six Proposals for the Reform of Literature in the Age of Climate Change',[41] Admussen, who teaches Chinese literature and culture at Cornell University, provides a set of guidelines and signposts which undertake the fraught attempt to tell writers, who are usually fiercely independent-minded, what to write and how to engage with their material.

Drawing their rationale from the example of a century-old Chinese treatise[42] by Hu Shi, the crux of Admussen's proposals, and the scaffolding of most of his arguments, is in the suggestion that consumption and production habits will change only if the culture changes, which means we need to tell new kinds of stories. Almost echoing LeMenager's assertions about social need, Admussen begins by arguing that our inability to visualize the unfolding disaster arises from a problem of our culture. That is, we are not writing and telling the right stories. Calling for doing away with progress-based narratives, Admussen argues that progress logic:

> transforms the struggle to dismantle a destructive system into an episode of *Scooby Doo* or a volume of the *Hardy Boys*, in which the broken waste pipe is discovered dripping green goo and the story ends with its owner in handcuffs. These narratives end before the real conversation should start: the one that prevents such crimes in the first place.[43]

He goes on to suggest that narratives centred on individualism are destructive as they erase 'radical dependence on each other and the environment'.[44]

Admussen's proposals also question stories about individuals and isolated actors, as they tend to shut out the suffering and experience of the collective. Further, he points out that romanticizing the poor while exporting industrialized nations' pollution to their nations is ethically wrong and that the voices of the underprivileged should be heard in the new fiction – narrating the ills that such a system promotes. This, as we shall see, speaks to Rob Nixon's[45] assertion about the role of the writer-activist in telling the stories of environmental 'slow violence' while also foregrounding justice issues in literature which we shall discuss in detail. Admussen's proposals finally emphasize connectedness and world-building in fiction, stressing on the need to focus on systems and not objects. He finishes by stressing on the necessary connectedness between 'knowing', art and ethics, closing with these important lines, 'Writing fiction must become more than an exercise in personal fulfillment, ambition, or hunger for fame. If there is no *Silent Spring* without *The Jungle*, if there is no American socialism without *Star Trek*, then artists have a calling and a responsibility that is much deeper, and more crucial, than the academy might have us believe.'[46]

From the need and means of engagement with climate change suggested by Admussen, we arrive at the absence of literature's engagement with climate change, pointed out by Amitav Ghosh. Ghosh devoted an entire part of *The Great Derangement*, his non-fiction work about climate change, to stories, mainly literary culture, where he flags how literature has failed to engage with the crisis. This turning away from one of the greatest challenges facing humanity today, he called the 'great derangement', going on further to discuss why and how this engagement didn't happen while noting several exceptions from the literatures of different regions of the world. However, as we earlier noted, this situation has been changing.

Now that we have arrived at an understanding about certain characteristics, purpose and role of climate stories, it is in order to dwell on some definitions encountered in the literature. However, the necessity arises here for a caveat.

Some of these definitions, as we shall see later, may not work for postcolonial texts, which while engaging climate change, do so by foregrounding a different set of concerns relevant to the postcolonial context. In fact, there is always the possibility of encountering stories in other genres that are not a good fit for these definitions, which only goes to show that the novelistic mode of cli-fi is ever evolving as creators with their varied tools, motivations, creative preferences and experiences try to grapple with and represent the climate crisis.

In an effort to structure the vast and growing number of works that deal with climate change, Gregers Andersen has suggested a definition of the genre. According to Andersen, cli-fi 'uses as a narrative element the scientific consensus that humanity's emissions of greenhouse gases cause global warming'.[47] Therein, he also notes that the importance of cli-fi 'as a tool for reflection' stems from the fact that it takes anthropogenic global warming as its point of departure.

Elsewhere, cultural critics Axel Goodbody and Adeline-Johns Putra, acknowledging the absence of a precise definition, describe cli-fi as:

> a distinctive body of cultural work which engages with anthropogenic climate change, exploring the phenomenon not just in terms of setting, but with regard to psychological and social issues, combining fictional plots with meteorological facts, speculation on the future and reflection on the human-nature relationship, with an open border to the wider archive of related work on whose models it sometimes draws for the depiction of climatic crisis.[48]

We can see how these two critics, while mentioning anthropogenic causes, leave wider room for a variety of creative experiments. Similarly, Trexler, in a pithy and useful characterization of cli-fi, writes, 'climate change novels are best understood as a force that interacts with climate change, remaking what we know about the climate and the novel at the same time'.[49]

More recently, cli-fi researcher Matthew Schneider-Mayerson, along with the climate consultancy Good Energy, has developed a test which they call The Climate Reality Check,[50] to examine climate representation in stories and films. They describe it as 'a simple tool to evaluate whether our climate reality is being represented in films, TV shows, and other narratives'. Based on the Bechdel-Wallace test for gender representation in film and TV, this test asks a simple question – whether in a given story, climate change exists and a character knows it.

Once again, it is perhaps possible to imagine stories where complex impacts of climate change, like migration, may be addressed without the characters or the narrative implicating carbon emissions. How helpful these stories will be from the representational and political points of view is a question we can leave for another day. I will step aside from this debate only with the comment that in the sometimes-contrary pulls between creative licence and theoretical certainties, my vote as an author is always for the former.

## A framework for approaching cli-fi

The number of books labelled by readers or marketed by publishers as cli-fi has been growing over the years. Right now,[51] the Goodreads list 'Cli-fi: Climate Change Fiction' has 416 entries, while many more works from the genre are included in other lists like 'Climate Dystopias' and 'Ecopunk Fiction'. Sifting through this substantial and growing bookshelf of cli-fi, it would be useful to employ certain strategies (Figure 2.2) or approaches to better comprehend the nature, thematic focus and possibilities of these texts. These strategies can be gathered and grouped under a three-pronged framework consisting of organizing principles or categories, creative-thematic challenges and the allied distinctiveness, and transformative potential.

A fancy name for the first set of strategies would be taxonomic approaches to cli-fi, the second set can be called analytical or creative-thematic (from an authorial perspective), and the third set constitutes a set of normative approaches that bring an activist lens to examine how cli-fi can influence change (Figure 2.3). These sets of strategies and

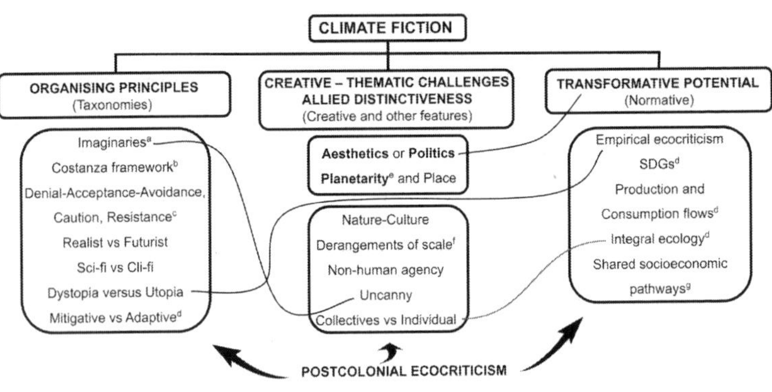


**Figure 2.2** A framework for approaching climate fiction.

Note: a) Gregers Andersen b) Robert Costanza c) Matthew Schneider-Mayerson d) Jeffrey Barber *et al.* e) Ursula Heise f) Timothy Clark g) Nikoleris et al. For detailed explanations of the items see chapters 1-4. The curved lines in the diagram provide some examples about the interconnections between the three sets of strategies and their constituents. The second box in the middle shows the major lenses (Politics, Aesthetics and Planetarity) used in the study while the 'minor' lenses are in the box below it. Rajat Chaudhuri, 2025.

their individual elements can be mutually dependent and inter-related (Figure 2.2). Thus, a particular creative-thematic challenge engaged by, or a distinctive feature encountered in, a text can determine which taxonomic category a work fits best with. Again, the handling of a creative challenge can have a bearing on a work's transformative potential.

For example, the 'imaginaries' approach of classifying climate fiction into different subtypes developed by Gregers Andersen has been linked by him to how certain types of stories evoke the uncanny[52] which is one of the creative-thematic features of cli-fi. Again, the organizing principle that divides cli-fi between dystopia and utopia can be mapped to its transformative potential, as some studies show utopian fiction and stories of hope tend to influence more people, while dystopian works can have the opposite effect. Similarly, the creative challenge of writing cli-fi, where a collective rather than a single hero is important, can have a bearing on its transformative potential, as we shall see when we discuss the integral ecology approach and related tools. Also, a focus on politics as a creative-thematic choice of the author is expected to have an added bearing on the transformative potential of a work if certain criteria, which we list as 'normative', are met. Closely meshed with our three-pronged approach to cli-fi (Figure 2.2) and undergirding the scholarship as well as the creative output of these books is the necessity to examine the genre's engagement with postcolonial writing and, in this context, dwell upon the commonalities and divergence between postcolonial writing and Western environmental texts.

In the following section, we will discuss organizing principles or taxonomies of climate fiction, which is the first of our three prongs or strategies to approach these stories. The next chapter will focus on the second set of strategies by delving into creative-thematic challenges and allied distinctiveness (distinctive features) of cli-fi. This second set of strategies will allow us to introduce the three major lenses for studying and analysing climate fiction. These major lenses will be further refined in the second part of the book and used in our in-depth readings of the chosen novels. This second set of strategies will also yield the minor lenses for analysing climate texts. In the

**Figure 2.3** Reading Climate Fiction. Illustration: 'Rough Weather' by Rajlaxmi Chaudhuri *c.*2025.

last chapter of this section, we will discuss the third set of strategies, where we will be looking at the potential of climate stories as agents of change. With these maps at hand, we will be ready to embark upon the adventure of reading those novels.

## Taxonomies of climate fiction

Taxonomic classifications are a convenient way to get introduced to a field without delving into too many details, specifics and individual examples. It saves us time while also allowing us to get an overall picture of a subject. The earliest known taxonomic work is attributed to the mythical Chinese emperor Shennong, who, sometime in 2700 BCE, created a catalogue of 300 medicinal plants. Later, the Egyptians and the Greeks were known to have taken up such classifications, among whom Aristotle had classified invertebrates into groups. But the figure whose name is inextricably linked to the field of modern taxonomy is the Swede, Carolus Linnaeus, whose system of classifying the living world remains relevant to this day.

Linnaeus's system gained precedence despite criticism from French naturalist Georges-Louis Leclerc, Comte de Buffon, who, among others, drew attention to its disregard for local circumstances, while other classifications and ways of knowing (as in Indigenous knowledge systems) remain less known to this day.[53] This shows how attempts at overly reductive taxonomies are fraught with the possibility of leaving out other ways of knowing.

To address such a possibility and generally to introduce a variety of ways of categorizing our material, we will be presenting a number of methods for classifying climate fiction.

Let us now examine some of these organizing principles. Climate scholars like Matthew Schneider-Mayerson, who we will remember also devised the Climate Reality Check, have noted an evident 'genre' democracy in cli-fi. His well-known empirical ecocritical study of nineteen cli-fi works was found to include realist literature, young adult fiction, noir, thriller, satire, post-apocalyptic fiction, science fiction, speculative fiction and weird fiction.[54] A nod to this can be found in Trexler, who argues that the Anthropocene presents certain challenges to generic conventions because of the narrative difficulties it presents. 'Literary novels,' he writes, 'bleed into science fiction; suspense novels have surprising elements of realism; realist depictions of everyday life involuntarily become biting satire. For these reasons, novels about the Anthropocene cannot be easily placed into discrete generic pigeonholes.'[55]

Nature writer Richard Kerridge, in his analysis of literary form and genre in the context of ecocritical approaches, and within the backdrop of the climate emergency and our attitudes towards it, argues that various techniques (like Modernist fragmented narratives) and genres serve different allied purposes. Commenting on the purpose of ecocriticism, he indicates the necessity for genre democracy when he writes:

> If the fundamental aim of literary ecocriticism is that environmental care should become stronger and more pervasive throughout literary culture, ecocritics will not be looking for a single form of literature that meets all the criteria at once; nor will they search only for a small number of new forms or genres specially adapted to environmental priorities. Rather, they will want to address all these various needs and audiences, and to bring environmentalism into all the influential forms of literature.[56]

The taxonomies we are going to present below, generally, but not always, acknowledge the genre-agnosticism of climate fiction noted above, instead focusing on the types of worlds these stories portray and what living in such a world means. These seven modes of classification do not constitute an exhaustive list, but between them they demonstrate the variety and evolving possibilities presented by literature's continuing encounter with climate change. They are based on the imaginaries framework, Costanza's approach, the approach focusing on denial, acceptance, avoidance, caution or resistance to the phenomena; the genre-based approach and tensions between sci-fi and cli-fi depictions; the approach examining present realist depictions versus futurist ones, the dystopian versus utopian division; and the approach separating mitigative and adaptive narratives (Figure 2.2).

The imaginaries framework, developed by Gregers Andersen, classifies a large number of works of Western climate fiction into five templates, or what he calls 'imaginaries'.[57] The word 'imaginary', as applied in academic discourse, can be traced back to Sartre's[58] theory of imagination which argues how an image is constituted from an object through the agency of an intention. The 'intention', so to speak, presents the whole picture of the object, unlike 'perception', whose field is limited. Later on, philosopher Cornelius Castoriadis[59] used the term 'imaginary' to designate the act of imagination which brings into existence a society which does not otherwise exist by itself. Both Sartre's intentionality and Castoriadis' act of imagining can be useful concepts to comprehend literary imaginaries of cli-fi where the author brings into being climate-affected storyworlds with their rules, laws, actors and their interrelations and dynamics.

Andersen's cli-fi imaginaries which have a bearing on how humans 'feel and understand their worlds'[60] include Social Breakdown, Judgement, Conspiracy, Loss of Wilderness and Sphere. Social Breakdown, whose cultural history he traces to the biblical story of Babel, consists of stories where anthropogenic climate change has led to wars or small-scale conflicts for limited resources. The Judgement imaginary covers stories where nature strikes back, so to speak, and we find non-human agency in play. He traces the cultural history of this imaginary to the *Epic of Gilgamesh* and the legend of Atlantis, among other texts. The Conspiracy imaginary blurs the realms of politics and science, telling a story where climate change is used as a tool of manipulation, tracing its history to the gods of the Greeks and their secretly orchestrated interventions in human life. Loss of Wilderness stories are those where nature as an entity of exceptional value is ruined or lost because of climate change, tracing their cultural coordinates to the biblical story of eviction from paradise. Finally, Sphere stories, tracing their roots to the story of Noah's Ark, present alternative 'terraformed' worlds or bubbles where people escape to, from a climate-ravaged world.[61]

Andersen provides examples of books and movies for each of these imaginaries. For example, Marcel Theroux's *Far North* is a story of Social Breakdown, Frank Schätzing's *The Swarm* fits with Judgement, Michael Crichton's *State of Fear* is a tale of Conspiracy, Jean McNeil's *The Ice Lovers* has a Loss of Wilderness imaginary and, finally, the

Sphere imaginary is to be found in Kim Stanley Robinson's trilogy *Science in the Capital* and other books.[62]

In his well-known 'Four Visions of the Century Ahead', ecological economist Robert Costanza devised a two-by-two matrix to imagine possible futures for the planet.[63] Costanza's framework suggests four possible visions for the future, comparing them to scenarios available in books or movies. While his matrix was not developed to study cli-fi specifically, we can repurpose it to divide cli-fi set in the future primarily into two types, those with a techno-optimist worldview which says technology (usually hi-tech) and science will solve climate change with access to almost unlimited energy (for example) and those whose worldview is techno-sceptic, implying technology won't solve climate change and there will always be a limited amount of energy and resources.

Next, following Costanza's method, we can predict that this techno-optimist vision can either come true, that is, technology (like geo-engineering, atomic fusion energy, among others) is able to deal with climate change or the optimists may be proved wrong, and climate change gets worse, pushing us towards dystopian scenarios and stories. This sort of a techno-optimist vision is present in Ian McEwan's *Solar*, with its promise of artificial photosynthesis, which, however, doesn't fructify because the novel takes a satirical turn. Techno-optimism once again fails completely as a geo-engineering experiment to cool the planet backfires in the *Snowpiercer* movie, pushing the planet into an ice age and the narrative into the realm of dystopia.

Similarly, the techno-sceptic worldview can generate two types of climate stories, neither of which depend on hi-tech solutions to climate change. In one of these, big authoritarian governments push for sustainability (carbon taxes, rationing, etc.) and in the other, social cooperation, including reduced consumption and greener production, helps to mitigate and reduce the impacts of climate change. In the first type, we can think of Saci Lloyd's *The Carbon Diaries*, where the story centres on the imposition of a carbon tax system, while among the second type, we can think about numerous hopeful stories in the solarpunk genre, where people come together in communities of mutual care, where low-tech and renewables fuel transformations to a better future.

In fact, this kind of an organizing principle for cli-fi can be further expanded by bringing in the sophisticated Shared Socioeconomic Pathways (SSPs) research[64] and the related IPCC climate models. These pathways chart out possible transformations in global society, economics and demographics till the beginning of the next century and are used as important inputs to climate models, thereby helping to predict how emissions will vary with each chosen pathway. The pathways, which are essentially projected narratives of the future, have been numbered and named as Taking the Green Road, Middle of the Road, Regional Rivalry, Inequality and Fossil-fuelled Development (Taking the Highway). Climate fiction can then be organized on the basis of which pathway(s) are closest to their storyworlds. Such an approach where literature and science are 'in conversation' can demonstrate the difference in the scientific and the literary approaches whereby 'climate futures become close and personal rather than distant and abstract.'[65] During the second wave of the coronavirus pandemic in India, we had the opportunity to work on a video game project – *Survive the Century* – which conceptually and literally demonstrated this conversation between literature and science.[66]

Our third categorization of cli-fi is based on the work of Matthew Schneider-Mayerson, who identified three broad themes in the climate fiction novel. The first of these is 'denial avoidance, and acceptance of climate change', the second 'cautionary fables of the Anthropocene' and the third is 'ecopolitics of resistance.'[67] In the first category, he places both Barbara Kingsolver's *Flight Behaviour* (acceptance) and Michael Crichton's *State of Fear* (denial); in the second is Cormac McCarthy's *The Road*, among others, while in the third category we find Kim Stanley Robinson's *Science in the Capital* trilogy alongside other books.

The divisions between realist and futurist cli-fi, our fourth organizing principle, are strong and well-fought. While realist descriptions and conventions do appear in these stories, the tilt towards narratives of the future seems to be pronounced among writers. Such stories can be set in the near (*The Ministry for the Future*) or far future (*Mara and Dann*), opening up their own set of creative and transformative possibilities. Realist narratives, on the other hand, can be expected to be more relatable for some readers because of their closeness and similarity to lived experience. In fact, research has shown that personal narratives of climate change, which we can expect to belong to the realist mode, do leave a deeper impression on a wide range of readers.[68]

As climate change becomes the lived reality of large populations, it is necessary to dig a little deeper into the realist mode of climate storytelling. Literary critic and professor of English at Duke University, Caren Irr, in her encyclopaedia entry on climate fiction in English, mentions the works of Amitav Ghosh (*The Hungry Tide*), Barbara Kingsolver (*Flight Behavior*) and T. C. Boyle (*San Miguel, When the Killing's Done*) as belonging to this realist stable.[69] However, she points out, these authors hybridize realist conventions with the use of myths, catachronisms and an apocalyptic sensibility among other strategies to tell the story of climate change.[70] This applies to a certain extent for Ghosh's more clearly cli-fi work *Gun Island*, the book we are going to study, which employs strong real-world correlates alongside myths and intrusions of the uncanny. In her reading, Irr focuses on two distinct tendencies of cli-fi, namely, those satirizing the conventions of the cli-fi novel and those which are realist hybrids. Taking up examples like Ian McEwan's *Solar*, Nathaniel Rich's *Odds Against Tomorrow*, Margaret Atwood's works, among others, she discusses how these works have 'disrupted the presumed heroism of the white male scientist' and, in the case of movies like *Snowpiercer*, have introduced non-white protagonists.

Still on realist depictions, the scientific realism of a climate novel like Ian McEwan's *Solar* has been critiqued by Trexler, who is of the view that this prevents the text from gathering agency and thus getting involved in the task of meaningful engagement. 'Through Michael Beard,' Trexler writes, 'a selfish, Nobel Prize-winning physicist, *Solar* suggests that the selfishness of human character, dictated by evolution, makes it extraordinarily unlikely that individual action or voluntary, collective movements will allow us to address climate change'.[71] In the concluding part of his book, Trexler indicates a lack of faith in realism as a form, as it 'is unlikely to imagine novel political affiliations because of its commitment to a desultory status quo', and instead puts his bet on the role of speculative future fictions in depicting the politics of climate change as this allows for 'inventing new ways of connecting diverse human beings'.[72] We will, however, argue that Trexler's assertion does not rule out the political agency of realist hybrids, like *Gun Island* or the social realism of Anita Agnihotri's *The Sickle*, whose departures from the realist mode through their examination of nature-culture entanglements, non-human agency and fictional representations of real political activism still provide room for hopeful imagination of novel political affiliations.

The next organizing principle is based on climate fiction's possible status as science fiction. Those supporting this argue that cli-fi, like sci-fi, employs what the theorist of science fiction Darko Suvin called a 'novum', which is a kind of novelty or newness that separates the reader's world from the world of the story. The novum of science fiction contributes to 'cognitive estrangement' – something which challenges our cognition.[73] Time travel, for example, is a novum of sci-fi which jars our understanding. In the case of cli-fi, it has been argued that the novum in these stories is embodied in climate change and the associated transformations resulting from its impact.[74] In this context, cli-fi writer Kim Stanley Robinson's assertion that 'We're in a science fiction novel now, which we are all co-writing together'[75] is also worth noting.

Another related argument in support of science fiction's representational apparatus stretching into the realm of climate change focuses on the speculative abilities of science fiction to depict climate-changed futures. Craps and Crownshaw, in their introduction to the climate fiction essays mentioned earlier, quoting Mark McGurl,[76] point out how

> seminal recent work has valorised the popular genres of science fiction and horror, and, by extension, weird and speculative fiction, by taking seriously the 'ludicrousness' of their 'posthuman comedy': their abilities to represent 'the inhumanly large and long'; that is, the vast scales of time and space commensurate with the planetary processes of climate change. Crossing the 'threshold' of habitual humanist literary purviews to dwell in those times and spaces, such genre fiction also imagines other species, the potential demise of our own, and the collapse of the idea that we are exceptional, and so projects an ecological vision of the consequences of climate change.[77]

Caren Irr, however, notices a difference in the ways sci-fi and cli-fi handle starting points and the dynamics of time in their respective narratives. Irr argues 'science fiction proper has often been concerned with either extrapolating technological development from existing social conditions or providing alternate histories that reimagine the supposed inevitability of the present', while climate fiction, especially of the prevalent post-apocalyptic near future type, 'often assume that the turning point for change occurred before our own historical moment'.[78]

The inclusion of all climate fiction within the house of sci-fi is also contested by the fact that we find tales of real-world, present-day happenings and social and scientific realism in the library of cli-fi. As the effects of global warming are increasingly visible and some writers have been drawing on these lived realities and real-world happenings, it is difficult to position climate fiction within the house of sci-fi, which needs a 'novum' or newness that is usually based on extrapolating or reimagining present-day technologies.

What climate change is actually doing is, it is bringing under stress our critical categories and genre conventions. One way to address this is to consider cli-fi as a kind of speculative writing which asks the what-if question (what if things got worse?), but this would still not include all kinds of stories in the genre. Better still would be to consider cli-fi not as sci-fi but as a supergenre covering all kinds of stories and not a sub-type of sci-fi at all. The above is supported, among others, by Andersen's imaginaries discussed earlier, which, however, has a speculative element to it, as well as the work of critics like Schneider-Mayerson, who, in his study of the influence of climate fiction, has found that these stories belong to all kinds of genres and could be labelled 'trans-generic'.[79]

Another simple way to categorize cli-fi would be to divide these stories between dystopian (or apocalyptic[80]) and utopian depictions. Acknowledging the fact that such a division may leave out certain kinds of stories, let us explore these two categories a little deeper.

It is difficult for many creative writers to ignore the allure of the apocalypse. Dystopia is attractive because of the possibilities of drama and also because readers like to get scared from a distance. Successful dystopian works spawn numerous inspired followers, as Michael Svoboda has shown in his study of ice-fi–cli-fi movies that imagine an ice-age-type dystopia.[81] So definitely dystopia is a legitimate sub-category of cli-fi besides having many takers, which will be evident from their numbers, compared to literary fiction, on a Goodreads list.

A few more words about dystopian depictions are in order. Researchers have found that dystopian tales, and specifically those incorporating catastrophe, lead to 'feelings of futility and low self-efficacy' and are less effective in motivating 'proenvironmental intentions'.[82] These stories, by portraying fearful scenarios, can reinforce helplessness in the face of climate emergency, leading to despair and inaction.[83] Still, despair as an emotion is not necessarily negative. For example, Jem Bendell, best known for his views about societal collapse and 'deep adaptation', had declared he is fighting against the 'tyranny of positivity' in environmentalism, pointing out that 'the range of ancient wisdom traditions see a significant place for hopelessness and despair. Contemporary reflections on people's emotional and even spiritual growth as a result of their hopelessness and despair align with these ancient ideas.'[84] Here he seems to be arguing that fear and despair can lead to positive outcomes.

In fact, the life of Gautam Buddha, especially the Four Sights that led him to leave home and seek out the roots of suffering, is an exemplar of the path from darkness to spiritual growth. We remember those four sights were those of an old man, a diseased man, a dead man and finally an ascetic. The first three sights were troubling, while the last had the germ of possibility. These sights instilled within him the motivation to seek the end of suffering (a daunting task, no doubt), and finally, after long meditations, he founded a world religion which charts a path out of the clutches of desire. Buddha's example shows us how suffering, darkness and despair, if rightly processed, can cleanse the mind and spur positive action. But how many of us have the strength and discipline required to reap the fruits of hope and action from the seeds of climate despair?

In this context, the non-fiction genre of ecological grief or climate grief, though different from cli-fi dystopias, represents a beacon of hope. These works, bearing witness to a familiar world slowly unravelling and becoming unrecognizable, stand on the logic that grief and darkness can lead to spiritual growth, resilience and action. Cli-fi author Liz Jensen's recent work, *Your Wild and Precious Life: On Grief, Hope and Rebellion* which followed the tragic and untimely death of her son at the age of twenty-five, stands out as a testament of hope where personal loss and grief is placed alongside planetary transformations caused by climate change, finally leading to the possibility of finding meaning from tragedy and loss.

Another argument that helps to dilute the criticism laid at the door of the dystopian sub-category can be noted in Schneider-Mayerson,[85] who has used theories of social psychology to show that dystopian or not, climate fiction, by diminishing the psychological distance of climate change scenarios, leads to low-level construals – which are detailed and specific – of the future which in turn can move people to action. Critics have also argued that people are able to filter the fear element of dystopia as speculation and will still act if there is a strong message. Sophia David makes this point, quoting Keira Hambrick, who 'suggests that readers have genre expectations and are more resilient to the apocalyptic depictions in climate fiction, since they decouple genre and reality. She (Hambrick) writes, "the speculative nature of apocalypticism becomes clearer in fictional texts, and readers may be less likely to feel immobilised by fear and eco-anxiety, and may respond favourably to the call-for-action"'.[86]

However, a problem with apocalyptic depictions and dystopia in triggering climate action is that they still, at least in the maximalist representations, remain far from reality. People enjoy getting scared from a distance without being involved. But, with the increasing frequency of climate disasters and the recent experience of the coronavirus pandemic, the comfort of distance that literary depictions of dystopia can provide may be eroding.

There are other critics of dystopia and apocalypse in fiction. Historian Barnita Bagchi has pointed out the absence of the apocalyptic vision in South Asian writing in her discussion of the works of Rokeya Sakhawat Hossain, Amitav Ghosh and Vandana Singh, linking this to the decolonization of the mind. Bagchi uncovers the existence of different critical temporalities in their works instead of a straightforward Western temporality involving the end of times and the apocalypse.[87] Amitav Ghosh has also critiqued dystopian depictions, saying they are a kind of fantasy, lamenting the fact that there is not a single novel about Hurricane Sandy, while there are so many about the future destruction of New York.[88]

Moving on to our sub-category of utopian climate fiction, we have to acknowledge that utopia or even hopeful imaginaries are subjective and notoriously difficult to define. Still, hope,[89] whether utopian or grounded in current realities, informs many works of climate fiction, and the visibility of such works seems to be increasing. Critics like Caren Irr, noticing an undercurrent of hope driving climate stories, have argued that these creative efforts 'unite around an expectation that humanity and the planet can survive the changes associated with the Anthropocene'.[90] Further supporting the hopeful turn of cli-fi, studies have counted the benefits of hopeful 'utopian' stories and how these can influence action.[91]

While humanity will always be split between the feelings of a savage John and the confidence of a Mustapha Mond,[92] there is a growing interest in cli-fi which imagines hopeful futures grounded in the present, which also embrace the messy realities of the world by, what Donna Haraway calls, 'staying with the trouble'.[93] Having had the opportunity to work on two international volumes of solarpunk fiction, one can say with some confidence that there is a rising readership and creative engagement with these hopeful stories which talk of multispecies justice, ingenuity, mutuality, kinship, the use of renewables and decentralized action for a more equitable and sustainable future.

It is indeed heartening to see more such utopian books being published every year, and that the solarpunk movement has been enjoying increasing visibility. Starting with international volumes, we now increasingly hear about local solarpunk publishing initiatives and growing research interest in the subject. As we watch these developments, Frederic Jameson's words about this capacity of utopian texts to generate new ones, which are improvements of the old, ring in our minds. 'Indeed, in the case of the Utopian texts,' Jameson wrote, 'the most reliable political test lies not in any judgement on the individual work in question so much as in its capacity to generate new ones, Utopian visions that include those of the past, and modify or correct them'.[94]

Beyond our simple binary of dystopian and utopian depictions, it is also possible to imagine 'critical dystopias' in climate fiction where a dystopian world has a utopian core[95] or locus which provides the possibility for emergence and radical change, serving thereby as a critique of the dystopian storyworld.[96] In my climate novel, *The Butterfly Effect*, which is generally dystopian, I imagined a secret utopian enclave hidden away in a valley of a South Korean mountain, held together by magic and spiritual powers, which welcomes the misfits of the surrounding high-consumption society. Such critical dystopias also clear the space for postcolonialist, ecofeminist and poststructuralist critiques of the simplistic idea of a singular technology-driven arrow of progress, where reason reigns supreme, nature-culture entanglements are disregarded and destruction of the environment is almost guaranteed.

Our final categorization of cli-fi follows Barber and others who divide climate fiction on the basis of narratives of adaptation or mitigation.[97] Narratives of adaptation constitute a large number of cli-fi works where people are affected by and adapt to climate change. A wide range of works can be accommodated within the adaptation umbrella, while narratives of mitigation tend to be fewer. Mitigative narratives would demonstrate humans directly intervening to reduce emissions, for example through a carbon tax, or by reducing the effects of warming through geoengineering efforts.

Here, *Snowpiercer* presents an interesting example. The movie begins as a mitigation narrative where nations come together to geo-engineer the climate by spraying an experimental cooling agent into the atmosphere using jet aircraft. However, this scheme horribly backfires; the whole planet goes into a deep freeze, and only a trainload of people survive. Thereon, it becomes a narrative of adaptation.

This completes our critical survey of the various organizing principles of the literature of climate change and what these categories mean. We end this chapter noting critical engagement with the evolution of the genre. In the next chapter, we take up the second component of our three-pronged approach to cli-fi which covers creative-thematic challenges and allied distinctiveness of climate fiction. There, we also discuss and develop the three major lenses for analysis of texts in part two of the book.

## An evolving genre

Looking ahead, critics like Schneider-Mayerson, Caren Irr and Jeffrey Barber, among many others, have commented about trends and possible or desired developments in the literature of climate change. Politically engaged commentators have often argued for the creation of critical dystopian writings and those that suggest clear solutions. Going a step further, Barber, in his work as a sustainability activist, has advocated for works that constitute real-life examples of change and has been working on a mechanism for a dialogue between activists and fiction writers.

At the end of the first decade of this century, Schneider-Mayerson noted two distinct thematic trends emerging in cli-fi.[98] One he called 'the imagination of and transition to life after oil' and the other 'climate injustice'. By now, there are already many novels written in those lines. Paolo Bacigalupi's *The Windup Girl* and Emmi Itäranta's *Memory of Water* being examples of the first type, while Anita Agnihotri's *The Sickle* is an example of the latter.

Meanwhile, Caren Irr, in her essay quoted earlier, noticed the movement away from 'science fiction hypermasculinity towards a more speculative multi-gender universe'.[99] There she also commented on satires of cli-fi which break well-established conventions, establishing the genre's arrival 'as a bona fide phenomenon'. Acknowledging a demand from critics for more experimentation in cli-fi, Irr also notes the centrality of the 'apocalyptic mood' and goes on to suggest that the strength of apocalyptic conventions may be the final determinant of the fortunes of cli-fi, whether they be in the realist, satirical or dystopian traditions.

In contrast, LeMenager has tended to focus on issues of 'slow-violence' and the quotidian experience of living through climate change and its attendant disruptions. Realist representations of climate change, as we find in Amitav Ghosh's *Gun Island*, being a good example of this. Speaking of fiction, LeMenager suggests, 'The everyday Anthropocene offers a setting or space-time for bioderegulation[100] and slow violence', saying this offers a corrective to the epochal discourse, 'which capitalises on the charisma of crisis … Epochs are not attentive to the wearing away of bodies, their slow depletion'.[101]

The focus on slow violence which, following Rob Nixon, acknowledges the continuing and almost invisible violence on the less privileged through effects of toxic waste, climate change, pollution and other 'toxic' realities of industrialized progress and neocolonialism, affords an entry point for literature to represent the postcolonial experience of climate change. By turning away from epochal discourse or apocalyptic imaginaries, it also clears the space for Indigenous peoples' narratives and narratives where one 'stays with the trouble' in novel configurations and kinships of humans and non-humans.

History is witness to the fact that Indigenous peoples' experiences of imperialist, colonial and now neocolonial violence, resource extraction and environmental degradation are of a much larger scale than the experience of non-Indigenous populations. This complicates the idea of dystopian and apocalyptic representations for them because what they have experienced and continue to experience is no different from the dystopias of fiction.

Indigenous philosopher and climate justice scholar, Kyle P Whyte stresses on this point, arguing that 'some Indigenous perspectives on climate change can situate the present time as already dystopian.'[102] Critiquing the literature of climate change written by non-Indigenous peoples, Whyte points out how Indigenous people are placed in historical categories therein, where allies appear as saviours protecting them from climate effects and colonial violence. This, he argues, is born of a denial about how the ancestors of these allies would have fantasized about the present, which prevents them from 'building coalitions with Indigenous peoples.'[103]

Indigenous peoples' perspectives continue to contribute valuable critical, research and fictional material in the fields of climate change, ecology, environmentalism and broadly in the ways we relate to the natural world and among each other. Alexis Wright's climate novel *The Swan Book* weaves myths, Indigenous peoples' values and powerful imagery to tell a dystopian tale with an Indigenous Australian girl at its centre. Another Indigenous author, Robin Wall

Kimmerer's non-fiction, *Braiding Sweetgrass*, connects the values of Indigenous wisdom with Western scientific knowledge to present promising insights and possibilities of our relationship with the earth. Closer home, Indigenous Adivasi author Hansda Sowvendra Sekhar's fictional world, in novels like *The Mysterious Ailment of Rupi Baskey*, or his young adult *Jwala Kumar and the Gift of Fire*, not only demonstrates how the culture of his ethnic Santhali people is 'deeply imbued with nature'[104] but also engages ideas of kinship, mutuality and respect for other beings.

The potential of weaving Indigenous futures, pasts and presents into stories, the focus on the quotidian lived experience and slow violence of climate change and the possibilities of acknowledging and building kinship with non-human beings are among the new and promising creative possibilities of cli-fi which demonstrate the evolution of the genre as the locus of literature's ongoing encounter with the climate crisis. It is important to note in this context that environmental justice, or for our purpose, climate justice, and its associated politics can be a useful lens to capture and analyse these new themes and issues in the evolution of climate stories.

These new directions of cli-fi not only call for continuously sharpening our critical apparatus for organizing and analysing this literature, but also warrant deeper studies of new works. Two of the novels we study later on in this book will allow us such an engagement.

3

# Michelangelo, mustard and Mother Earth

## *Recipes for climate stories*

Still in my ragged sneakers, I had returned from Sweden and carried on with my chastising, preaching and sharing for the environment, gathering friends and enemies in equal numbers. During this time, we founded a small environment group which used to publish a journal on sustainable development that was quite well received. Having cut down on conferencing and international travel, those years also allowed me to devote more time to my fiction writing and reading of new stories.

Those years, I was taking trains to small towns in Bengal, Odisha or Rajasthan, talking with farmers about environmental impacts and livelihoods, questioning industry representatives in Delhi or Mumbai about compliance with laws, getting to know what others are doing while implementing small projects. But I had also begun to publish and write more regularly around this time, and over the years, my first climate novel had begun to take shape. While the book was well-received and I basked for some time in critical acclaim, partly because of this, and maybe also because of my articles appearing in the media, a new issue cropped up, which I was not sure how to handle.

Friends involved in party politics, considering me a fellow traveller, had begun asking me to participate and write for their publications. I remember sitting through a meeting or two in the dimly lit conference room of a political party and sharing tea from clay cups as we discussed the slow dance of our great democracy. But party politics was never my thing, and so I went back to my books and environmental activism, inventing stories to ward off the possibility of contributing to political pamphlets.

Still, having taken up writing climate fiction, which I believe is primarily a literature of commitment, I could really not avoid the politics. It continued to creep up into my stories as I struggled to keep track of the plot, besides honouring the aesthetic impulse. This struggle between the aesthetic and political, not to miss the science, is a shared experience of many climate fiction writers, whatever sub-genre they may be writing in. To get a better idea of their dynamics within the novel, we have to dwell for a while on the history of the debates surrounding their purpose in fiction. This is also necessary because the political and the aesthetic, and their inherent tension,[1] constitute two important creative-thematic features (Figure 2.2) to be used as strategies for our readings of climate novels. To focus upon this tension, we can begin by directing our attention to the work of the nineteenth-century French poet and novelist, Théophile Gautier.

'The most useful part of the house is the privy',[2] Gautier wrote in the preface to his novel *Mademoiselle de Maupin* (Figure 3.1), the sexually daring story of an unconventional woman which was partly inspired by the life of French opera singer Julie d'Aubigny. Gautier was arguing how need and usefulness are divorced from beauty. 'What is the use of music? or painting?' He goes on to ask, 'Who would be foolish enough to prefer Mozart to Monsieur Carrel, Michelangelo to the inventor of white mustard?' finally delivering that famous line which was eventually turned into a war cry for the art for art's sake movement, 'Nothing is really beautiful but that which cannot be made use of; everything that is useful is ugly.'

As we go on to discuss the creative-thematic challenges and distinctive features of cli-fi, we can in no way ignore this contentious issue that informs, among others, the literature of climate change. This is the tension between beauty and usefulness, or to look back

**Figure 3.1** Mademoiselle Maupin de l'Opéra, *c.*1700. Used with permission from Bibliothèque nationale de France.

at another illustration from Gautier, between the church and the windmill. Obviously, it would not have been possible for the poet to foresee the increasingly important role that wind energy will be playing in a scorching planet suffering the consequences of the carbonophilia of a species possessed by the idea of a planet-denuding progress.

## Aesthetics, politics and the *littérature engagée*

Carbonophilia and planet-denuding progress bring us back to the realm of climate stories and the inherent tension between beauty and benefit (realized through political agency of the text) or the aesthetic and the political within the narrative. By political, we broadly mean the sphere of human action for justice (including, in certain contexts, multispecies justice), equality, resistance and change. So the story of the flag-bearing climate activist fighting against deforestation will be as much a representative of the political in a climate novel as will be one where the quest for climate justice and equity are the driving themes of the narrative.

Near the beginning of his seminal work on literary theory, Terry Eagleton, noticing the disinterest in the political among the Romantics, comments, 'such a detachment from history reflected the Romantic writer's actual situation'.[3] The Romantics are worshippers of beauty, and aesthetics which provides a framework for understanding beauty, is evidently a more contested concept. Aesthetics draws on several philosophies, ideas and movements, including German idealism,[4] Romanticism (and the concept of 'sublime'[5]) and the work of the Romantic poets, and the ideas of Russian formalists, including its echoes in New Criticism. It also stands on the concepts of symbol, harmony and form, while focusing on literary devices, language and emotions. If we read Gautier's uselessness of beauty with these ideas, then the works of literature which are aesthetically pleasing and therefore beautiful would consequently be politically useless.

However, this 'useless' beauty also came to be associated with high art and the aesthetic experience. In the case of literature, 'literary works' or literary fiction bear the crown of high art, granting it an aura of exclusivity not granted to 'genre fiction'. Genre fiction, on the other hand, has attracted the charge of being too focused on the story and sensational plots and in general was found to lack in several departments, including depth of characterization, style, use of symbols, imagery, language and formal experiments.

This separation between genre and thè literary is partly predicated, at least in common usage, on the aesthetic experience conveyed through the elements mentioned above. The separation is also explained in the context of the separation between Nature and Culture (human) and the consequent purification project of modernity, wherein certain 'hybrid genres', dealing with both the human sphere of culture and the sphere of science that is nature and natural laws, were consigned to the outhouses of serious fiction.[6]

The Nature Culture divide (another creative-thematic feature which we shall discuss in a later section) and the chasm that it opens between 'serious' fiction and cli-fi is significant in our case because climate fiction, just like science fiction, happens to be a hybrid genre engaging both the sphere of the natural and the human. Thus being 'impure', it is pushed to the ghettos of genre and is considered lesser than literary novels which live in the mansion of serious fiction. So climate novels, being genre fiction, are not only impure and inferior, but they also, by the fact of this association with the less-serious genre fiction, are compromised in their ability to convey the aesthetic experience and thus be considered literary art (Figure 3.2). We will examine this charge in our reading of *Memory of Water*.

Science fiction has also had to face a similar treatment, but there have been conscious efforts from within the genre to engage with these charges, while not deviating from their thematic focus, and write differently. The New Wave movement in science fiction which began in the sixties, experimented with literary techniques and language use and absorbed modernist influences, bringing it, if one may say so, closer to literary fiction. It will be our effort to demonstrate later that climate novels are also beginning to chart this

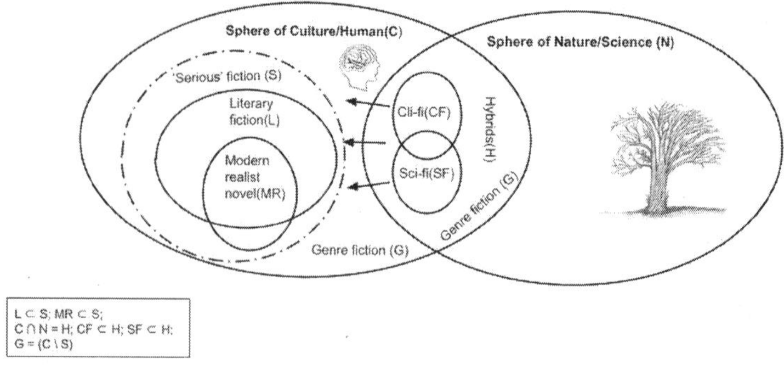


**Figure 3.2** Climate fiction, literary genres and the aesthetic impulse.

course of experimentation (Figure 3.2), followed by science fiction, which blurs the aesthetic boundaries through the use of language, literary techniques, character development and other features of literary fiction.

Later, during our analytical reading of *Memory of Water*, we shall elucidate and specifically employ the concept of 'literariness' (besides a few characteristics of literary fiction) borrowed from formalist critics as a touchstone of 'the aesthetic experience' derived from a climate text. 'Aesthetics', or the aesthetic experience, one of the creative features of cli-fi, will be one of the three major lenses we shall employ to study a climate novel.

Now, if we also subscribe to the view that one of the responsibilities of cli-fi is political, that climate fiction is a *littérature engagée*,[7] that these books should be useful in changing thoughts, beliefs, ideas and influencing action and change, then the question arises – is it possible to communicate political messages without sacrificing aesthetic value? As the reader will note, this is a question equally applicable to other 'genres' of the novel.

Sophia David extensively addresses this question by contrasting the views of Marxist philosopher György Lukacs with those of social theorist and leading member of the Frankfurt school, Theodor Adorno.[8] Lukacs, she points out, gives importance to art as a driver of political resistance, but he holds that politics can be emitted from the work not because the author desired but because of the work's 'subtle mirroring of society'.[9] Adorno, on the other hand, was of the view that art born of political intention 'fails as an artwork'. This would imply that climate fiction, if it stresses on political engagement, will fail aesthetically. If we look back at Admussen's 'Six Proposals', clearly his stress is on such politically engaged climate fiction. Then the challenge, for a literary-minded author, is to write a book, which, while retaining aesthetic value, also demonstrates political commitment.

Joining related debates about politically engaged literature and independent artistic merit, Kerridge writes about schools of radical literary criticism and their rejection of the Arnoldian and Leavisite traditions,[10] which focused on high culture and independent literary value. Still, he notes a persisting tension in these radical schools between two kinds of quality of the text – the relative, which they emphasize, and the general. The relative is geared towards political agency as it determines how the text stands up relative to the challenges of the present moment, while the general quality approximates what we have called the aesthetic; it asks the question 'how well' a text is doing what needs to be done. According to Kerridge, 'Neither [question] can be relinquished, yet neither is sufficient to determine literary quality. The second question may be answered in aesthetic terms, by a criticism that looks for inspired artistic control of literary form, while the first must be answered in ethical and political terms.'[11] In our focus on the formalist concept of 'literariness' as a marker of aesthetics, we will be trying to capture such an 'inspired artistic control' that Kerridge alludes to.[12] Alongside this, we will also probe what, according to Kerridge, is the 'relative' quality of a climate text using a lens of politics framed through justice.

Axel Goodbody, who teaches at the University of Bath, in his study of cultural and aesthetic alternatives in climate fiction, has addressed the transformations of the climate novel from the thriller model to one where 'use of poetic language, symbols, myths, settings and cultural traditions'[13] are significant. In his study of four works, two of which (*Memory of Water* and *Gun Island*) we also discuss in this book, he has found such aesthetic approaches enabling an 'awareness of nature's agency and attentiveness to the environment'. Goodbody's findings provide us with further justification to employ a lens of aesthetics, sharpened with the tools of formalist critics, in our reading of climate novels.

The tug-of-war between the aesthetic and the political and their workings and impact on the text has indeed been a long-fought one. Recognizing the importance of these creative-thematic features and the possible roles they can play in influencing minds about the urgency of the crisis while delivering reader satisfaction, we use aesthetics and politics as two of the three major lenses to study climate novels. To avoid any confusion, we have to make a clear distinction here between our three-pronged approach to understanding cli-fi (Figures 2.2 and 2.3) discussed earlier and the triad of major lenses (Figure 3.4) which are developed from the second (creative-thematic challenges) of the three prongs aimed to engage climate fiction. Just as the lens of aesthetics will be sharpened using the formalist concept of literariness, the lens of politics will embody ideas of climate justice. For two of the novels, postcolonial concerns, which are closely enmeshed with climate justice issues, will also be addressed.

In the course of discussing the first of many creative-thematic challenges (Figure 2.2) of writing climate fiction, which arises from the tension between aesthetics and politics, or in Gautier's words, between Michelangelo and mustard, we have now introduced two major lenses for our subsequent analysis. These will be sharpened and developed further in part two of this book before the analytical readings. In the next section, we introduce 'planetarity', another creative-thematic challenge, which will yield the third and final major lens for our purpose. The section that follows it will address the remaining creative-thematic challenges, namely Nature-Culture entanglements, Derangements of Scale, Non-human agency, the

Uncanny and depictions of collectives in climate fiction. These will constitute the minor lenses for our reading of the novels.

## Planetary networks of climate crisis

A little Mexican girl, Josefina, arrives with her family in Feathertown, Tennessee, where she meets Dellarobia, a housewife who is curious about their arrival. Earlier, Dellarobia's community had unexpected visitors in the form of thousands of monarch butterflies who had been roosting in the valley below their little Appalachian town:

> 'If you don't mind my asking, why didn't you stay there?' Dellarobia asked.
>
> 'No more. It's gone.'
>
> Dellarobia leaned forward, hands pressed between her knees, strangely dreading what might come next. Miracle or not, this thing on the mountain was a gift. To herself in particular, she'd dared to imagine. Not once had she considered it might have been stolen from someone else.
>
> 'Do you mean the butterflies stopped coming?' she asked. 'Or just the tourists stopped coming?'
>
> 'Everything is gone!' the girl cried, in obvious distress.
>
> 'The water was coming and the mud was coming on everything … *Un diluvio*'. … Josefina nodded soberly, her body shrinking into the sofa. '*Corrimiento de tierras.*' The mother lifted the girl onto her lap, folding both arms around her protectively.[14]

We will return to Josefina's story shortly, but first a little background about planetary networks is in order. Anthropogenic climate change is a widely dispersed phenomenon unfolding over large time scales and across geographies, affecting the human and non-human world alike in myriad ways. However, all these disparate phenomena and their effects are driven by the heat-trapping greenhouse gas emissions from production and consumption activities of humans. There are of course other factors and interactions relating to earth systems, which work together in complex systemic combinations and networks with the heat-trapping effect of emissions, via positive and negative feedback loops, and across looming tipping points to present the totality of climate change phenomena and its impacts on all beings.

The five 'earth systems' are the geosphere, biosphere, cryosphere, hydrosphere and atmosphere. These systems continuously interact with each other, giving rise to climate and weather phenomena. Climate change, arising from anthropogenic emissions, interacts with and affects these earth systems, and its manifestations and effects are also thereby impacted. For example, the Atlantic Meridional Overturning Circulation (AMOC), which is like a giant conveyor belt across the ocean that transports warm water northwards near the surface and brings back colder water south, is a major circulation system operating within the hydrosphere, which is getting affected by climate change (warmer oceans and melting ice).

The AMOC has a significant impact on the weather of landmasses bordering the Atlantic. If climate-related effects result in a serious weakening or collapse of the AMOC, this will be a tipping point leading to extreme impact on weather on the European continent and elsewhere. In fact, Kim Stanley Robinson's climate novel *Fifty Degrees Below*, part of his *Science in the Capital* trilogy, envisages such a possibility. The solid scientific work around planetary boundaries[15] which has focused on a safe operating space for humanity across a number of earth-system processes, also highlights these interconnections between human action and planet-wide effects like climate change, ocean acidification, freshwater change and changes in biosphere integrity, among some others.

Obviously climate change is planetary, although the variety of its impacts is experienced by individuals at a more local scale. The displacements that were partly responsible for triggering the recent conflicts in Syria have been implicated by some scholars[16] to water scarcities and droughts which in turn had a climate connection. Similarly, the melting of polar ice caps because of climate change is leading to rising sea levels and disappearance of small islands in the Bay of Bengal and elsewhere, weakening the AMOC, disrupting weather patterns in Europe and affecting fisheries, habitats and associated livelihoods worldwide among a vast network of effects flowing from climate change. A literary work grounded in scientific facts and socio-economic and environmental realities, while engaging climate change, can do well to address such connections and networks of effects and the associated risks across extended geographies, thereby demonstrating a 'sense of planet' as Ursula Heise[17] describes it in her groundbreaking work.

In Barbara Kingsolver's *Flight Behaviour*, which we quoted at the beginning of this section, the monarch butterflies change their migration patterns and appear in Feathertown because of climate effects. This not only disrupts the livelihood of Josefina's father in Mexico, who used to take tourists to see the roosting monarchs, their community is further affected by the *corrimiento de tierras* or landslides, which uproots them, turning them into migrants while also stopping the arrival of the monarchs. The landslides[18] are also an effect of climate change which makes these people homeless, besides affecting their livelihoods, finally bringing Josefina's family to the United States. The plot of this novel demonstrates the planetary scale of climate change with which economies, cultures and livelihoods are closely intertwined through networks of dependency and interconnection.

Heise, arguing for the importance of this sense of planet, in contrast to the emphasis on the 'local' in North American environmentalism, directed our attention to the global nature of political, economic, ecological, social, cultural and technological connections and networks and how these should influence environmentalist thinking by shifting cultural imagination away from the territorial to a more planetary and systemic perspective. Climate change and its associated risks, in the nature of a massively distributed hyperobject,[19] are evidently a globe-spanning planetary network operating through a vast number of interactions and connections with the human and non-human spheres, the effects of which are experienced and addressed at the level of the human and other beings.

In Amitav Ghosh's *Gun Island*, we shall see how 'planetariness' is addressed in the story through its handling of different time periods and, more importantly, distant geographies with the intertwined human stories and experience of climate disasters. Again in *Flight Behaviour*, where place is initially focused upon in the manner of a modern realist narrative, the connections of one place with another, between Feathertown, Tennessee and little Josefina's Mexican hometown, are gradually foregrounded through climate impacts on humans and non-humans, and become central to the plot. This telescoping from the particularities of place to the wider planetary depictions of impacts and effects on humans and non-humans through complex connections and networks of effects allows certain climate imaginaries of fiction to better depict the global reach of climate change and the interconnected human and non-human worlds with which it is entangled. The modern realist novel, with its fixation on 'place', is at a disadvantage while representing these planetary connections, thus making such place-based narratives less suitable for certain forms of climate storytelling.

Heise was among the first to point out the significance of this planetary sense or planetarity in the environmental imagination. This shift in the imagination is not only supported by science, as we noted earlier, but also validated by the growing global networks and interconnections facilitated by globalization, technological development, geopolitics and other factors. As we observe the unfolding climate crisis in its varied manifestations across vast geographies and among distant societies, we increasingly realize the value of this planetary sense and systemic perspective in literary representation. This then leads us to the third major lens of planetarity, which centres the planet, or in St Francis' memorable words, 'our Sister Mother earth',[20] in the reading and writing of climate stories. We will be employing this lens in examining Amitav Ghosh's *Gun Island*. We will further dwell on Heise's work as we refine this lens of planetarity before our reading of Ghosh's novel. In the section that follows we discuss the remaining creative-thematic challenges (Figure 2.2) and allied distinctiveness of climate novels. All of those will be used as minor lenses to examine the three climate stories we have chosen for this book.

## Creative-thematic challenges of representation

While writing my first climate novel, *The Butterfly Effect*, I had to negotiate a set of challenges that I hadn't encountered till then in my career as a fiction writer. This was going to be my fourth work of fiction, but because of the themes I had chosen, I was, at least in the early days of planning, completely at sea.

I had been trying to tell a near-future story where climate effects had aggravated to an extent where social order is breaking down, and humanity is staring at imminent collapse. Although it was possible to quickly take my narrative from the present to such an apocalyptic setting, being fed on a balanced diet of modern realist fiction, I didn't have the stomach to experiment with the time leaps that this narrative journey would entail. Therefore, as a workaround, I decided to use a science-fiction plot[21] about genetic engineering experiments going wrong as the engine to speed up the narrative while weaving the climate effects on that scaffold. For this, I needed a scientist, and he became one of the important characters of the story.

The writing of climate fiction, as we have been noting all through, is fraught with many such challenges. This is because this genre of writing has to tread the less trodden route of representing nature-culture entanglements, often on a planetary scale, while also attempting to capture the psychological, real, cultural, political and socio-economic impacts of climate change over long time periods. As I was speeding up the narrative of my novel, I had not only taken the help of a fast-evolving sci-fi novum but also had to be sensitive to the attendant considerations of representing nature-culture entanglements, the agency of non-humans, and if possible, the role of collectives in the story as well as representation of the uncanny.[22]

In general, the problems encountered by literature in its engagement with climate change are manifold, but much of it arises from the intransigence of the material presented by the climate crisis, where human action intersects and interacts with natural processes. Anthropogenic global warming, climate change and its manifestations are spread out over vast geographies, unfold over extended time spans, affect collectives of people, involve nature-culture, the agency of non-humans and are often manifest as improbable events which evoke the uncanny.

The contemporary novel, as Amitav Ghosh[23] discusses, is ill-suited to handle much of this. According to him, the modern 'realist' novel focuses on 'place' (while concealing continuities and connections between places) and 'period'; it narrows down and directs its narrative energies to the level of the individual (and not collectives) and their 'moral adventure' and ensures that narrative leaps and improbabilities are concealed with intrusions of the everyday and the ordinary, or what literary historian Franco Moretti calls 'fillers'. These fillers, according to Moretti, paralleled the easy-flowing certainties of bourgeoisie life.

About the bourgeoisie and their stamp on the novel, Moretti had this to say:

> regularity, not disequilibrium, was the great narrative invention of bourgeois Europe. All that was solid, became more so … whereas the aristocracy had shamelessly idealized itself in a whole gallery of intrepid knights, the bourgeoisie produced no such myth of itself. The great mechanism of adventure was being eroded by bourgeois civilization and without adventure, characters lost the stamp of uniqueness that comes from the encounter with the unknown.[24]

This encounter with the unknown and the improbable is once again at the forefront of representational goals as literature confronts the unprecedented changes brought about by a warming planet. To do this, many works of climate fiction, among other strategies, have been rediscovering 'the great mechanism of adventure' that stories from an earlier time possessed and had consequently lost in their engagement with bourgeoisie civilization.

Let us begin our exploration of creative-thematic challenges of representation by examining nature-culture entanglements and their artificial separation. The history of this idea goes back far, but one of the inflexion points in its career came in the last century in the form of a well-known article by the British novelist and scientist C. P. Snow, which appeared in the *New Statesman* on 6 October 1956. There Snow wrote:

> Not to have read *War and Peace* and *La Cousine Bette* and *La Chartreuse de Parme* is not to be educated; but so is not to have a glimmer of the Second Law of Thermodynamics. Yet that case ought not to be pressed too far. It is more justifiable to say that those without any scientific understanding miss a whole body of experience: they are rather like the tone deaf, from whom all musical experience is cut off and who have to get on without it.[25]

The argument is crystal clear. There indeed exists a yawning gulf between the literary arts and the natural world of science. Snow further developed these ideas in his 'The Two Cultures and the Scientific Revolution' lecture delivered at Cambridge the following year, where he delved deeper into this division between the sciences and the humanities and the resultant impact on society. But the roots of this estrangement, which climate change has brought back into public discourse, stretch further back in time.

The history of the division between the sciences (and nature) and the human sphere of culture and politics is long and can be traced as far back as classical antiquity. Two important figures, who had between them solidified this separation, appear on the scene of the European Enlightenment in the figures of Thomas Hobbes and Robert Boyle. Boyle, who is best remembered as the founder of modern chemistry and for his eponymous law of gases, was focused on the development of the scientific method. Meanwhile, Hobbes' political philosophy concentrated on the sphere of human action and politics. Between them, they had embarked on a project of 'purification' which led to further solidification of an artificial divide.

But the realities presented by climate change, where the natural and the human (cultural) spheres are evidently entangled, have exposed the artificiality of this division while emphasizing the need for studying nature-culture entanglements. In our analysis of the texts, and following feminist scholar and cultural critic Donna Haraway, we will be often using the more expressive and analytically appropriate term 'natureculture'[26] to mark and represent such entanglements of the 'natural' and the 'cultural'.

In recent times, scholarly work has repeatedly addressed the importance of recognizing these entanglements. Bruno Latour[27] had called attention to the partitioning project of modernity wherein Nature, which consists of the natural world and is the preserve of science, has been separated from the realm of culture which includes literature, and has gone to great lengths to expose the artificiality of this separation in his work. The eminent historian Dipesh Chakrabarty, in his 'Climate of History: Four Theses', has likewise averred 'anthropogenic explanations of climate change spell the collapse of the age-old humanist distinction between natural history and human history'.[28]

In the field of literature, the roots of this separation and the attendant purification project have been sunk deep and are manifest in the labelling of certain kinds of texts, which are hybrids of nature-culture themes, as a kind of genre fiction (Figure 3.2). Amitav Ghosh[29] points out how this has led to the relegation of those literatures which can be called nature-culture hybrids to the outhouses of 'genre' fiction, while 'serious' literature (and high culture) remained 'pure' and untainted by nature and science. The genre label may have, in fact, dissuaded some writers to write such hybrid literature like cli-fi, while others have refused to acknowledge[30] that they are. However, there are notable exceptions from the past and the present, for whom labels didn't matter, and their numbers keep growing.[31]

Besides nature-culture entanglements and the creative challenges discussed in the previous section, there are many other ways (Figure 2.2) that literature's encounter with climate change transforms how we create, read and comprehend stories. The next challenge we address is 'derangements of scale'.

It is not difficult to imagine how the contexts, meanings and the agency of a story, set in the present, can change drastically as we read it against the backdrop of longer (and wider) time periods (and geographies) like centuries, millennia (and planetary) and so on. Readings over such extended temporal (or geographical) scales are pertinent when literature engages climate change because the associated processes, politics, histories, as well as species-level interventions and effects unfold over these long scales.

In 'Telemorphosis: Theory in the Era of Climate Change', Timothy Clark, writing about derangements of scale, draws our attention to the scalar subjectivity of literary works.[32] In a critical analysis of Raymond Carver's short story 'Elephant', Clark points out how that text can be read against three different scales, starting from the immediate cultural-human, through the national on to the planetary, stretching over centuries. To address this issue of different scales and material, Clark advocates a multi-modal approach towards the critical study of the climate novel.

The human dramas that drive most stories, especially the modern realist novel, are easier depicted within shorter and condensed time scales, while the scale at which anthropogenic climate change (and other historical climatic changes like the Little Ice Age) unfolds is much longer and widely spread. Such impediments, once again, make the modern realist novel ill equipped to handle the material presented by climate change and so writers and critics have to discover ingenious ways to engage with the subject. A novel that juxtaposes the narratives of characters from different time periods, as Janice

Pariat does in *Everything the Light Touches*, a story that allows a river to speak of its past, or a narrative of future history where a different species looks back at the climate crisis, something I attempted in a children's book,[33] is expected to enjoy an advantage in handling the derangements of scale that Clarke has pointed out.

In my recently published climate novel *Spellcasters*, blinding smog that envelops the city of Delhi (Aukatabad in the story) becomes an important actor, driving the flow of the narrative. Later in the book, a billionaire industrialist who has a world domination agenda meets his end in his castle hotel, struck by lightning in the presence of the ghost of a woman he had murdered. Also in the same story, an unnatural deluge allows one of the important characters to seek out an adventure that takes the plot in a new direction. All of these are examples of the agency of the non-human, of the natural and the inanimate, which play important roles as actants[34] in the story because of climate and other anthropogenic effects. Non-human agency is the next creative-thematic feature we take up in our study.

The argument that non-humans are without agency is strongly rooted in Descartes' idea of the *cogito* – that established the thinking man's unique agency compared to the non-humans who are considered mindless machines. His was a mechanistic concept of the universe where everything in the natural world works according to mechanical laws. But even in the time of Descartes, there were contrary views. The great essayist and Renaissance figure Michel de Montaigne, who passed away a few years before Descartes was born, didn't subscribe to the dichotomy between humans and non-humans. In his essay 'An Apology for Raimond Sebond', Montaigne presenting a compelling case against such a dichotomy wrote, 'what is there in us that we do not see in the operations of animals? Is there a polity better ordered, the offices better distributed, and more inviolably observed and maintained, than that of bees? Can we imagine that such, and so regular, a distribution of employments can be carried on without reasoning and deliberation?'[35]

That Finnish tale of old about why the trees stopped talking,[36] the Creation myths of Indigenous peoples, and to cite a specific example of Indigenous wisdom, the beliefs of the Achuar people of Amazon who, as Phillippe Descola found in his research, grant personhood to plants, animals and other beings, treating them as subjects with 'souls, consciousness, language, and culture',[37] all indicate a long but ignored tradition of belief in non-human agency.[38] While developing his argument that for many of these belief systems the outward form is what differentiates humans from non-humans while the inner substance remains the same, Descola writes, 'we have seen, these Indians of Colombian Amazonia define as masa (people) many plants and animals that are endowed with a soul that is identical to their own'.

The reality and impact of anthropogenic climate change have upended the idea of unique human agency. In the realm of theory, fields like science and technology studies and new materialism have slowly established the importance of the agency of non-humans and the interconnections and dependencies between humans, non-human animals, objects, concepts and technology. Today, we know that nine out of ten cells harboured by a person are microbial cells that influence our moods and health, we realize how social media influences our behaviour, and we accept that our vehicles are powered by the liquefied remains of dead algae and zooplankton. Sometimes such non-human agency is more plainly visible, as in the ability of certain crows to fashion tools or in the tireless work of pollinators like bees which improves local biodiversity and impacts our diets.

These interactive relationships and interdependencies between humans and non-humans are well elucidated in Actor-Network Theory (ANT) developed by Bruno Latour,[39] Michel Calon and John Law. ANT as a method has some kinship with earlier philosophies of process that stretch from Henri Bergson and his idea of the *élan vital*[40] or vital impulse, through mathematician Alfred N. Whitehead's Process philosophy,[41] which between them had focused on relations between objects, creative acts and the idea of 'emergence', where complex properties and behaviour can arise from simple interactions. In this context, a valuable contribution of ANT is in the understanding that actors are not independent 'starting points of action'[42] but are linked in networks of dependencies with other actors and their actions. Climate change and its encounter with humans, non-humans, ideas and technologies, both in the real world and in stories, can be better comprehended by studying these networks and interactions and the allied ideas of entanglement and non-human agency.

In Frank Schatzing's novel *Swarm*, we find whales attacking ships, and similarly in other books we come across clear demonstrations of the agency of non-humans. Some of these works can be slotted under Andersen's Judgement imaginary discussed earlier, where non-humans emerge as actors in the plot, and it is as if nature is striking back. The cli-fi movie *Into the Storm* has a memorable scene which blends non-human agency with the climate uncanny. Amitav Ghosh's *Gun Island* and Emmi Itäranta's *Memory of Water* also evoke the 'uncanny' in scenes where the agency of non-humans like serpents (in Ghosh) is important.

Uncanny is the creative-thematic feature we are going to explore next. We finish our exploration of non-human agency with a few observations in the context of climate change and its representation in literature. The non-human objects of cli-fi and their real-world counterparts gather their agency because of human interventions, thus making them a sort of hybrid[43] where the non-human (natural) and human (social) categories co-exist. The unnatural deluge or the smog of my novel displays their agency and propels the plot because of human interventions in earth systems through emissions and pollution. This then is another illustration of nature-culture entanglements we discussed earlier, where none of these categories of nature and human society are independent of each other. Also, as we shall see now, these entanglements and the consequent agency of the non-human often evoke in the storyworlds of cli-fi the sense of a specific kind of uncanny or eeriness, as familiar 'objects' behave 'unnaturally'.

A deeper discussion about uncanny, our next creative-thematic feature of cli-fi, and its close connection with non-human agency is in order, and for this I present below, with some changes and additions, parts of my essay that appeared in *Scroll* magazine.[44] Besides exploring two kinds of uncanny encountered in climate fiction, the following discussion also employs the concept, along with non-human agency, to forge a conceptual connection between planetary madness and mental health and its representation in fiction.

Gregers Andersen has employed the concept of 'uncanny' to characterize the climate-related transformations of our inner (mind) and outer worlds that we often encounter in fiction.[45] He goes on to elaborate how the concept occurs in the writings of both Heidegger and Freud. As psychology students would know, Freud's well-known essay 'Das Unheimliche'[46] introduced the uncanny as a sensation an observer feels when repressed fantasies imbue objects with life, often triggered by phenomena like ghosts, spirits, doubles or doppelgängers. According to Freud, the 'uncanny element is actually nothing new or strange, but something that was long familiar to the psyche and was estranged from it only through being repressed'.[47] According to Andersen, this kind of uncanny pervades climate fiction and can be understood as the eerie feelings an observer experiences when they witness inanimate objects inexplicably come to life. Here the observer could either be the reader or the character experiencing the agency of the inanimate object first-hand.

In the movie *Into the Storm*, the storm chaser Pete is sucked up high in the sky by the funnel of a tornado, and in that eerily memorable scene, the funnel slowly turns him around, and he is bathed in a strange golden light. It seems the funnel is sentient, and it is observing this human subject before flinging him down to his death. A scene like that, steeped in Freudian uncanny, sends shivers down our spines.

Such animated objects of climate or environmental uncanny, with their apparent agency (non-human agency), are what Bruno Latour, following a term used by Michel Serres, would call quasi-objects[48] which are formed out of a fusing of 'object-discourse-nature-society'[49] or, to look at it in another way, lie 'in between and below the two poles'[50] of nature and society. This in the climate context would mean the ferocious wildfires of California or the scary increase in lightning strikes during the Indian monsoon, for example, are not mere natural 'objects' or phenomena but are infused with human and discursive elements. We can also say that such quasi-objects, often tinged with the uncanny, are infected by human greed and faulty policies and are objects no more but have turned into monster hybrids of the natural and our desires.

The concept of the uncanny also appears in the writings of Martin Heidegger. While the Freudian uncanny is an 'affective quality' or feeling emerging from the familiar becoming unfamiliar, the Heideggerian uncanny is about modes of being and our inner worlds. Andersen refines this other sense of the uncanny, incorporating insights from Hermann Schmitz, one of Heidegger's disciples, to explain the transformation in the characters caused by observing the unimaginable destruction of the surrounding environment caused by climate change. In this other sense, however, the uncanny feeling 'merge(s) inner and outer experience',[51] thus connecting both the unfamiliar, unhomely aspects of the transformed surroundings with the fear and insecurity of the inner world of the character or observer. We find this 'Heideggerian' uncanny in scenes from climate novels like Cormac McCarthy's *The Road*. There the father and son duo trudging across a devastated American landscape are in the grip of (as evidenced from the dialogue, actions and evocative use of language) this other kind of affective uncanny, triggered by the unimaginably transformed surroundings. A similar uncanniness is evoked in Octavia Butler's *Parable of the Sower* and also in many scenes of Doris Lessing's *Mara and Dann*, as the brother-sister duo cross a climate- and war-ravaged future Africa pursued by a potential murderer.

An important distinction needs to be made. While both the Freudian and Heideggerian uncanny can be found within the pages of cli-fi, where the uncanniness is connected to climate change and disaster, uncanny is also experienced in other genres of literature, for example, in ghost stories. However, the uncanniness manifest through the actions of ghosts is different from the 'climate uncanny' encountered in cli-fi, because in the latter, the uncanny surroundings that influence us are the result of non-human forces unleashed as a result of human action, they are, in fact, as we mentioned in our discussion of quasi-objects, human greed and unsustainable living, manifest as transformed 'nature'. Ghosts, on the other hand, as Amitav Ghosh points out, marking this distinction, while being non-human, are 'projections of humans who were once alive'.[52]

Before concluding this discussion about uncanny[53] as a creative-thematic feature of cli-fi, let us try to explore a possible connection between uncanny manifestations and mental health effects of climate change using the concepts of transference and mirroring.[54] The first of these is based on the Freudian idea of 'transference', which, simply put, is the phenomenon where a psychoanalyst gets affected by her patient because the patient unconsciously transfers some of her past feelings about another person towards the analyst. This feeling could be anger, mistrust, hate, love, among several others. Now, if we frame climate change impacts on mental health with an analogy of planetary madness, we can see how this parallels the 'transference' described by Freud. It is as if the planet, or Gaia,[55] or let us say the earth systems as a whole, is redirecting negative feelings towards its inhabitants.

But there is a major difference here which should not be missed in the analogy. It is obvious that the earth is not redirecting or transferring past feelings about another entity towards us. What we are seeing is actually payback time. It is our exploitative relation with the planet that is getting reflected back at us through unfolding disasters and the attendant mental agony. Therefore, instead of transference, we can call this 'mirroring', where our faces, contorted by greed and our avaricious minds, held in thrall by the mantra of endless growth, are being transformed and reflected back at us as an uncanny laced with human ferocity.

While 'transference' helps us analyse this phenomenon with a psychological lens, we need to call it mirroring, albeit through a distorting circus mirror, which captures the character of the reflection and its transformation into a darker and even more grotesque echo of our individualistic actions. And yet it is still a kind of transference because the over-consuming subject or groups (populations with maximum per capita emissions and largest ecological footprints or the Global North) are the ones making the planet sick, while the worst sufferers of climate effects are, and will be, non-humans and people of the Global South, whose impact on the planet is much less.

Let us look for a parallel in literature. The character of the psychotic teenage patient Bethany Krall in Liz Jensen's climate novel *The Rapture* demonstrates a similar mirroring of the agonies of the planet that we explained above. The violent and delusional Bethany begins to predict a string of disasters, including a deadly earthquake in Istanbul, a cyclone that flattens Rio, and finally a submarine landslide and a 'methane gun' incident triggering runaway global warming. It is as if the agonies of the planet transferred to wrath are reflected in the mirror of her 'deranged' mind before they appear as disaster. At one point, the author writes about Bethany, 'her despair is earth-shaped'.[56] Here the apparent insanity of the planet, especially the anthropogenic climate disaster which marks the turning point of the story, is sharply mirrored by Bethany in a strange and uncanny fashion. Climate novels often incorporate scenes that not only evoke the uncanny but also depict such mirroring in subtle and creative ways.

The final creative-thematic features we are considering are collectives and their role in climate stories. Cli-fi, which foregrounds large groups instead of what Admussen would label as narratives centred on individualism, is a challenge to put together, but we find writers doing this too. Collectives like communities, villages, civil society groups and other kinds of associations not only help depict interconnections, dependencies, shared responsibilities and joint action, but they can also help articulate ideas of mutuality, cooperation, care and common cause which are all important for adapting to the present crisis while imagining transformative futures. Anita Agnihotri's *The Sickle* is an example where collectives and collective actions are as important as the actions of individual characters, thereby also demonstrating how narratives about collectives allow the representation of climate injustice and suffering. Similarly, some of Kim Stanley Robinson's novels, with their ensemble casts and community involvement, also address this need for telling stories about aggregates.

We are almost at the end of our exploration of the creative-thematic features (Figure 2.2) of climate stories which began with aesthetics and politics and ends with the role of collectives. While discussing these features, we noted how the focus on place, shorter time periods and individual experience puts the modern realist novel at a disadvantage while representing scale effects, nature-culture entanglements, non-human agency and some other creative-thematic features pertinent to climate fiction. So new creative techniques are necessary which situate humanity not as separate but part of the natural, while also acknowledging its role as a geological agent.

In looking for creative solutions, we have to, however, draw a distinction between the modern realist novel with its representational disadvantages vis-à-vis climate change, and the literary techniques that were developed during the period of literary Modernism. According to Kerridge, certain techniques developed by the Modernists seem to be more suitable in addressing some of the representational problems of an ecological imagination. We believe such techniques should be equally applicable for climate fiction.

Kerridge writes:

> A philosophy that dissolves unitary selfhood must expect to have difficulty in finding expression in conventional narrative. Who is the protagonist? What is the narrative point of view? Literary forms in the Modernist tradition – dispersed, ventilated, fragmented, multivocal, dialogical forms without stable narrative viewpoint, or impersonal forms replacing the single narrative or lyric voice with cut-up and collage – would seem more adaptable to ecocentric and New Materialist approaches.[57]

In fact, David Brin in *Earth* has employed fragmented narratives and montage quite successfully. Striking a note similar to Kerridge, Sophia David has argued about the potential of avant-garde works 'which push and subvert boundaries, and constantly renew styles in order for a continued reflection and attentive reading, can be part of creating a more ecological form of the novel'.[58]

A deeper problem that an author faces while telling stories about climate change is with the deficiencies of language itself. Ghosh[59] points out with examples of Buddhist pagodas in Burma and 'thinking forests' how images and forms and text-image hybrids could be better vehicles to convey the stories of climate change to readers. In response to this necessity of a new hybridized storytelling where image and text co-exist, we have been seeing graphic and illustrated climate stories being published in increasing numbers. Among Indian writers of climate fiction, Sarnath Banerjee's *All Quiet in Vikaspuri* is a step in that direction.

This completes our exploration of all the creative-thematic features of cli-fi which are born of challenges peculiar to the genre. In the course of this discussion, we have first introduced the three major lenses (Figure 3.4) of politics, aesthetics and planetarity that we will be further sharpening and using throughout the book to study the three novels, one for each. We have also examined those other creative-thematic challenges like nature-culture, uncanny, non-human agency, derangements of scale and the role of collectives which will be employed as minor lenses to read those same novels.

We will now briefly examine the connections between the sets of major and minor lenses which are based on the creative-thematic features of climate fiction. This, besides providing us with a simple and useful method to read and analyse cli-fi in future, will also justify the adoption of the major lenses. For this exercise, we will now enlist the services of a Franciscan friar of the High Middle Ages.

## The major and minor lenses

William of Ockham[60] was born in England in the late thirteenth century, where he received his theological training. Because of his openly heterodox views, Ockham was asked to answer charges of heresy and summoned to the Papal court at Avignon, wherefrom he had to eventually flee on account of serious contradictions with the views of the pope. Today, he is best remembered for the theory of 'nominalism', which argues against universal concepts, and even more for the famous 'Ockham's Razor' which advocates ontological parsimony. In simple terms, the principle of Ockham's Razor suggests that the simplest and usually correct explanation for something is thc one that requires a minimum of explanations and assumptions.

Ockham's Razor is a useful, but not infallible, tool which can be applied in day-to-day contexts as well as in complex decision-making. What we try to do now is to examine if it is useful for our purpose, specifically by trying to shave off a number of our minor lenses by subsuming some or all of them in the major three lenses of our study.

Such an exercise will not only offer added justification for the use of three major lenses for reading climate texts, out of a possible set of eight (Figure 3.3), but will also help readers notice how the lenses are connected and interdependent, thereby providing new and less complicated ways of reading climate texts. In our case, however, because one of the purposes of this work is to present various ways of reading climate fiction, we shall still use all the major and minor lenses in the second part of the book, albeit with different degrees of emphasis and with a focus on the major three.

First of all, my reader will remember that each lens, major and minor, between them represents a creative-thematic challenge (Figure 2.2) of depicting climate change in fiction which bestows certain distinctive features to these stories. The three major lenses are aesthetics (primarily literariness), politics (primarily climate justice) and planetarity, while the five minor ones we discussed are nature-culture entanglements, derangements of scale, non-human agency, the uncanny and the role of collectives.

In the previous sections, we have already hinted at how nature-culture entanglements, non-human agency and the uncanny are connected. This dependency can be explained through Latourian quasi-objects and actor-network theory, which argues that no actor is independent. That is, in our context, non-human agency or the agency of the 'natural' and that of the human (cultural), because of nature-culture entanglement, act upon each other, and this interaction drives climate phenomenon, including its uncanny manifestations and affects, while also informing literary representations. We have already explained how this climate uncanny, both in its Freudian sense of animated objects (the 'sentient' funnel of the tornado with the storm chaser Pete caught in it) and the Heideggerian sense (the unsettling settings of *The Road* and how it affects the father-son duo) which connects inner and outer worlds in a climate-affected setting, is an affective quality which emerges from the fact of nature-culture entanglements and the perceived agency of the non-human.

The interdependencies of nature-culture, non-human agency and the uncanny, we will now argue, can be captured by the concept of planetarity, or the sense of planet. Heise's concept of the 'sense of planet' and the associated idea of 'eco-cosmopolitanism' 'attempts to envision individuals and groups as part of planetary "imagined communities" of both human and nonhuman kinds'.[61] This, we argue, implicitly acknowledges the entanglements of nature and culture (non-human and human), projecting them to a planetary scale

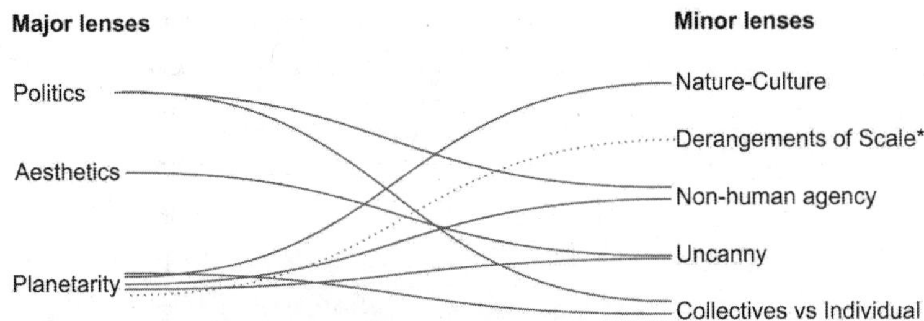


**Figure 3.3** Planetarity, politics and aesthetics in climate fiction.
*Timothy Clark coined the term 'derangements of scale'.

while focusing on the need to foreground these in the environmental imagination.

Therefore, the sense of planet and the associated eco-cosmopolitan imagination on a global scale can serve as good scaffolding for imagining and acknowledging these nature-culture entanglements that stretch across geographies. These entanglements, as we have seen through the real-life experience of the global impact of the novel coronavirus, are animated by the agency of the non-human. In fact, theorists of interspecies cosmopolitanism, acknowledging this agency or the 'non-human power', have argued how these should determine the configurations of transformative projects in the Anthropocene.[62]

We can therefore say that Heise's planetary sense and the associated idea of eco-cosmopolitanism can be employed as a broader framework (or lens) through which the specificities of nature-culture entanglements, non-human agency as well as the uncanny, which is related to the first two, can be captured. Or in other words, nature-culture, non-human agency and the uncanny, three minor lenses of our study, can be nested under a more capacious, yet simple, sense of the planetary which includes the associated concept of eco-cosmopolitanism, especially when we are talking of projects (novels) of a global scope (Figure 3.3). It should also be noted that nature-culture entanglements and non-human agency have a bearing on issues of rights and multispecies justice and thus can also be addressed through our major lens of justice. Further, in a later chapter, we shall see how the climate uncanny can be evoked through aesthetic strategies, aesthetics being one of the three major lenses we employ.

This is, however, not to overemphasize these relationships by trying to subsume important features of the climate imagination under broader frameworks. Rather, this is an attempt, inspired by Ockham's razor, to explore the possibility of simplification by focusing on a broader lens and fewer conceptual tools for studying climate fiction. In attempting this simplification, we are conscious of the focus of Heise's original intention[63] and how our attempt builds on that for our specific purpose.

We have now established connections between three of our minor lenses and the planetary imagination and eco-cosmopolitanism. The two remaining minor lenses are the derangements of scale and the role of collectives in the context of climate change imagination. The role of collectives in transformative change is closely allied to politics and justice, and so the lens of politics can subsume the importance of the role of collectives in climate imagination and action. In this context, we will remember Nick Admussen's 'Six Proposals', where he writes, 'Individualism is an intervention we make into our environment. It is a destructive and atomizing act of imagination. It erases our radical dependence on each other and on the environment.'[64] The lens of politics, as we have hinted earlier, is also closely related to the transformative potential (Figure 2.2) of cli-fi which provides signposts and indicators of potential change.

Finally, derangements of scale, following Timothy Clark, arise from the fact that climate change unfolds over long timescales and across vast geographies. This asks for new kinds of narrative and ecocritical approaches which can better represent and engage the wide spatial and temporal dimensions of climate change. Heise's planetary imagination, among others (like the epic mode of storytelling), enjoys a certain advantage in better grasping these scale effects because of its acknowledgement of these extended spatial dimensions of the global, thus opening a route for studying and imaginatively representing climate change and the Anthropocene. Heise has in fact engaged with Clark's idea of derangements of scale as well as Ghosh's critique of the modern realist novel, where she argues that science fiction presents models and methods (species narratives, time leaps and time travel, among others) that are well-suited to represent derangements of scale and other aspects of the Anthropocene.[65] As we shall see, 'planetary' novels like *Gun Island* enjoy the advantage of using their geographically spread-out narratives (among other techniques), thereby addressing scale effects to a certain extent.

From this discussion, we can say that a planetary sense could be one of the strategies, which, while not comprehensive, can engage with certain (e.g. spatial), but not all, scale effects of climate change. Unlike the other lenses, 'planetarity', as theorized by Heise, is not meant to grasp all the scale effects and their associated complexities. However, planetarity, in its connotation of vastness, can be used as shorthand to imagine spatial and temporal scales across which climate change manifests.[66]

The Ockham's Razor approach that we have applied to explore how the major and minor lenses connect has now helped us to subsumc most of the minor lenses within the three major lenses or frames of aesthetics, politics and planetarity. This is represented in Figure 3.3. It is important to restate the fact that this exercise is not meant to freight the three major lenses (born of three creative-thematic

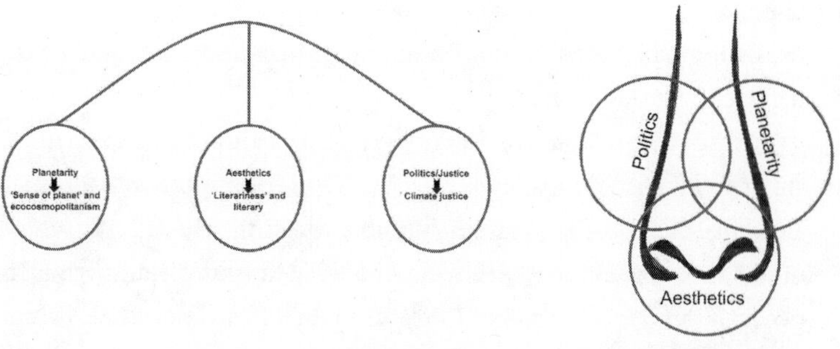


**Figure 3.4** The three major lenses: A nose for sniffing signals.

features) with the burden of multiple concepts, thereby diluting the theoretical rigour behind those concepts which form the bases for presenting certain distinctive features relating to the unique challenges of depicting climate change in fiction. Besides, we are not enamoured by the prospect of having to flee like William of Ockham for committing academic heresy. The sole purpose of this exercise is to present easy shorthand for critically analysing climate stories, which can be employed by researchers and storyteller-activists as a reference point for fine-tuning their adoption of texts while serving their representational and climate communication goals.

In fact, the three major lenses of politics, aesthetics and planetarity, focusing primarily on climate justice,[67] literariness and a planetary sense (besides geological time scales) can be used as a simple triad for reading climate fiction. This method of reading, akin to triangulation used to locate mobile phones, can pick up these three kinds of signals from a climate story, telling us about its representational, aesthetic and transformative values and potentials. This simplified strategy used to 'sniff' for positive signals, and because of its resemblance to the exploratory function of triangulation, has been represented by a human nose and labelled the 'nose model' in Figure 3.4.

The purpose of using Ockham's razor in our case has therefore been twofold. First of all, it allowed us to further justify our choice of the three major lenses which are used later to study different climate texts. This exercise also provided a simplified method to engage climate fiction which might be beneficial in the ongoing work of designing climate communication and critical approaches using the vehicle of stories.

In the next chapter, we shall focus upon the influence of these stories on our minds and how to gauge the potential of such narratives as tools for sustainable transitions to a better future. For doing this, we will follow the elements listed under transformative potential in our approaches to the climate novel (Figure 2.2). There we will also comment upon colonialism and its impact on the climate and environment, and how postcolonial and Western ecocritical approaches diverge, and how they might come together on the issue of justice. As we will be talking mostly about the power of books and their influence on our minds, we begin the next chapter with the story of a famous novel and its author and a meeting that took place between her and an American president in the backdrop of the Civil War.

# 4

# The little woman's great war

## *Stories in action*

A story is often told about a meeting between Abraham Lincoln and Harriet Beecher Stowe, the famed author of *Uncle Tom's Cabin*. This was in the winter of 1862. A few months before this, early in the morning of April 12, a mortar had roared through the air over the Union-held Fort Sumter in South Carolina, followed by volleys of gunfire from Confederate positions and floating batteries around the Charleston harbour. The defending forces inside the fort were totally outmanned and outgunned by the assault. By next afternoon, Sumter had fallen to the Confederates, marking the beginning of the American Civil War which was fought, among other things, on the issue of the abolition of slavery.

Stowe's meeting with Lincoln happened a few months later, on a damp and chilly day in Washington. As the story goes, Lincoln was seated in a cosy room going through some papers when the visitors arrived. A fire was crackling away, and the president had propped his feet up on the mantle. As he saw his visitors, he put away his papers and hauled himself up to greet the author, saying, 'Why, Mrs. Stowe, right glad to see you!' and added, 'So you're the little woman who wrote the book that made this great war! Sit down please.'

Lincoln's alleged greeting which appears in some biographies of the author, cemented the well-known fact about the impact of Stowe's book on the movement for abolition of slavery which in turn precipitated the Civil War. *Uncle Tom's Cabin*, which portrays the horrors of slavery and was the second best-selling book after the

Bible, is one of those great works of fiction which exemplifies how stories can have a decisive impact on history.

Stowe's involvement with the movement for the abolition of slavery did not stop with her famous novel. Her well-known 'Reply to an Address from the Women of Great Britain'[1] is another important document that energized the abolitionist and feminist movements. It had a far-reaching impact, and according to one of her biographers:

> created a sensation in the United States, as well as in Great Britain. Its effect was intensified when, later in the year, Henry Ward Beecher made an extensive speaking tour of the British Isles and frequently quoted from his sister's work. The British Government was placed in an exceptionally uncomfortable position. An attempt might have been made to ignore or discount the Emancipation Proclamation, but the barrage of publicity incited by Mrs. Stowe and her brother made this impossible. President Lincoln later attributed Britain's failure to extend diplomatic recognition to the Confederacy to three factors: *Uncle Tom's Cabin*, Mrs. Stowe's 'Reply', and the Reverend Henry Ward Beecher's British tour.[2]

The writer's activism against slavery is further borne out through numerous letters written to influential people that appear in her biographies. In one of these, addressed to the Duchess of Argyle, Stowe writes, 'Slavery will be sent out by this agony. We are only in the throes and ravings of the exorcism. The roots of the cancer have gone everywhere, but they must die – will … Your mother will live to see slavery abolished, *unless* England forms an alliance to hold it up.'[3]

The point we are making here is obvious. Books can have an impact on changing the world while being further aided by facilitating circumstances and helped, as we have just seen, by the author's activism. There are several examples of stories which have had a significant influence on laws and beliefs in the field of environment and politics.

Upton Sinclair's account of the working conditions of Chicago meat-packers in *The Jungle* was instrumental in the formulation of the first food safety laws in the United States. In fact, Jack London described Sinclair's book as 'the Uncle Tom's Cabin of wage-slavery'. Another famous example, this time from the field of environment, is Rachel Carson's 'A Fable for Tomorrow' in her *Silent Spring*, which is known to have energized the environmental movement.[4] And to those among us still not convinced, we remind them of the continuing influence of *The Communist Manifesto* and the three volumes of *Das Kapital*.

But here we are concerned with fiction and more specifically climate fiction. So let us now explore how stories that engage climate change can impact beliefs, thoughts and ideas. What factors in their storytelling, characterization, themes and concerns engender the possibility of changing minds and thereby influence the politics of change?

## Climate stories and their transformative potential

Stories are sticky; they remain with us for a long time. They can also be good vehicles for conveying complex ideas. Moreover, well-told stories connect with us at a deeper level which dry scientific summaries or sensational reports in popular media may not.

The messages, ideas, science and scenarios that climate fiction conveys are expected to help in building awareness and imagining hopeful futures if they congeal around generally accepted principles and goals of justice and sustainability while also engaging production and consumption flows and emissions. Not delving further into the debates around dystopian cli-fi and whether or not it embodies a certain potential for influencing change, we will now take a look at some of the granular aspects of plot, content and other features of cli-fi in general, which can help deepen awareness about climate change while also making an impression on readers.

There are many approaches that have been developed to look at this transformative potential of climate fiction. Besides empirical research, there are goal-oriented and SSPs-linked strategies[5] to test the content and potential of climate stories. Here we shall look at the content, delivery and reception of messages through climate fiction by discussing five normative approaches (Figures 2.2 and 4.1) for reading these stories.

The first three approaches that we are going to discuss have been developed in part and employed by a team of researchers, including my colleague Jeffrey Barber in their study[6] of science fiction movie trailers. The fourth approach employs science-based narratives, while the fifth is an empirical ecocritical research method used by Matthew Schneider-Mayerson, Denis Baden and others in their studies of climate novels. It needs to be mentioned here that these analytical tools can be used individually or in combination for a better and in-depth appreciation of the potentials of cli-fi. The five approaches (Figure 4.1) we are now going to present are based on Sustainable Development Goals (SDGs), Production and Consumption Flows, Integral Ecology, the SSPs and Empirical Ecocritical studies. We will employ a number of these approaches in our readings of the stories in Part Two of the book.

There are internationally agreed definitions and goals of sustainability and climate action enshrined in the seventeen global sustainable development goals or SDGs,[7] the Paris Agreement climate goals and other documents. For example, Goal 13 of the SDGs asks

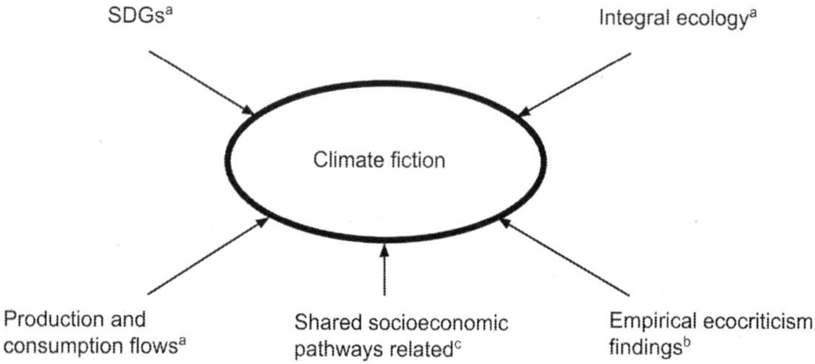


**Figure 4.1** Transformative potential of climate stories.

Note: Some approaches to probe the transformative potential of climate fiction. See a) Jeffrey Barber et al. b) Studies by Matthew-Schneider Mayerson et al., Denis Baden among others. c) Nikoleris et al., and the accompanying discussion.

countries to 'Take urgent action to combat climate change and its impacts by regulating emissions and promoting developments in renewable energy.' Other SDGs, like number 12, deal with Responsible Consumption and Production, number 11 with Sustainable Cities and Communities, number 7 with Affordable and Clean Energy, which, among others, have obvious implications and linkages with the climate goal. These goals have, in turn, been linked with a number of verifiable and measurable indicators.

While analysing climate fiction, a convenient approach to test its advocacy and awareness potential is to check for the text's familiarity with these goals and directions, either directly or indirectly. Such awareness could be discovered in the plot, dialogue, themes or implicit messages. This does not mean that the text has to explicitly mention or advocate for these goals. It should, however, through the story, plot or dialogue convey the importance of one or more of these objectives as they relate to climate change.

The second approach deals with Production and Consumption flows. In its very basic form this looks at how a particular cli-fi work frames climate impacts by defining the problem and identifying its roots – which always lie in unsustainable production and consumption and presenting possible solutions, strategies and policies. Here we can also look at the balance between scientific accuracy versus artistic license.

If we look at *The Road* through this lens, we can see that impacts have been identified in the book, but the roots are hardly mentioned and only hinted at. In fact, the story is silent about the origins of the disaster and we can only guess. Also there is nothing specific in the plot about solutions, and the only quest there is to survive. In contrast, Kim Stanley Robinson's *Pacific Edge* clearly identifies solutions, strategies, policies (wage ceiling, green housing), obstacles (developers, New Federalists) and the roots of the problem, but climate change is not directly identified in that novel. However, many of his other novels, including the *Science in the Capital* trilogy, clearly mention the climate change problem, identify the associated production and consumption flows and suggest mitigative (like 'carbon coin' in *Ministry for the Future*) and adaptive strategies and instruments through the plot.

The third approach for probing the transformative potential of cli-fi employs the conceptual framework of Ken Wilber's integral theory.[8] Integral theory is a meta-theory (a theory about theories) which integrates various streams of Western thought and Eastern traditions into a unified framework. Jeffrey Barber and others[9] have applied integral theory in the aforementioned study of science fiction movie trailers, using insights from Esbjörn-Hargens and Zimmerman's[10] integral ecology approach and Chris Reidy's application of integral futures to study visions of the future in the climate action movement.

Reidy, summarizing his study of the climate action movement using an integral futures approach, mentions how this approach can 'help movement leaders to develop the ability to see and inhabit multiple perspectives' and 'perhaps provide the starting point for a more inclusive movement that respects and holds multiple visions as a source of strength and appeal, rather than seeking to manufacture agreement around a single core vision'.[11] Besides the study of movements, this approach can be equally useful for studying changes within the storyworld.

Using integral theory and Wilber's well-known four-quadrant model, Barber and others have examined sci-fi storyworlds from movie trailers and how these stories portray change in individuals as well as collectives, both internally – psychological and cultural (worldviews) change – and externally, that is, change with respect to the behavioural (practices) and social realms covering economic, political and the natural environment.

Their analysis generates a four-quadrant (two-by-two matrix) view of the storyworld, its embedded values, behaviours, practices, systems and change. We can adopt this model and apply it to study the storyworlds of cli-fi, which can then allow us to examine holistically how the text addresses the problems and solutions of climate change and what kind of values are embedded in the societies that the author portrays. This can then help policymakers and activists to 'inhabit' these storyworlds and draw lessons about inclusiveness and possible trajectories of the future, which could be useful in designing change. Because of the elaborate nature of this approach, we will use it only once to probe the first of the three novels we analyse, Amitav Ghosh's *Gun Island*. However, this will have enough detail for the reader to be able to easily replicate this approach for other books.

The fourth approach to studying the transitional potential of cli-fi builds upon the transition pathways research that we find in the narratives of the SSPs. The SSPs, which project five possible trajectories for the future, have in fact been employed to study climate fiction. This research, as indicated earlier, allowed a parallel comparison of climate fiction storyworlds or literary imaginaries and the narratives of the SSPs or scientific imaginaries, allowing the researchers to 'make links between larger societal trends and personal accounts of climate change'.[12]

The authors of this study have demonstrated what literary scenarios can do when juxtaposed with SSPs by answering two questions, namely, 'how they affect the understanding of challenges to mitigation and adaptation and how they affect engagement with climate change as an issue'. Their research places the storyworld of Liz Jensen's *The Rapture* close to SSP 3 which is the possible future pathway of regional rivalry (The Rocky Road) and that of Ian McEwan's *Solar* somewhere between SSP5 and SSP3, that is, between the pathways of fossil-fuelled development (Taking the Highway) and The Rocky Road, among several other books. It is important to note here that such imaginaries of the future found in novels or video games,[13] and their dialogue with scientific imaginaries, can be used not only to visualize potential futures but also as tools[14] for anticipatory governance and backcasting exercises which can help guide policies for a sustainable future. While we won't apply this approach in our reading of the novels, readers might want to look at the studies mentioned here and the work on anticipatory governance referred to above.

Finally, the fifth approach provides another way to gauge the influence of climate fiction on environmental belief and behaviour using empirical ecocritical methods of reader surveys which generate qualitative and quantitative data. There is an increasing number of studies using similar and allied methods to test the impact of climate fiction on readers. Schneider-Mayerson, who devised the Climate Reality Check, used a reader-response[15] approach with data about nineteen cli-fi works from 161 American respondent-readers to investigate 'who its readers are and what they make of their reading experiences'.[16] This study found that readers of climate fiction were younger, more liberal and more concerned about climate change than those who didn't read this genre. Also, there was a large percentage of millennials among cli-fi readers.

While these books did not help to shape the views of all readers, 'Nevertheless, climate fiction did not just help some readers picture potential futures but focused their gaze on subjects that had previously been unknown.' It was also found that liberals, rather than conservatives, are more likely to be nudged by cli-fi from their 'cautious' to a 'concerned' position or from 'concerned' to 'alarmed' about climate change. Besides influencing dialogue, this study also demonstrated that techniques of 'character identification' and 'personal connection to setting' often have a greater effect and that character identification can lead to empathetic responses. However, Schneider-Mayerson's study noted the inadequacy of the behavioural change triggered by environmental anxieties for a number of respondents and that 'these new behaviors barely contribute to climate mitigation, collective adaptation, or the pursuit of climate justice'.

Another study of the immediate and delayed impacts of climate fiction on readers' beliefs and attitudes found 'significant positive effects on several important beliefs and attitudes about global warming'.[17] Character identification and transportation by the story were found to be mediating factors for these positive effects of cli-fi. However, the study found that these impacts wear away fast, which is why the researchers flagged the importance of repeated exposure to climate messages from different sources.

Other studies of the impact of climate fiction have found that solution-focused stories and those that inspire hope through positive role models have a greater impact in influencing pro-environmental intentions. Denis Baden of the University of Southampton, who also runs the solutions-focused Green Stories Project, found that 'stories with a solution focus were more effective in motivating pro-environmental intentions than catastrophic stories. Analysis of textual data indicated that being able to identify with a positive role model who provides examples of pro-environmental behaviours that are easily imitable was inspirational for most readers.'[18] Baden's romcom climate novel *Habitat Man*, which has many embedded ecological themes and solutions, was tested in a reader-response study of fifty respondents which found attitudinal change in a large percentage of readers, and adoption of green alternatives.[19] Another such study found[20] that personal stories played on the radio can shift climate change beliefs and risk perceptions through the mediating role of emotion, while others[21] have often flagged the role of hope in influencing positive behaviour.

We now have a fair understanding of five approaches and associated tools that can be employed to examine how a certain work of cli-fi can fairly represent the climate crisis and the potential of these stories in changing minds and behaviour. Here we noted the importance of sustainable development goals, scientific understanding of production and consumption flows, transformations of storyworlds and culture, hope, solutions, character identification, role models and scientific imaginaries, among other factors that have a bearing on the transformative potential of these stories.

In the second part of this book, we shall see how some of these tools can be employed in studying the awareness-raising potential and influence of climate novels. In doing this, we have to remember how the politics of a climate novel, one of our major lenses and creative-thematic features, is connected to this set of five approaches for probing the transformative potential of cli-fi. Meanwhile, in the next section, we will discuss 'ecocriticism' or environmental studies and its differences, commonalities and interface with postcolonial writing.

This focus on 'postcolonial ecocriticism' is necessary for a number of reasons. First of all, colonialism, environmental degradation and the present realities of climate change are intricately connected, and a proper engagement with the crisis through imagination and action cannot ignore these connections. This will allow us newer ways of reading and comprehending postcolonial climate texts beyond the adopted methods of a Western ecocriticism. An allied logic that also applies in our case is provided by Scott Slovic, who, in his introduction to *Ecocriticism of the Global South*, writes, 'The complex relationship between literary texts from developing regions of the world and the threatened environments that produced them suggests the need for new practices of reading both the texts themselves and the place of humans in nature more generally.'[22]

Because of socio-economic and geographical reasons, many postcolonial nations, which have overlaps with Southern or developing nations,[23] are more vulnerable to climate effects while having fewer resources to adapt to the same. This positions climate fiction set in postcolonial nations as an important area of study. Last but not the least, as this book will be examining two postcolonial climate novels, a comprehensive analysis of those requires that we are conscious and engaged with the intricacies of the connections between postcolonial writing and the field of ecocriticism, which has been traditionally associated with the West.

## Postcolonial concerns and the literature of climate change

Around the middle of the eighth century of the Common Era, the Anglo-Saxon missionary Boniface, who was then carrying on with his relentless efforts to convert the Germanic tribes to Christianity, had cut down a sacred oak tree venerated by the Pagan inhabitants of the Hesse area of Germany. This incident is recorded by George W. Robinson, who translated Willibald's biography of Boniface, who describes it thus:

> the saint attempted, in the place called Gaesmere, while the servants of God stood by his side, to fell a certain oak of extraordinary size, which is called, by an old name of the pagans, the Oak of Jupiter. And when in the strength of his steadfast heart he had cut the lower notch, there was present a great multitude of pagans, who in their souls were earnestly cursing the enemy of their gods. But when the fore side of the tree was notched only a little, suddenly the oak's vast bulk, driven by a divine blast from above, crashed to the ground, shivering its crown of branches as it fell; and, as if by the gracious compensation of the Most High it was also burst into four parts[24]

In Emil Doepler's painting[25] from the early twentieth century depicting the incident, we find Boniface holding aloft a white crucifix with the fallen oak at his feet. One of his attendants can be seen praying while another holds an axe. In the background, standing around the trees, are members of the tribe for whom the oak was sacred. Almost cowering, their mouths fallen open, they have an incredulous expression on their faces. It is a painting done in bright colours, barely communicates the gravity of the act and the far-reaching implications it holds for an age when humanity's disassociation with nature has visited upon the planet a crisis of planetary proportions.

The felling of the sacred Oak of Jupiter is one of many symbolic subjugations of nature and the natural before the human, in this case through divine sanction.[26] Another such sanction can be found in these words from the book of Genesis, which says, 'fill the earth, and subdue it',[27] thereby cementing a stronger connection between Christianity and anthropocentrism[28] which later fed into the logic for colonialism entailing the domination and exploitation of non-humans as well as the colonized 'others', who, presumed to be lacking reason and being close to nature, were considered less than human.

The European Enlightenment which established the primacy of reason, fuelled among others by Descartes' *cogito*, further enabled this separation of the human from the non-human (culture from nature), thus establishing an anthropocentrism which combined with a Eurocentrism in the logic of colonialism. In their book on postcolonial ecocriticism, Helen Tiffin and Graham Huggan explain these connections by drawing on the work of environmental philosopher Val Plumwood, who has argued:

> The western definition of humanity depended – and still depends on the presence of the 'not-human': the uncivilised, the animal and animalistic. European justification for invasion and colonisation proceeded from this basis, understanding non-European lands and the people and animals that inhabited them as 'spaces', 'unused, underused or empty'. The very ideology of colonisation is thus one where anthropocentrism and Eurocentrism are inseparable, with the anthropocentrism underlying Eurocentrism being used to justify those forms of European colonialism that see 'indigenous cultures as "primitive", less rational, and closer to children, animals and nature'.[29]

This shows us how attitudes and sanctions for dominating the environment and the 'natural', via anthropocentrism, are closely connected with the colonialism that followed. As postcolonial studies and imagination are ways of engaging and critiquing colonialism in the past and its newer neocolonial avatars, the above arguments allow us to uncover a connection between attitudes towards the environment and the colonial (and neocolonial) project, thereby laying the critical foundations for examining the linkages between environmental studies and postcolonial studies.

Let us take a closer look at the two disciplines of postcolonial studies and environmental studies (or ecocriticism) to further analyse their connections and differences. One of the simplest and oft-quoted definitions of ecocriticism comes from Cheryll Glotfelty, which says it is 'the study of the relationship between literature and the physical environment'.[30] Glotfelty, acknowledging that it has been 'predominantly a white movement', believes it will become more multi-ethnic when social justice and environment issues are better connected.[31] On the other hand, postcolonial writing and criticism is an attempt to expose the colonial and neocolonial systems of power from the past, present (and imagined futures) that remain embedded in social, economic, cultural, political and other domains.

But these two critical domains are not homogeneous. As Tiffin and Huggan[32] point out, postcolonialism has Marxist and poststructuralist divisions. Similarly, in the field of environmental studies, which we will often substitute with the term 'ecocriticism' despite a nuanced difference in meaning, there are divisions between an environmental focus on one hand and animal rights activism on the other. Ecocriticism has also been mapped, by Reed,[33] on the basis of a number of schools or approaches which include conservationist, ecological, deep-ecological, ecofeminist and environmental justice, while acknowledging overlaps.

The differences and possible meeting points between the Northern (North American[34]) ecocritical and postcolonial (as well as Global South) approaches, at the level of text and practice, have been examined by many environmental thinkers and practitioners. Focusing on this difference, the noted Indian environmentalist and public intellectual Ramachandra Guha and Catalan economist Joan Martinez-Alier have articulated the idea of the 'environmentalism of the poor' which is markedly different from the environmentalism of the rich (North), for whom it is often a post-materialist environmentalism. Using examples like the Chipko movement and Narmada Bachao Andolan from India, they have shown how 'the "environmentalism of the poor" might be understood as the resistance offered by ecosystem people to the process of resource capture by omnivores: as embodied in movements against large dams by tribal communities to be displaced by them, or struggles by peasants against the diversion of forest and grazing land to industry'.[35]

The Narmada Bachao Andolan, which is a movement involving Adivasis (Indigenous peoples), farmers and activists against the threat of displacement by large dam projects on the Narmada River in India, as well as the non-violent Chipko movement,[36] spearheaded by women to save trees in the Himalayan region from logging, are classic examples of this environmentalism of the poor. In contrast, environmentalism of the rich Northern countries appears within the context of a post-materialist, post-industrial society. Later in this book we shall see how the climate imagination of author Anita Agnihotri in her novel *The Sickle* represents the environmentalism of the poor, where climate change alongside systemic faults acts as a pivot, driving and aggravating exploitation and displacement.

Rob Nixon of Princeton University, who started out as an activist, has proposed the concept of 'slow violence', which captures the slow and almost invisible environmental violence inflicted on poorer (and weaker) nations, regions and people through the dynamics of waste export, toxic drift, climate impacts, deforestation, biomagnification and the thawing cryosphere, among a plethora of other effects. Nixon defines slow violence as 'a violence that occurs gradually and out of sight, a violence of delayed destruction that is dispersed across time and space, an attritional violence that is typically not viewed as violence at all'.[37] This is another compass which can guide our understanding of postcolonial environmental problems and the representational role played by 'writer-activists', who are closer to the ground, in comprehending and communicating the same.

Going deeper into the divisions between environmental and postcolonial literary studies, we find Nixon pointing out four distinct schisms between the dominant concerns of each discipline.[38] First of all, ecocritics, by which he means those practising environmental studies in the North, have focused on 'discourses of purity' where 'virgin wilderness' and protection of 'uncorrupted' places assume significance. On the other hand, postcolonial writing has tended to emphasize 'hybridity and cross-culturation'. Next he points out the focus on literature of place in environmental studies, while postcolonial studies have been exercised by the story of displacement. The third and related difference pertains to spatiality or its absence, where Nixon points out how environmental writing is strongly connected to a national (American) and also often nationalistic framework, whereas postcolonial studies engaged with the transnational and the cosmopolitan. Finally, the fourth difference is temporal, with environmental studies attaching importance to 'timeless, solitary moments of communion with nature' where history has been suppressed, whereas postcolonial writing aims to dig out the 'marginalised past' and write 'history from below', which is 'often along transnational axes of migrant memory'. Later in our reading of climate novels, we will see how Amitav Ghosh's *Gun Island*, as a postcolonial text, digs out forgotten stories from Sundarbans and Venice while twining them around a narrative of migration.

Nixon's framework, Tiffin and Huggan argue, may lead us to think that postcolonial writing is anthropocentric and environment writing, while 'privileging the white male western subject',[39] is not quite attentive about cultural differences. However, as these two authors point out, this is not quite the case as contrary examples can be found in the literature and there 'is a long history of ecological concern in postcolonial criticism'.[40] As a way out of this critical bottleneck and to create the possibility of a sharpened analysis of postcolonial texts, Tiffin and Huggan suggest, 'that the proper subject of postcolonialism is colonialism, and therefore to look accordingly for the colonial/imperial underpinnings of environmental practices in both "colonising" and "colonised" societies of the present and the past'.[41] Such an effort naturally opens up for critical examination, the intersections of environment and society or more accurately environment, society, politics, economics and rights.

This can be done using a lens of environmental justice, which is a tool well honed for the field of postcolonial ecocriticism. The pioneering environmental thinker Lawrence Buell, in his analysis of the two phases of ecocriticism[42] and the consequent shift from nature writing to a more involved writing which acknowledges how nature and the built environment are mixed up, stresses on the importance of justice when he writes, 'Literature-and-environment studies must develop a "social ecocriticism" that takes urban and degraded landscapes just as seriously as "natural" landscapes. Its traditional commitment to the nature protection ethic must be revised to accommodate the claims of environmental justice – or (more broadly) "the environmentalism of the poor"'.[43]

This lens of justice (including multispecies justice) can then be used to address ecological imperialism going right back to the Columbian exchange,[44] which entailed the transfer of flora, fauna, diseases and ideas between the Old World and the New, often with devastating consequences. Such a lens of justice can just as well be employed to examine and expose the neocolonial systems and networks of power embedded in the existing order and its socio-cultural and economic systems.

This last is exactly what an 'environmentalism of the poor' and other critiques of top-down 'development' engage with. This is not to say that the only role of postcolonial ecocriticism, including postcolonial literary texts with their focus on justice, is one of advocacy to change the world. Postcolonial ecocritical texts can and do also serve the imaginative and representational functions, but compared to ecocriticism, it is the politics that tends to animate its critical and creative apparatus. Tiffin and Huggan, supporting this view, write, 'While it would be a mistake to see ecocriticism as being more concerned with inhabiting the world than with changing it – as being fundamentally more interested in phenomenological than political processes – it is clearly the case that postcolonial ecocriticism tips the balance towards the latter.'[45]

Addressing the possible role of these texts, Anne Maxwell has pointed out that postcolonial criticism has found it difficult to critique the 'aggressive phase of capitalism known as "globalisation"' and that 'engaging with ecocritical discourses is one way to overcome this crisis'. She goes on to suggest, 'An area of study that is especially promising for postcolonial critics, is analysing apocalyptic dystopias that speculate on the dire social and physical consequences of global warming.'[46] Elsewhere, Adeline Johns-Putra, in her study of two such dystopian cli-fi novels, Alexis Wright's *The Swan Book* and Chang-rae Lee's *On Such a Full Sea*, discusses how 'they are postmodern in their sensibilities in as much as they question the dominance of master-narratives. They are also postcolonial in their identification of this dominance as both a cultural and a speciseist imperialism'.[47]

Postcolonial scholar Dipesh Chakrabarty, acknowledging the fact that with global climate change, humans have now become geophysical agents, argues that this necessitates a fleet-footed thinking across multiple scales where the human is both a bearer of rights and an agent in planetary-scale upheavals. This situation, according to Chakrabarty, where global climate change and our agency therein intersect with globalization, challenges the ways we envision the human at the level of rights, justice (including climate justice) and post-structuralist[48] critics of the human subject. 'This is why', Chakrabarty writes:

> the need arises to view the human simultaneously on contradictory registers: as a geophysical force and as a political agent, as a bearer of rights and as author of actions; subject to both the stochastic forces of nature (being itself one such force collectively) and open to the contingency of individual human experience; belonging at once to differently-scaled histories of the planet, of life and species, and of human societies … in an age when the forces of globalization intersect with those of global warming, the idea of the human needs to be stretched beyond where postcolonial thought advanced it.[49]

As the climate crisis is experienced through our 'anthropological differences', Chakrabarty further argues there can be no unified political response at the level of the human. This, however, opens up the space for 'the politics of climate change', which in turn explains its openness 'to science and technology' as well as to 'rhetoric, art, media, and arguments and conflicts conducted through a variety of means'.[50]

The continuing encounter between climate fiction and postcolonial writing and criticism, modulated by what Chakrabarty labels as our anthropological differences and complicated by our role as geophysical agent and bearer of rights, is expected to beget new and interesting variations of the climate novel. As a subset of postcolonial environmental writing, this encounter will no doubt be informed by the features and critical impetus that we expect from postcolonial ecocriticism, with its focus on power, justice and the environmentalism of the poor. However, it will also be nuanced by the creative-thematic challenges of climate fiction that we addressed earlier, giving rise to new varieties of creative engagement.

It is beyond the scope of this work to critically engage and analyse the dynamics of these interactions between the creative-thematic features of climate fiction and the political preoccupations of postcolonial writing. However, many such experiments in the field of creative imagination are afoot, and in our readings of the postcolonial climate works of Amitav Ghosh and Anita Agnihotri, we will have ample opportunity to examine these interactions in action.

Finally, there is another related point about difference. We had noted earlier that postcolonial writing attempts to expose colonial and neocolonial systems and networks of power embedded in the existing order. Because of this, postcolonial writers of climate fiction will often tend to focus on social justice and the workings of power and exploitation on the ground, which are intertwined and intersect with climate effects, without necessarily expending much effort to foreground the connection with emissions. As a result of their focus on justice, rights, hegemony, power, political action and forgotten pasts, among issues specific to a postcolonial engagement, it might sometimes be difficult to categorize a postcolonial climate novel as a work of climate fiction if we depend on some of the tests and definitions of the genre discussed earlier. This, however, shouldn't detract from their status as works of postcolonial climate fiction.

But all this is in a flux, as with the worsening climate situation, place-based environmental writing and criticism develops a planetary sense, and postcolonial texts engage globalization with concepts like slow violence and the tools of ecocriticism. This encounter between the postcolonial, the ecocritical and the specificities of the climate imagination is resulting in a churning within the genre which is expected to beget newer and more interesting stories in the days ahead.

## Gathering the maps

We have now arrived at a nuanced understanding of climate fiction. This has encompassed category-based divisions as well as a fair idea about the various creative-thematic challenges posed by the material that bestows certain distinctive features to these stories. In the course of this chapter we have also examined the transformative possibilities of climate fiction and the dynamics of the engagement of postcolonial writing with environmental and climate texts.

In the preceding chapters, we have also adopted the major lenses of planetarity, aesthetics and politics (climate justice), which we will use, after further refinement and focusing, in the second part of this book. Readers must have noted that two of these lenses, planetarity and climate justice, are specific to climate change fiction. These lenses are expected to grant us insights as to how the books we will be reading have engaged with planetarity and justice, thereby allowing the work to represent certain important aspects of climate change in fiction. The third lens of aesthetics, which is a broader probe also applicable to other genres of fiction, will help to reveal the 'literary' value of a climate novel and whether it furthers any specific representational goals of cli-fi.

In the next three chapters, we will be reading *Gun Island*, *Memory of Water* and *The Sickle* using planetarity, aesthetics and politics (climate justice) as the respective major lenses. As hinted earlier, we will follow a structured approach to examine each of the three climate novels chosen for this book. We will begin with a personal note introducing the creative-thematic focus, followed by a review of the novel which will include a detailed story outline. Next we will further develop the specific major lens used to read that particular work, drawing on relevant theories and research, examples, visualizations and in some cases activist insights to present a well-rounded understanding of the major lens we are going to employ. This will be followed by an analysis of the novel using that major lens to reveal how that particular work embodies either planetarity or climate justice or stands out for its attention to aesthetics.

This analysis of each novel with a single major lens will be followed by an examination of the text using the categories (taxonomies) of climate fiction. Then we shall briefly explore how the novel stands up to the scrutiny of the two remaining major lenses as well as the minor lenses which between them constitute what we have called the creative-thematic challenges (Figure 2.2) of cli-fi. This will give us an idea about the work's effectiveness as a literary representation of the climate crisis. Next we shall examine the transformative potential of each novel by probing the text with reader-response insights of empirical ecocriticism, as well as the advocacy and policy frameworks of SDGs, Production and Consumption Flows and in case of Ghosh's novel, the Integral Ecology approach. Following a section that applies a postcolonial ecocritical perspective to briefly examine the story (for the two postcolonial novels), the full analysis for each novel will be gathered in some concluding remarks.

It is necessary to restate the fact that this combination of three sets of probes (Figure 2.2) is a novel approach for studying climate fiction not commonly encountered in the literature. While we have excellent studies that have looked at a particular work through a specific lens, 'planetariness' for example, there are hardly any works which have applied multiple perspectives in an extensive reading of climate fiction. This multi-focal approach is expected to provide the reader a more nuanced and in-depth understanding about the ways of reading and appreciating the possibilities of these stories. This would be, to recall that famous parable, akin to having the blind men conversing to arrive at a consensus about the nature of the elephant that is the evolving genre of climate fiction.

Now that we have gathered the maps for our journey, it is time to embark upon the adventure of reading the stories. The routes that we uncover while exploring these texts will offer a blend of the reviewer's art with theoretical interludes and cross-practice nuance, opening vistas of meaning that reach out into the heart of climate fiction. Our journey begins in a café at the United Nations, which provides a window to the planet.

# Part Two

# Routes

# 5

# The Vienna Café

## *Climate and planet*

The Vienna Café in the basement of the United Nations Headquarters in New York is a warm and friendly place. If you have visited, you would know how this brightly lit space turns into a microcosm of the planet, or at least its human inhabitants, with delegates, journalists, activists and visitors from all corners of the world.

There is friendly banter exchanged between government officials and civil society representatives over steaming hot lattes; you find groups of activists wielding highlighters poring over texts emerging from negotiation rooms, tired delegates taking a break after hours of debate, or journalists munching on pastries while hooked to their laptops.

As you weave your way through this milieu to seek out a corner table, you may catch discussions ranging from carbon trading and climate adaptation funds to human rights and multi-stakeholder partnerships, often woven in with personal stories and experiences in the fields of policymaking and grassroots action.

It is in places like these that the planetary nature of issues like climate change or ozone depletion is immediately obvious. Otherwise, it is difficult even for grassroots activists to grasp the planetary scope and interconnected nature of climate change. While well-argued ideas and media reports from across the world do leave an impression, this first-hand experience and engagement of hundreds of delegates shared at such venues give us a clearer understanding of the global reach, impact and systemic interconnections of the climate crisis, which could otherwise get diluted in our quotidian focus on the 'local'.

Well-told stories, narrated from the vantage point of experience and an understanding of planetary connections, can help to correct this anomaly of understanding, where, despite the science and the reports, we tend to forget how our actions in the form of production and consumption connect across vast geographies and earth systems to manifest as the fearsome realities of the climate emergency.

And this is true about many aspects of the environment. In my first climate novel, *The Butterfly Effect*, I had tried to plot these global connections with the story of a transcontinental environment and health disaster, triggered by 'bad' science, which is aggravated by climate change. While writing that book, supported by generous grants that allowed me to research and situate my novel across multiple geographies, I had realized how necessary it is to address a widely spread crisis both at the global and local levels. Later on, of course, the Covid-19 pandemic drove home the ferocity of global disaster refracted and amplified through networks of international connections where economics, ecologies, global travel, politics, technology, culture and policy response all played significant roles.

While planning this book, I had been on the lookout for a novel which grappled with the planetary dynamics of climate change and its connections with global networks and flows in a well-told story which demonstrates a planetary consciousness. I found a number of books conscious of these connections, out of which Barbara Kingsolver's *Flight Behavior* and Amitav Ghosh's *Gun Island* left the strongest impression.

Kingsolver's novel, as mentioned earlier, makes these connections, twining the story of climate-induced change in migration patterns of the monarch butterfly with a natural disaster-related displacement of a family from Mexico to Feathertown, Tennessee, in the United States. However, her novel is mainly set in Feathertown and does not travel to other far-flung geographies as much as Ghosh's story does.

This is in addition to the fact that as a postcolonial Indian writer, Amitav Ghosh presented a more interesting choice for me as I set about to explore the planetariness of his fiction and how it connects to the stories of distant places like Bengal, Italy and the United States. Ursula Heise's work about planetary consciousness provided an appropriate lens for this examination.

But before we dive into Ghosh's novel, I have to tell you one more story. This is about my friend, the Dutch activist Manus van Brakel, whom I first met at the Vienna Café of United Nations headquarters in New York. Warm, affable and with an endearing smile, Manus was heavily involved with sustainability work for the Friends of the Earth when our paths had crossed.

One evening, Manus and I were on our way back to our hotels from the United Nations when we stepped into a street, right next to the glittering Plaza Hotel, where roadworks were in progress. Unmindfully, I had stepped on the hot tar, and my Khadim sneakers, already showing its age, got stuck in the molten asphalt. I extricated myself with some difficulty, with my shoes intact, when Manus breaking into his mischievous smile quipped, 'You have to be careful, otherwise you pull up the whole world with your feet.' These words of my dear departed friend still ring in my ears as every passing day reminds me of the need to tread softly, the need to be kind and the need to care as we go about navigating the stormy seas of the Anthropocene.

## Sundarbans, Venice and the planet – reading *Gun Island*

The Indian edition of Amitav Ghosh's *Gun Island* comes in a black dust jacket with a hamadryad coiled around the lettering, with stylized calotropis[1] blossoms completing the design. It is an intriguing artwork which, helped by the title, draws you immediately into the pages of this climate novel by this distinguished author, who has also published the widely acclaimed non-fiction work about climate change – *The Great Derangement*.

In *Gun Island*, Amitav Ghosh makes a spirited foray into the domain of climate fiction, a category still not well represented by postcolonial writers, though things have been changing fast.[2] The novel is in two parts – part one is titled The Gun Merchant and part two, Venice. The first part has ten chapters named Calcutta, Cinta, Tipu, The Shrine, Visions, Rani, Brooklyn, Wildfires, Los Angeles and Gun Island. Part two (Venice), which has twelve chapters, begins with The Ghetto and follows up with Rafi, Strandings, Friends, Dreams, Warnings, High Water, Crossings, Winds, The *Lucania*, Sightings and finally The Storm.

Written in the first person, that imparts immediacy to the narrative, the story of this novel begins in Kolkata, where New York-based antiquarian Dinanath Dutta, Deen to his friends, had been wintering at his family home. Quite by chance, he is introduced to the story of Bonduki Saudagar or the gun merchant, a forgotten figure straddling legend and history who is said to have drawn the wrath of a goddess for refusing to become her devotee and had escaped to a place called 'Gun Island'. But misfortunes had followed him to his refuge. The story of this legendary trader, Deen finds, has many parallels with the Bangla verse epics about Chand Sadagar and Manasa, the Hindu folk goddess of snakes, who is also central to the gun merchant's story. He learns that the gun merchant has a 'dham' or shrine in Sundarbans, the mangrove-covered deltas of south Bengal.

In between and quite by chance, we are introduced through a flashback to the glamorous and brilliant Italian historian Giacinta Schiavon or Cinta. Deen had first met Cinta at a library of a Midwestern university in the United States, wherefrom he had graduated, and later in Kolkata, where she had arrived to research the historical spice trade of Venice. Between these two meetings, Cinta comes across as a character who values experiences and phenomena that are beyond the pale of reason, and soon she tells Deen about a strange premonition she had before her husband and daughter were killed in a car accident.

While wintering in Kolkata, Deen meets Nilima Bose, founder of Badabon Trust, a charitable organization in the Sundarbans, and Piya Roy, a marine biologist who runs it. Egged on by Nilima, Deen journeys to the deep interiors of Sundarbans, where he would be introduced to Tipu, the son of trust employee Moyna, and Rafi, who is the last of a family of Muslims looking after the gun merchant's shrine.

Tipu, an insolent young man who had gotten mixed up with the wrong sort of crowd in America and has consequently gotten involved with human traffickers, needles and annoys Deen as they take a motorized launch to the shrine. Deen says, 'Moyna's description of her son had led me to expect an abject, morose young fellow. But it was evident at a glance that Tipu was a creature of an altogether different kind; he had the probing eyes and darting movements of a hungry barracuda' (52).

Tipu and Deen arrive at the shrine where they would meet Rafi. They find friezes with strange symbols on the facade of the structure which form bits of the puzzle around the gun merchant's story. But the visit ends with Tipu being attacked by a king cobra which almost kills him.

It won't be out of place to note that Piya and Nilima are two of a few more characters who recur from Ghosh's ecofiction *The Hungry Tide*, which was set in the Sundarbans. In this world of mangroves and murky waters, time is measured from one cyclone to another, from one disaster to the next:

> Sometimes, said Moyna, it seemed as though both land and water were turning against those who lived in the Sunderbans. When people tried to dig wells, an arsenic-laced brew gushed out of the soil; when they tried to shore up embankments the tides rose higher and pulled them down again. Even fishermen could barely get by; where once their boats would come back loaded with catch, now they counted themselves lucky if they netted a handful of fry.
>
> (49)

Climate-related environmental strife and disaster in the Sundarbans area (Figure 5.1) is the spinning core of *Gun Island* from which characters like Tipu, Rafi or even the gun merchant in another time are hurled outward, into other stories, by the violent centrifugal force of climate disaster overlapping with other reasons. Chased away from the punishing land they called home, these characters get drawn into other dreams, to other refuges, propelled by promises, towards other stories of life in the West, which constitute another set of interwoven narratives of this novel, where characters like Deen, Piya or the charismatic Cinta play important parts.

However, and because climate change effects know no boundaries and can spring surprises and unleash 'violence' at a place of its choosing, and also because stories connect with stories riding microscopic filaments of probability and chance, the characters of *Gun Island* find how an angry planet stitches them together in the present, as it had in the past, when the gun merchant was running away from a wrathful goddess.

The trials and tribulations of Tipu and Rafi drive the plot at one level, as it travels from Sundarbans to Venice, like many other climate refugees, who, taking great risks, cross land borders and oceans in search of a better life in Italy. Here in Deen, Tipu and Rafi's stories and their experiences, we perceive climate change as a hyperobject manifesting and influencing the plot, in places far removed from one another, through poisonous sea snakes, raging wildfires, killer cyclones, freak weather, fist-size hailstones and shipworms eating up the foundations of a city and more.

Returning to the story, we find that after being attacked by the cobra, Tipu goes into delirium, and he asks the others to warn Piya about 'Rani' who, it is soon revealed, is one of a pod of Irrawaddy dolphins that Piya had been researching for many years. Soon Deen and Piya will discover that Rani's pod had beached on an island

**Figure 5.1** A jetty in the Sundarbans. Photograph by Indranil Sinha Roy.

named Gorjontola for reasons that could be connected to changes in habitats and the effluents from a refinery in the region.

Now Deen returns to his home in Brooklyn, where he is possessed by anxiety and listlessness while Tipu strikes up an internet conversation with him which continues for days. Tipu asks him strange questions about ghosts and shamans and the different meanings and connotations that these words have. The young man informs him that he had heard shamans can communicate with animals, trees and mountains while also warning Deen that he might see a snake on his way to LA, where he was heading for a conference.

Tipu tells Deen that he is now in Bangalore while also surprising him with the information that he knows about his friendship with Cinta, insisting cryptically that Deen should listen to what she has to say. As Deen travels to LA for the conference, he indeed sees a snake in the talons of a bird above a wildfire-scorched landscape, and later on, the conference venue itself is threatened by advancing forest fires and has to shift to a safer location.

It is at this conference, with the wildfires raging outside, that a speaker brings up the history of the Little Ice Age (LIA) and the worldwide socio-political changes that it led to. Cinta is also a speaker there, and through her speech and the conversations that follow, the unexplained parts of the legend of the gun merchant and the mysterious symbols on his Sundarbans shrine are explained. The gun merchant, it is revealed, got his name because while fleeing from the wrath of Manasa Devi, he had taken refuge in Venice which in Arabic is 'al-Bunduqeyya' (from the Byzantine 'Banadiq'), where bunduqeyya is also the word for guns, or 'bundook', in India.

Cinta, using her knowledge of history, unravels the missing parts of the gun merchant's story for Deen, and it is revealed that the trader was sold by Portuguese pirates to a Jewish captain named Nakhuda Ilyas, who is with him for most of his voyages. We soon come to know that the drought and floods plaguing the gun merchant, manifesting as the wrath of the goddess, are the effects of the climatic disturbances of the LIA.

The first part of the novel ends with Deen's return to Brooklyn, from LA, where he sinks into worries about his future and finances while also receiving an invitation from Cinta's cousin's daughter, Gisa, to visit Venice. The city has many Bengalis, and Deen will be working as a translator, helping Gisa on a project.

The second part of the novel is set in Venice, where Deen luckily escapes an accident at the Ghetto and completely by chance meets Rafi again. Rafi now works part-time as a mason in Venice, and he introduces Deen to Lubna, who is from Bangladesh, and whose stories of climate strife and displacement from that country easily connect with Deen's own Bangladesh background, wherefrom his parents left during the Partition of India.

As Deen goes about his interviewing duties in Venice, he gathers more of the Gun Merchant's story from Rafi and comes to know of the part when the merchant took refuge in the gun foundry of the Venice Ghetto and was bitten by a poisonous spider. Meanwhile, Deen also has encounters with poisonous spiders, which have extended their geographical range with climate change, while he receives a phone call from Gisa, who tells him about a boatful of refugees, perhaps including some Bengalis, coming across the Mediterranean from Sinai in Egypt and heading towards Sicily. This Blue Boat soon becomes a political issue between the right wing, who want to stop the refugees, and those who are ready to welcome them.

Meanwhile, Piya receives an anonymous message predicting a beaching of dolphins in the Sundarbans which surprisingly comes true. While there, she makes inquiries about Tipu and gradually begins to uncover the story of his migration. Tipu, it seems, has set off on a dangerous journey through Pakistan, Iran and Turkey, and he is probably headed for Venice but is stranded somewhere in between. The possibility that he had sent the anonymous message also crops up as Piya reports all of this over the phone to Deen, and they realize how the stranding of Tipu parallels the strandings of the dolphins.

There is this definite sense from the story so far that just as the poison from refineries is affecting marine life, visible in the beached dolphins, so also the 'poison' of carbon emissions and the resultant climate change has been a factor leading to migrations and severe hardship for displaced people like Tipu. This poison, the author seems to say, is nothing other than human greed manifest through unsustainable production and consumption, which is affecting all beings.

Meanwhile, Deen is seized by this ever-growing feeling that there was a hidden pattern in his encounters with Tipu and Rafi, and he struggles to put this away as mere chance.

> I sat in bed as if paralysed, staring at the wall ahead. What was happening to me? To us? There seemed to be a pattern in my encounters with Tipu and Rafi. Yet that pattern was not of our own designing; it was as if something or someone had taken possession of us for reasons beyond our understanding.
>
> (187)

Soon afterwards Deen comes to know from another refugee, Bilal, that Rafi has been beaten up by a *scafista* (trafficker) for defaulting on a loan he had taken for a friend who, like him, was trying to come to Italy through the migrant routes. Bilal now tells Deen about his own dangerous journey to Italy, and from Bilal's account of the strong bonds that develop between friends on such dangerous voyages, it becomes obvious that Rafi had loaned money to help none other than the stranded Tipu.

As Deen waits for Cinta's return to Venice, he steps one day into the Querini Stampalia library, where he has a strange encounter with the Renaissance classic, *Hypnerotomachia Poliphili*. The incunabulum[3] is about a man who sets out in search of an always-absent lover and ends up in a forest of savage animals where he dreams a dream in which voices and messages emanate from these beings. Now Deen has an uncanny feeling that fantastical creatures – spiders, cobras, sea snakes – were dreaming about him, and they and he had become 'a part of each other's dream' (208). From an illustration of wreathing snakes in the Hypnerotomachia, Deen realizes that the Gun Merchant had seen this book and this is where he must have seen the face of Manasa Devi while sheltering in Venice. As he tries to open the glass case containing the book, he is surrounded by security but is later released.

With Cinta's return to Venice, Deen has long debates with her about how climate change is affecting all beings, where he leans towards scientific explanations and her words are framed with the ideas of demonic possession that human beings are under a spell which is why climate action is not taking off the way it should. Cinta, however, believes that Deen is undergoing a kind of awakening (through his uncanny encounters) – 'You are lucky, Dino – some unknown force has given you a great gift' (217).

Next, Cinta and Deen visit the Santa Maria della Salute with its statue of the Black Madonna of La Salute, or Madonna the Mediator. 'It is she who stands between us and the incarnate Earth, with all its blessings and furies' (223), Cinta explains, telling Deen that the statue came from Heraklion in Crete which is famous for the Minoan goddess of snakes. At the Fondamente Nove, Deen and Cinta have an accident as Cinta slips over a mass of squirming shipworms as parts of the pier they were standing on begin to fall off and get flooded. Luckily, Bilal, who is nearby, saves them, but Cinta has to be hospitalized.

Now Rafi begins to tell Deen the story of their (his and Tipu's) difficult journey on the way to Italy and how the two got separated while trying to enter Turkey. Tipu had managed to enter Egypt, which is the last news Rafi has had from him, so the possibility that he might be on the Blue Boat with refugees increases. Meanwhile, Lubna, along with other activists, is planning to meet the refugee boat, and Deen decides to join, and so does Rafi.

Soon Piya, Cinta and Gisa also join Lubna and the team of activists, and on a day marked by strange weather and tornadoes, they set out on the *Lucania* to meet the refugee boat. More uncanny events accumulate in the narrative as Gisa narrates an incident when she seems to have heard Cinta's dead daughter's voice, and Cinta says that *she* is with them. As more news about the Blue Boat arrives, it is learnt that the group of refugees had managed to free themselves from the traffickers because of a tornado that had struck the area in the Sinai (Egypt) where they were being kept captive.

As the Blue Boat with the refugees comes into view and bands of right-wing charter boats surge ahead to stop them, the Italian navy is also pressed into service. But now a strange phenomenon begins to unfold. Millions of birds appear in the sky, and in the water, different species of dolphins and whales are seen, and they begin to circle the refugee boat. As these miraculous scenes unfold, the admiral of the Italian navy, ignoring orders, takes a decision to welcome the refugees. Tipu is on that boat with the other refugees.

While the Admiral is getting interviewed, Cinta falls sick, but she says she is well and tells Deen he has given her a great gift. Finally, Cinta passes away on the *Lucania*, leaving Deen with the realization that 'the possibility of our deliverance lies not in the future but in the past, in a mystery beyond memory' (286).

From this poignant climax and her role throughout the plot, Cinta stands out as an important character who frames the novel with insight and a connection to the unknown. She is the one who helps Deen with the detective work necessary to get to the bottom of the gun merchant's story. She, as we have seen, is also the person who hears voices and seems to be able to communicate with the spirit world. Cinta is present near the beginning of this book, stirring up the plotline, and she is there again in these closing scenes aboard the activists' ship – a magnetic presence, balancing the real and 'unreal' worlds of *Gun Island*.

## Footwear, planetariness and eco-cosmopolitanism

Imagine we are travelling on a metro in Paris. Well, it could be any other city of an affluent nation. A shy person like me, to avert the gazes of strangers, will be looking down at the floor or doom-scrolling on the mobile. As you might have by now realized my obsession with shoes, and the absence of a really sturdy pair, you wouldn't be surprised if I tell you that my attention will soon be drawn towards the footwear of co-passengers sitting across from me. There, I wouldn't be surprised to find many well-known multinational brands of sneakers, sports shoes and of course rain shoes that I crave. Examining the footwear alone and shutting myself off to conversations of co-passengers, it would be difficult for me to tell which part of the world I'm in right then. The idea of place or the 'local' will have become 'deterritorialized' in my focused gaze.

Now I might begin to wonder where these shoes came from – China, Vietnam, Indonesia, Bangladesh or places further afield? What journeys have they undertaken, over rough seas, in oil-guzzling container vessels, trucks and freight trains, and how much carbon dioxide has been emitted in bringing them here, I would be asking myself. Quite probably, many of these were made with cheap labour in a developing nation where the forces of globalization have been able to dilute labour rights. Do some of these shoes hold a store of the dangerous sulphur hexafluoride in their soles,[4] a greenhouse gas which is more than 24,000 times powerful than carbon dioxide? What will happen when those shoes end up in landfills and the gas is released? I will also be questioning myself about the other materials and technology used in the manufacture of footwear, how much pollution they have caused and whether the factories where the raw material was processed or sourced from had displaced Indigenous peoples or destroyed the habitats of endangered species in a distant land.

As these questions crowd my mind, I will be attempting to comprehend trans-border systems and processes where ecology is twined with politics, technology, economics and world trade. In doing this, I will be opening myself to a systemic understanding of planetary processes where the human sphere of action, interests and adaptations overlap and intersect with earth systems as well as the sphere of the non-human flora and fauna of distant places. Thereby I will be expanding my ecological consciousness to a much broader and more systemic 'sense of planet' in which far-off places, peoples and other beings are interlinked through chains of causations in a planetary aggregate which will provide me with a better apparatus to question and comprehend multidimensional planetary crises like climate change.

This visualization provides an outline of the ideas developed by Ursula Heise in her paradigm-shifting work *Sense of Place and Sense of Planet: The Environmental Imagination of the Global.* Let us briefly examine her arguments which will help us sharpen the lens of planetarity we are going to use in this chapter. In her book, Heise begins by exploring how place or the local came to occupy a position of primacy in the environmental imagination, especially in the United States.[5] Flowing from various historical and intellectual streams as also in reaction to the nomadic sensibilities of Americans, the central idea of this outlook is that place or the local is the crucible of meaning and whatever is far and distant is outside the reach of ethics and action.

Aldo Leopold's 'land ethic'[6] and Zygmunt Bauman's idea of 'proximity'[7] are among several of these intellectual strands which, according to Heise, had solidified the primacy of place in the environmental imagination. In developing her arguments for the necessity of a planetary sense, she points out how writers like Mitchell Thomashow,[8] while acknowledging processes that stretch far beyond the local, through such experiences as migration patterns of birds that appear in the neighbourhood, still end up privileging perceptions and experience rooted in the local as the gateway to comprehending much larger processes and systems. This is despite various criticisms of this sense of place arising out of problems related to scale, the fact that place is culturally constructed, and how technology and globalization have created 'non-places', like airports, where the local has lost character.

Against this problematic privileging of the local, Heise, following sociologist John Tomlinson[9] and others, focuses on the concept of 'deterritorialization'. Tomlinson (quoted by Heise) writes, 'what is at stake in experiencing deterritorialized culture is not, crucially, level of affluence, but leading a life which, as a result of the various forces of global modernity, is "lifted off" its connection with locality' (52).

Deterritorialization and the severance of the connection with the local are evident in our day-to-day life. Public spaces like airports or subway stations (as also our metro example) present instances of such deterritorialization, where often it may be difficult to connect these places with national or local contexts. Similarly, the plethora of consumer goods, exotic vegetables and food items on my neighbourhood superstore shelf erodes the sense of the local from my consciousness.

However, these deterritorialized experiences can help to expand our environmental consciousness. Heise goes on to state that 'This deterritorialization of local knowledge does not necessarily have to be detrimental for an environmentalist perspective, but on the contrary opens up new avenues into ecological consciousness' (55). These new avenues of consciousness lead us on to a sense of planetary connections growing out of the plethora of experiences that are not connected with a 'familiarity with the local environment' (56). Therefore, while familiarity with the local can itself grant an entry into a sense of global connectedness, experiences not rooted in the local can also be an entry point to a planetary and a more systemic perspective which is underpinned by trans-border political, ecological, economic and other forces.

Stressing on the importance of these deterritorialized entry points of knowledge, Heise writes, 'In a context of rapidly increasing connections around the globe, what is crucial for ecological awareness and environmental ethics is arguably not so much a sense of place as a sense of planet – a sense of how political, economic, technological, social, cultural and ecological networks shape daily routines' (55). Therefore she goes on to state 'The challenge for environmentalist thinking, then, is to shift the core of its cultural imagination from a sense of place to a less territorial and more systemic sense of planet' (56).

Before we attempt to examine the 'planetarity' of *Gun Island*, it would not be out of place to mention that the author of that novel has elsewhere (*The Great Derangement* and *Smoke and Ashes*) demonstrated a keen awareness of these connections between places in his analysis of the modern realist novel in the context of climate change. There Ghosh has shown, with examples from well-known texts, how focusing on place and particular settings was important for those novels and how climate change, because of its global reach and manifestations, has made it difficult to tell tales that are corralled by the particularities of place while being blind to interconnections and continuities.

Prior to our analytical readings, we need to dwell for a while on another related concept, which is 'eco-cosmopolitanism'. Heise, in her book, contends that the planetary outlook she has elaborated on needs to be grounded in an environmentally oriented 'cosmopolitanism' or 'eco-cosmopolitanism' which while acknowledging planetary processes also examines the connections between humans and the other-than-human in communities that are affected or at risk.

To return to our metro ride, we have already seen how the origins of the shoes connect the passengers not only to global forces but also to far-off communities of human and other-than-human flora and fauna, who would have been affected or be at risk by the manufacturing and journey of this consumer product of a multinational company. Now, being an environment activist, my thoughts about the shoes and their impact on far-off human and non-human communities can make me contemplate upon the need for a cross-border intervention that engages the imagined community of final consumers, factory workers, displaced Indigenous people and affected flora and fauna all taken together. Furthermore, and thinking like an activist, I might also like to recruit my co-passengers in a community of awareness and action where their choice of footwear is conscious about trans-border systems and processes and the implications of the same on distant communities of humans and non-humans.

This would then be an imaginative leap, a sense of larger community driven by a planetary outlook and underpinned by an eco-cosmopolitan imagination. Heise writes, 'Eco-cosmopolitanism, then, is an attempt to envision individuals and groups as part of planetary "imagined communities" of both human and nonhuman kinds' (61). We will soon explore how the author of *Gun Island* demonstrates such an eco-cosmopolitan awareness while examining the 'planetarity' of his novel, both in the mythical and the realist layers of the story.

The climate crisis, being a global phenomenon of causes, effects and risks that operate through complex networks, bringing together earth systems, ecology, technology, culture, economics and society, can be engaged with a creative imagination that centres this 'sense of planet' we have described. In her discussion on climate change and eco-cosmopolitanism, Heise, analysing a number of novels, finds, 'All of these works, implicitly or explicitly, highlight the imbrication of local places, ecologies and cultural practices in global networks that re-configure them according to a logic that recent theories of globalization label "deterritorialization"' (210). She goes on to say that these texts 'thereby participate in the search for the stories and images of a new kind of eco-cosmopolitan environmentalism that might be able effectively to engage with steadily increasing patterns of global connectivity, including those created by broadening risk scenarios' (210). We will now see if and how Amitav Ghosh's story fits into this characterization, thereby arguing that this is a climate novel with a planetary consciousness.

## Climate and planet in *Gun Island*

Let us explore how the planetary consciousness of the author imbues the plot and the characters of *Gun Island* with a layer of meaning that is not only pertinent for a climate text but also allows the reader a better understanding of the systemic interconnections between place and planet that underlie global climate crisis. We will see how, through stories, journeys and the agency of characters both human and non-human, Ghosh has woven an engaging tale connecting distant places and peoples. This emerging sense of planet, we shall argue through examples, is a significant characteristic of this novel.

It is obvious from the multiple settings of Sundarbans, Kolkata, Venice, California, Brooklyn and the Mediterranean that this is a global novel that is not easily confined by territoriality or any long-running attachment to place. Supporting this view, Edwin Gilson, in his paper on 'planetary Los Angeles', argues that the novel's 'plot, characters and ... settings should be understood as products of a realist mode that prioritizes planet over place'.[10] While in that essay Gilson examines Los Angeles as symbolic of this planetary outlook, we will examine how a number of places (including LA) spread across continents, imparts what Heise, in her book, characterizes as an attempt to imagine the 'less territorially defined forms of inhabitation' (207).

*Gun Island* is narrated across a wide global canvas encompassing past and present, but this is not only a surface spread. The settings of the novel are active, and the entanglement of the story with the culture of peoples spread geographically apart, as well as with the lives of nonhuman beings, goes deep and far. It is therefore a work which engages with what has been called a 'cultural perspective of the global' (207).

Just as the settings stretch far and wide, the characters of the novel too come from very different places, and we find the author flavouring the text with words and phrases from Bangla and Italian. Antiquarian Deen is from Kolkata, educated in the American Midwest, and living in Brooklyn; Cinta is half-American, half-Italian and lives in Venice; Tipu and Rafi from the Sundarbans migrate to Italy; Lubna, who helps Bengali migrants to settle down in Italy, is from Bangladesh, while Piya lives between Kolkata and the United States.

The Bengali migrant community settled in Venice has an important place in the plot, as do communities of migrants and activists (pro- and anti-migration) from Asia and Europe, respectively. Besides this, the story and its settings also impinge upon and transform the lives and habitats of dolphins in Sundarbans, shipworms and spiders in Venice and serpents in Sundarbans and America. This wide variety of characters with different backgrounds and cultures enriches the cultural perspective of the novel. And all these different peoples, individuals and groups, including non-humans, are somehow or the other affected by climate change in its several manifestations and effects.

In her book, Heise emphasizes on the importance of bridging 'the gap between stories of individuals and accounts of global transformations' as one of the main challenges of the 'cultural representation of climate change' (208). We have seen Nick Admussen focusing on this aspect of connections in his Six Proposals for the Reform of Literature in the Age of Climate Change, where he writes, 'In the stories we need, though, nobody exists outside of some reference to social and physical contexts. Life touches at life from all points on the globe at all times.' *Gun Island*'s plot easily telescopes from the individual, Tipu and Rafi, to the collective story of the journey of migrants, the risks, dangers and hardships on the way and in their adopted home, and the efforts and counter-efforts of activist groups gathering to help or thwart them. And once again we cannot ignore the fact that the journeys of these migrants (and that of the Gun Merchant) in the mythic narrative from the past are often triggered by climate change (present or past) and the forces of globalization (mainly in the present) – manifest 'as a better life' and transmitted through networks of social media and the internet.

Digital social networks are another strand of connectivity that allows us to focus on planetary connections. Heise, in her work, mentions 'digital networks' while discussing the global imagination of David Brin's novel *Earth*. 'Digital network', she writes, 'indeed, is the counterpart and in some sense the master trope for the ecological connectivity with which it fuses at the end' (209). We find in *Gun Island* how chat channels, mobile phones, social media and the internet pervade the story. Tipu often talks with Deen over a chat channel when Deen is in the United States, trans-continental mobile phone conversations between characters move the story along and Tipu is found to have done extensive research on the internet about Venice before setting out on the dangerous journey to the West.

On their first meeting, Tipu reveals to Deen how he has been using the mobile phone in his illegal business of sending climate-affected villagers to the West. 'The Internet is the migrants' magic carpet; it's their conveyor belt' (61), he declares. Explaining it further, he tells him how the mobile phone is instrumental in transmitting images and the accompanying lure of a better life to would-be migrants:

> Where d'you think they learn that they need a better life? Shit, where do you think they even get an idea of what a better life is? From their phones of course. That's where they see pictures of other countries; that's where they view ads where everything looks fabulous; they see stuff on social media, posted by neighbours who've already made the journey – and after that what d'you think they gonna do?
>
> (61)

Let us now take a closer look at the story to see whether a systemic sense of planet and an eco-cosmopolitan sensibility inform the narrative. Close to the beginning of the novel, we are presented with a flashback of Cinta's visit to Kolkata, where at a folk theatre she is introduced to the goddess of snakes and poisonous insects – Manasa Devi. The goddess, as we have seen earlier in the story summary, will come to play an important role throughout the book. In fact, in the gun merchant's story, she is the manifestation of non-human agency or, as the author writes, their *portavoce* or 'voice carrier' (152), thereby connecting the human and non-human worlds of *Gun Island*.

Later in the narrative set in Venice, when Deen visits the church of Santa Maria della Salute (the Madonna of Good Health), who is supposed to have wrought a miracle during the plague of the seventeenth century, Cinta takes him up to the altar of the Black Madonna of La Salute. Also known as Madonna the Mediator, 'it is she', says Cinta, 'who stands between us and the incarnate Earth, with all its blessings and furies' (223).

The parallel between Manasa and Madonna the Mediator cannot be missed, as their roles of voice carrier and mediator are very similar. This also strengthens the planetary connections in the mythical layer of the story, which thereby helps to advance the plot. Interestingly, the non-human connection between Manasa and the Madonna becomes even more prominent when it is learnt that the icon of Madonna the Mediator was brought from the city of Heraklion which is famously associated with the name of the Minoan goddess of snakes.

In the Indian myth, Manasa Devi goes after the gun merchant who refuses to be her devotee, assailing him with floods, famines, droughts and storms. He is captured by Portuguese pirates on the Bay of Bengal and sold off as a slave in Goa, where a ship captain (Nakhuda Ilyas) buys him, and they set off on journeys to many lands (later revealed to be Maldives, Egypt and Istanbul). But Egypt and Istanbul are in the midst of political turmoil and climatic disturbances, and so they finally take refuge in Bonduk Dwip (Venice) or Gun Island, where too the merchant cannot escape the wrath of Manasa Devi, who appears before him, and later he is bitten by a poisonous spider.

The merchant escapes from Gun Island, but their ship is attacked by pirates, and he is taken prisoner to be sold off, when Manasa Devi appears before him again. Only when he swears he will become her devotee and build a shrine for the goddess in Bengal, she comes to his aid in the form of various creatures of the sea and sky which attack the pirates. On his way back the merchant does many lucrative trades and returns with such a vast fortune that they call him Bonduki-Sadagar or the Gun Merchant because he had been to Gun Island. This Gun Island, as the book later reveals, is the city of Venice.

The shrine to Mansa Devi that the Gun Merchant finally builds after returning to the Sundarbans is dated between 1605 and 1690, which would imply that the storms and natural calamities that the goddess unleashes to punish him happened around that time. This timeframe of natural calamities in the tale of the Gun Merchant overlaps with the LIA, a period of worldwide climatic disturbances. So the myth, which is embedded in local culture, is also the implicit carrier of a story where the experiences of an individual – the Gun Merchant – connect with 'planetary transformations' (206) of the LIA. The myth as framed by Ghosh therefore clearly demonstrates a planetary sense.

This period of worldwide climatic change known as the LIA, among other things, resulted in extreme cold weather in parts of Europe. We have earlier noted how one of Andrew Marvell's poems may have been influenced by these climatic changes. These changes were also recorded in Continental Europe by authors, diarists and artists like Pieter Bruegel the Elder and Hendrick Avercamp, who took to drawing winterscapes (Figure 5.2). In *Gun Island*, the LIA is a significant driver of the plot, besides being intellectually engaged with by the character of a professor at the lecture in Los Angeles, which Deen attends.

**Figure 5.2** Winter Landscape with Ice Skaters by Hendrick Avercamp c.1608, Courtesy Rijksmuseum, Amsterdam.

The author's engagement with the global through various real-life experiences or myths that are connected with planetary risk scenarios (storms, droughts) of climate change is observed throughout the book. The snakes (of Manasa) appear not only in Sundarbans where it bites Tipu, but also on a Californian beach. One particular reptile, a 'yellow-belly', which kills Gisa's dog Leola, appears far from its natural geographical habitat, having been displaced by a warming planet.

Again, the appearance of spiders on two occasions in Venice is an indicator of planetary processes at play. The first spider springs upon Deen and Rafi, while the second one, a poisonous 'brown recluse', appears in Cinta's home, scaring Deen. Soon Deen comes to learn through Piya and an expert that the appearance of the brown recluse can be explained by a warming planet which has enabled it to expand its range and appear in Venice.

As we mentioned earlier, a poisonous spider also appears in Venice, in the Gun Merchant's story. Despite the fact that he had sheltered in a room with iron walls, the spider managed to sneak in and bite him. This is when the merchant realizes he can no longer remain in Venice because there too he is unable to hide from Manasa Devi. It is clear that the disrupted planetary processes of the LIA are making their presence felt in the form and shape of non-human agents, which appear in the story, altering the flow of the narrative.

This is true as well for the timeline of the novel set in the present, where we repeatedly see climate change leaving its impression on the plot. The brown recluse spider that scares Deen is another manifestation of global climatic processes at play. The careful reader, as well as Deen himself, will not fail to notice how creatures like snakes and spiders appearing far from their natural habitats dilute the sense of place (of California and Venice), connecting our experience to the larger global process of climate change at play. We can easily draw a parallel with our earlier thought experiment of the footwear of the metro passengers because here too the local losing its specificity (although for somewhat different reasons) becomes deterritorialized in our experience, expanding our ecological consciousness to a broader and more systemic 'sense of planet'.

There are other instances, settings and plot points in this novel that demonstrate deterritorialization and planetary connections in the context of a planet affected by climate crisis, and we will now address a couple of these. The author draws a clear visual parallel between two important settings of the novel – Sundarbans and Venice. As Deen's plane begins its descent into Venice, he marks the similarity of the two from the air:

> when I turned to look out of the window I found myself gazing down at a sight that reminded me of the patch of Bengal countryside that I had glimpsed on my last flight out of Calcutta, a little more than two years before: an estuarine landscape of lagoons, marshes and winding rivers.
>
> From that height it was possible to mistake the Venetian lagoon for the Sundarbans.
>
> (147)

Through this visual comparison, Ghosh subtly nudges the reader towards an appreciation of the connections and the underlying climate change-related dynamics of the two settings.

Though separated by thousands of kilometres, the waterworlds of Venice and the deltaic Sundarbans have a few things in common which are revealed by the story. There are two important but related strands to these similarities and connections. These are through direct climate change effects and non-human agency, on one hand, and between people and culture, on the other.

Let us first explore this connection through climate effects and non-human agency. In its early chapters, the book, through backstories of Horen, Neelima and others, fleshes out the increasing climate-related stress and events that assail the ecologically fragile Sundarbans. So we find mentions of real cyclones like Bhola and Aila and their accompanying floods, saline water affecting agricultural land, the altered behaviour of species like orcaella dolphins (of which Rani is an important character), and the beaching and death of fish, crabs and a pod of orcaellas.

Likewise, in the Venice scenes too, we have an unprecedented tornado, hailstorms, the high water or *acqua alta* and the billions of shipworms that have been eating into the foundations of the city. In bearing witness to the climate-related phenomena and effects, Venice and Sundarbans (and also California) stand out as signifiers of global climate crisis refracted through their individual geographies, ecologies, economies and cultural peculiarities.

We have already discussed non-human agency through the role played by spiders and poisonous snakes in the story. Similarly, the behaviour of other creatures like dolphins and shipworms between these two places also indicates the agency of the non-human in the flow of the narrative. We learn that the dolphin Rani in Sundarbans begins to make eye contact with Piya, with something of a look of gratitude, after she frees her from a nylon net, and about Piya later rushing to witness the beaching of these creatures. In Venice, the shipworms that are eating into the foundations of the city are also instrumental in an important scene that puts Deen and Cinta in mortal danger. Poignantly, Rafi makes a planetary connection between Venice and Sundarbans by comparing the sounds made by those shipworms with the sounds of the crabs burrowing inside the embankments of the Sundarbans. These manifestations of non-human in Sundarbans and Venice not only drive the narrative of *Gun Island* but also make the global impacts of climate crisis apparent to characters like Deen and Piya.

The second strand of connectivity between these two settings is revealed at the level of the human through phenomena like forced migration, its associated risks and deterritorialized experiences of culture, as in Deen's noticing of the use of Bangla among migrants in Venice. In fact, Deen is saved by inches when someone shouts a warning (*sabdhan!*) in Bangla as a block of masonry from a construction site crashes next to him on a Venice street. Also, Deen meets Rafi first in Sundarbans and then by chance in Venice (after that close shave) and then again in the course of doing research for Gisa as an interpreter, thereby getting connected to the community of Bengali migrants of the city.

While in Venice, Deen makes this observation:

> I began to listen carefully now and soon I was hearing echoes of familiar words and sounds all around me. I wandered down the street, starting conversations in Bangla almost at random: the idea that it might be possible to do this in Venice was, for me, something so novel as to be astounding. For even though Bangla is spoken by a great number of people – more than twice as many as speak German or Italian, for instance I was not accustomed – to thinking of my mother tongue as a 'global language'.
>
> (163)

Through his encounter with the brown recluse spider, far from its usual habitat, and with his growing connection with the Bengali community in Venice, Deen's experience, by then, is not only deterritorialized, but he is also discovering the planetary connections of global climatic, economic and political forces that have played a role in this dilution of the sense of place.

As the plot progresses, both Tipu and Rafi are displaced from Sundarbans, an area severely impacted by climate change. They embark on a dangerous journey headed west to escape poverty and driven by the allure of a better life. Similarly, many other Bengali migrants in the story have been displaced by climate change and economic factors.

'Every time there was a flood – which was happening more and more – they would try to move the boundaries' (192). Bilal, another migrant, tells Deen revealing how natural forces, greed, the threat of violence and the insidious working of power, ultimately forced them to leave. The migration of these Bengalis (among other people) who, displaced by climate strife, conflict and violence in their homeland, embark on dangerous journeys in search of a better life, are not only important drivers of the narrative, they also signify planetary forces at play.

Arriving in Italy to help with Gisa's research, Deen finds Henry James' Venice novel *The Aspern Papers* in Cinta's home. He soon realizes how different the time (late nineteenth century) of that book is from the Venice of the present, and also from the time of the Gun Merchant, when the sense of place and fixed bearings had been blown away by global forces at play:

> It wasn't just that the novella was about another time; it depicted a Venice in which it was impossible to imagine evocations of Madaripur, or a reunion with someone from the Sundarbans. It struck me that the Venice I had encountered today harked back to a time before that of The Aspern Papers – it was closer in spirit to the city that the Gun Merchant would have seen in the seventeenth century, another era when unaccustomed forces were churning the earth. Except that now it was unimaginably more so; it was as if the very rotation of the planet had accelerated, moving all living things at unstoppable velocities, so that the outward appearance of a place might stay the same while its core was whisked away to some other time and location.
>
> (166)

Incidentally, Madaripur is a place where the Bangladeshi character Lubna, who helped immigrants with work and advice, came from, another place which had been affected by cyclones and climate chaos, forcing people to migrate.

These uprootings and migrations, the support of the community of activists who try to help the refugees and the resistance from right-wing anti-migration groups, entangle climate with culture, politics and economics, building up to the memorable final scenes of the novel on board the ship *Lucania*. This thread of the narrative deftly connects individual places, culture and politics in a broader planetary framework which allows a deeper appreciation of the wide-ranging impacts of climate change.

The final chapters of the book which are set aboard the rescue ship *Lucania* not only consolidate the planetary consciousness of the author, but also, by weaving in the non-human world, again demonstrate what Heise has called an eco-cosmopolitan outlook, which 'is an attempt to envision individuals and groups as part of planetary "imagined communities" of both human and nonhuman kinds' (61).

As the *Lucania* with Deen, Cinta, Piya and others sails out into the Adriatic to meet the Blue Boat carrying Tipu and other displaced persons trying to reach Italy, there are two parallel narrative threads that join up in a memorable scene which foregrounds an 'imagined community'[11] of displaced humans and migrating non-humans, articulating the eco-cosmopolitan vision of this novel.

The first of these threads has to do with the politics surrounding refugees and migrants. Deen and others aboard the *Lucania* soon find other chartered ships with right-wing anti-immigrant activists heading out to stop the refugees from setting foot in Italy. This opposition leads Deen to reflect on the international networks and systems of migration right from the days of chattel slavery through colonization and the forced displacement of indentured labour to far-off lands, and on to the present when climate change, wars, aspirations and poverty drive people to foreign shores. Here again, Ghosh demonstrates a planetary outlook which connects distant places through the movement of people and the economic, technological, climatic and other forces that are implicated in these journeys.

The other thread of events observed by the characters on the *Lucania* and all other boats and ships in their vicinity is an almost miraculous crossing of migration paths of dolphins, whales and millions of birds. The possible climate connection to this unusual event is mentioned by Piya, but what is significant here is the fact that this magical scene with the somersaulting dolphins and whales slapping their tails on the waves and the 'storm' (281) of birds funnelling down and forming a halo around the Ethiopian leader of the refugees on the Blue Boat influences the admiral of the Italian navy to decide that the refugees will be welcome. The Admiral says it's a miracle, and this scene indeed demonstrates a momentary coming together of the human and the non-human in a planetary 'imagined community' of the sort Heise mentions in her conceptualization of eco-cosmopolitanism.

It would not be out of place to mention here that researchers like Nidhi Angurala, on the contrary, have noted what could be interpreted as resistances to the eco-cosmopolitan outlook in the novel.[12] Angurala has pointed out that the hostility of the sea snake or the cobra is an indicator that the eco-cosmopolitan project is far from complete till a universal inter-species communication system fosters the forming of imagined communities.

While there is a surface rationality to such an assertion, one cannot deny the fact that there are moments and scenes in the book where non-verbal communication between humans and other species seems to be taking place, and there are indications, most strongly in the scene with the 'storm' of birds that the author points to a possibility of community and communication between humans and non-human others is possible. Moreover, the hostility of non-humans that these researchers point out does not necessarily demonstrate the untenability of imagined communities, rather these demonstrate the complex entanglements between species and how these have been further complicated by anthropogenic climate change. That a tiger attacks a honey-gatherer doesn't necessarily mean that the dream of a cross-species imagined community has fallen apart; it is just a reaffirmation of the importance of imagining such multispecies communities and that of negotiating the complexities of multispecies justice,[13] within contexts of caring and kinship which acknowledge shared modes of existing and surviving without ruining the planet.

To re-emphasize this possibility of an imagined community and how climate fiction can bring this to life, within a planetary framework, it is best to conclude this section with this evocative description of the pivotal moment when the halo of birds begins spinning around the Ethiopian woman leading the Blue Boat of refugees from distant lands:

> She stood absolutely still for what was perhaps only a moment, with a halo of birds spinning above her, while down in the water a chakra of dolphins and whales whirled around the boat. And then an even stranger thing happened: the colour of the water around the refugee boat began to change. In a few moments it was filled with a glow, of an unearthly green colour, bright enough that we could see the outlines of the dolphins and whales that were undulating through the water.
>
> 'Bioluminescence!' cried Piya. 'I don't believe it!'
>
> For a few moments more we were transfixed by this miraculous spectacle: the storm of birds circling above, like a whirling funnel, and the graceful shadows of the leviathans in the glowing green water below.
>
> (282)

## Where to place this story?

Where does a planetary climate novel fit in with our categories of cli-fi? Does its planetariness imbue it with certain characteristics which make it easier for us to slot it into one or more of the types of cli-fi we discussed earlier? Having studied the novel with the major lens of planetarity, we will now examine it using these categories (Figure 2.2) discussed in an earlier chapter.

First of all, let us begin by saying that Ghosh's climate novel easily passes the Climate Reality Check and fits with the other definitions of climate change we discussed in an earlier chapter. Now, let us revisit our organizing principles for climate fiction. These, as we might recall, included the five Imaginaries, the modified Costanza framework, the three-way division between novels of Denial-Acceptance-Avoidance, Caution and Resistance, a possible slotting between Realist and Futurist works, the sci-fi, cli-fi and Supergenre contentions, the division between Dystopian and Utopian depictions and the classification on the basis of Mitigative and Adaptive narratives.

On the surface, the sense of planet does not seem to have much of a bearing on the possible categorization of the novel based on the above. However, Ghosh's book is quite clearly cli-fi, rather than sci-fi, and its engagement with eco-cosmopolitanism (flowing from its sense of planet) speaks to Costanza's sub-type of works where the role of collectives and community is strong. Let us look a little deeper into the story and its driving concerns, putting them under the scanner of the taxonomies of cli-fi.

We first try to apply the imaginaries-based classification of Gregers Andersen to our reading of this book. The novel's story world is definitely not a Conspiracy imaginary nor is it a Sphere story of alternative safe zones or terraformed bubbles of refuge from climate strife. It, however, contains elements of the other three imaginaries: Loss of Wilderness, Judgement and Social Breakdown. The increasing climate stress on the Sundarbans is a major plot point of the book, driving its story forward, and letting the reader experience how climate change and other concatenating factors are affecting this mangrove-covered deltaic region, leading to loss of tree cover from cyclones, increased salinity of the rivers, growing oceanic dead zones, habitat loss and more. So Loss of Wilderness is a significant imaginary for portions of the book. The Judgement imaginary also informs the narrative through the story of the Gun Merchant's encounter with punishing storms and droughts unleashed, per the legend, by the wrath of the goddess but really caused by climatic changes of the LIA. Judgement as a climate imaginary is also prominent in the ways the Sundarbans landscape seems to be turning against its inhabitants[14] driving women to the sex trade, snatching away livelihoods and causing migration. The following passage is poignant:

> Sometimes, said Moyna, it seemed as though both land and water were turning against those who lived in the Sundarbans. When people tried to dig wells, an arsenic-laced brew gushed out of the soil; when they tried to shore up embankments the tides rose higher

> and pulled them down again. Even fishermen could barely get by; where once their boats would come back loaded with catch, now they counted themselves lucky if they netted a handful of fry.
>
> (49)

And though society hobbles along through the pages of this novel, there is always the possibility of imminent breakdown as intolerance towards displaced peoples grows in places like Italy, and more and more young people leave their homes from regions like Sundarbans, dislodged by climate change and propelled by dreams of a better life. So the Social Breakdown imaginary does lurk in the background at the borders of possibility. In fact, in the narrative of the Gun Merchant which unfolds during the climatic disturbances of the LIA, there is socio-economic turmoil in the countries he visits before seeking refuge in Venice. So each of those three imaginaries is manifest to different extents in this novel, with Loss of Wilderness playing a pivotal role in the narrative.

The second taxonomic frame based on the Costanza framework hardly applies to *Gun Island* as the story is not set in the future and technological fixes to climate change are not addressed. However, as we noted above, there is a narrative thread dealing with activism and community engagement to mitigate the suffering of climate migrants, which tilts the novel towards a belief in activism.

Looking at the third taxonomic frame, we can say the story is both a tale of acceptance, in the category of Barbara Kingsolver's *Flight Behaviour*, and resistance. The text, including some characters, is conscious of the origins and impacts of climate change and engages with it through dialogue and action. This action is visible in the intellectual engagement of the California professor, Cinta's conversations with Deen and Piya's work with dolphins. But most significantly, resistance and action are visible in the activism of those who try to help the refugees. *Gun Island* is also not a cautionary tale presenting vivid depictions of future catastrophes but is rooted in the present climate emergency and its significant challenges.

The fourth perspective addresses realist and futurist narratives. The novel is evidently not set in the future. Following Caren Irr, who has discussed satirical and realist-hybrids, we would place *Gun Island* in the category of realist-hybrid works. While there are many pages of realist description here, we also encounter myths as a major storyline as well as a conscious political engagement (not 'emitted' in the Lukacs sense) of the plot. Also, in a departure from the modern realist novel, the fearsome spectacles and uncanniness of climate change, including the role of non-human agency and the unimaginable, are ever present. Moreover, because of the presence of ghosts and the supernatural in the narrative, we can say the book demonstrates intrusions of the fantastic or rather a dialogue between the human, the non-human and the spirit world.

We will remember that Irr has noticed apocalyptic tendencies existing alongside realist depictions in the fiction she calls realist-hybrids – 'they fuse realist prose style with apocalyptic sensibilities'.[15] While apocalyptic tendencies can be read in the depiction and agency of the cyclones, floods and fire of *Gun Island*, Ghosh has remarked that his book is 'not apocalyptic' and that he is 'leaving hope as a possibility',[16] which the reader would notice in the scenes culminating in the rescue of the refugees on the Blue Boat.

From the perspective of the fifth frame, we can easily conclude that this book is not sci-fi. We don't encounter any consistent sci-fi novum in the text. The book rather takes up the substance of myth (the Gun Merchant's story) and the reality of fossil fuel exploitation by humans and projects it into the realities of a climate-changed present.

The sixth taxonomic division addresses dystopian and utopian cli-fi. *Gun Island* is clearly not dystopian despite the occasional scenes with wildfires, freak weather and hailstorms. The world in the present timeline of the novel is not different from our lived present, and unless we agree the present to be dystopian, we cannot label the book as dystopia. The timeline of the past, set in the period of the LIA, can look dystopian because of the focus on dystopian elements in the merchant's story, also because this period is known to have experienced (as the novel also mentions) worldwide environmental and socio-political chaos. But that time was not much different from the present if we think of anthropogenic climate change and its effects, wars and the pandemic.

While the book ends with hope, there is no discernible effort to work out a utopian imaginary in detail. The story however addresses the politics of environmental justice and the slow violence of toxic waste mentions oceanic dead zones and engages climate-mediated migration. Le Menager's articulation of the 'everyday Anthropocene'[17] which 'offers a more granular and personal account of near catastrophic change' and that cli-fi 'does not need a compelling apocalyptic drama', seems to be borne out by this novel, where critical, but not apocalyptic, events connect through probability and chance, laying out the complex plot of the story.

Finally, if we focus on the seventh taxonomic frame, this is more a novel of adaptation than mitigation. Mitigative strategies where people directly address emissions sometimes come up in dialogues about causes of global warming, but otherwise, most of the relevant narrative is about affected people managing, adapting and carrying on with their lives or looking for better opportunities in distant lands.

## Climate and the imagination in *Gun Island*

How does a planetary climate novel like *Gun Island* navigate the other representational challenges of climate fiction? Does the planetary scope offer an extra advantage to the story, as our Ockham's razor-inspired approach suggested, while it negotiates some of these creative-thematic challenges (Figure 2.2) of cli-fi?

We have earlier noted how the distinctive features of cli-fi are inseparable and connected to the creative-thematic challenges of depicting climate-changed worlds. These, embodied in the major and minor lenses of our exploration, pertain to nature-culture entanglements, derangements of scale, non-human agency, the uncanny, the role of collectives and most importantly politics, aesthetics and the idea of planetarity. Out of these, aesthetics, politics (justice) and planetarity are our major lenses, among which we have already discussed planetarity of *Gun Island* in a preceding section. Depending on the type of story the author is trying to tell, some of these features may be more significant for certain texts while others may recede into the background.

The nature-culture divide in literature, which has its roots in the partitioning project of modernity, is something that Ghosh has himself discussed at length in his non-fiction work about climate change, *The Great Derangement*. There are several ways that his novel challenges this artificial division, presenting a story where culture or the human sphere smoothly dovetails with the natural, non-human world. Ghosh does this primarily by bringing culture, personified by Deen with his antiquarian trade, in close contact with the complexities of the Sundarbans' ecology and myths and the scientific attitude of marine biologist Piya. In other settings of the book, like California and Venice, we find the natural world seeping into the story in the form of sea snakes, spiders, shipworms and also through a character like 'Horen' in Sundarbans, about whom Deen says, 'Storms, I soon discovered, were Horen's measure of time' (54).

Moreover, Ghosh superimposes the character of the scientist, marine biologist Piya, in the landscape of myths – the Sundarbans – which is under stress from human activity. We come to know of the beaching dolphins and the discharge of effluents by a refinery in the area, all of which connect in the plot, through Piya's concerns for the dolphin Rani and her pod, and the clairvoyant Tipu's predictions of their beaching. We begin to see once again how science and the natural world are inextricably entangled with the human and the cultural, in a complex network of effects that influence the drift of the narrative, thereby revealing a more nuanced picture of a planetary crisis.

There are other plot elements, instances and themes in the book where the connections between nature and culture are visible. It is not possible to examine each of these within the confines of these pages, but one major thematic element, which subsumes these particular instances, is climate change, past and present. The climatic changes of the LIA and the anthropogenic climate change of our time, are mirrored in Ghosh's narrative as it juxtaposes the gun merchant's trans-continental flight from the wrathful Manasa Devi, the *portavoce* of nature, who unleashes upon him storms and droughts, with the misfortunes, trials and tribulations of climate-displaced characters like Tipu and Rafi setting out on dangerous journeys drawn by the allure of a better life in the West.

The role of Manasa Devi as the *portavoce* of nature pursuing the Gun Merchant across continents during the crises-ridden years of the LIA is a clear instance of the climate novel's planetarity, foregrounding nature-culture as one and indivisible. A comparison can also be made between the increased geographical range of the brown recluse spider or the yellow-belly snake and the migrations of Tipu and Rafi, in both of which anthropogenic climate change can be implicated. All these plot strands reveal how closely enmeshed the natural world and the planet are with that of the human, while not denying other factors like the economy that also play an important role in this enmeshment.

Although nature-culture as a distinctive feature is important for the representational goals of climate stories, this, at times, irrespective of any author, comes at a cost. Because of the powerful legacy of the separation of nature from culture, many readers have not been trained to appreciate hybrid genres and the ways in which nature-culture becomes unified in literary representations of climate change. Such readers may find some of these seepages, 'intrusions' and enmeshments jarring, and feel as if there is a tear in the fabric of the story and something unexpected, and uncanny, is peeping out from it.

On the issue of scale, Ghosh, by introducing the centuries-old myth of the Merchant, which also reveals patterns of similarity to the wrath of climate change, opens up the temporal scale of the story to give the reader a better perspective of climate change happening over long time periods. At a more expository level, a character questioning the speaker at the Los Angeles conference mentions the beginning of the use of coal by Londoners in the seventeenth century as the inception of humanity's dependence on fossil fuels, thereby engaging with the longer temporal scales of climate change. Therefore, recalling Timothy Clarke's arguments about derangements of scale, we can say Ghosh's novel is conscious of scale effects and provides some opportunities for multi-modal reading across time and geographical scales that Clark advocates.

Ghosh, by turning his gaze back by a few centuries through the myth of the gun merchant (the LIA is also mentioned) in Sundarbans, by mentioning the use of fossil fuels and through the history of Venice, transports us over these much-longer temporal and spatial scales through which the climate crisis assumes clearer meaning and significance. And back in that past too, the reader encounters 'disasters', 'burning winds' and 'poison-spitting' monsters, most of all Manasa Devi, the goddess of snakes who can be read as a symbolic representation of non-human agency, or their 'voice', plaguing the protagonists of the myth.

*Gun Island*, as we have already seen, depicts non-human agency and non-human characters twined to its quest plot, right from when Tipu is bitten by the hamadryad which makes him delirious and to an extent clairvoyant, through Deen's episodes with the spider, the narrative stream about Rani (a chapter is named after her) the dolphin, Cinta's encounter with her daughter's spirit, the episode with shipworms that are devouring Venice's foundations, the incident of the water snake killing a pet dog and finally the poignant climax where millions of birds funnel down from the heavens and whales and dolphins circle the refugee boat carrying Tipu.

In many of these incidents, the agency of the non-human, in the ways they affect the flow of the narrative and the thoughts and actions of the characters, is plainly evident. For example, Tipu, becoming delirious after being bitten by the hamadryad and his apparent clairvoyance thereafter, from which he alerts Piya that Rani may be in danger, sends Rani and Deen to look for the dolphins. Tipu's warning turns out to be right. Deen's encounter with the brown recluse spider, itself an agent of planetary upheavals, at Cinta's home gives him a panic attack, and he consequently finds out that rising temperatures have led these creatures to increase their geographical range. More importantly, it is the bite of a poisonous spider which makes the gun merchant realize that he is no longer safe in Venice and has to leave. The climax of course is the most poignant depiction of non-human agency because it is the miracle of the birds and the sea creatures which finally convinces the Admiral to welcome the refugee boat.

We will remember from Actor-Network Theory that actors are not independent starting points of action and are linked through dependencies with other actors. This conceptual understanding is well played out in many of the scenes of the novel where human and non-human actors, along with ecologies and global forces, interact through networks of dependencies. So the Admiral does not take his decision to welcome the refugees on his own but is influenced by the migration of the birds and the sea creatures, while the refugees themselves are not independent actors but are driven by global forces of climate change, economic conditions, and war, which in turn are driven by other actors and ideas. The migration of the sea creatures also has a possible climate connection.

All of these weaken the edifice of independent human agency in the story, foregrounding the interconnected roles of non-human actors. Yet one cannot completely escape the feeling of foreignness of the text, a kind of estrangement on the surface, which could be a symptom of our lack of preparedness for the falling apart of the conventions of the modern realist novel. Non-human agency, like the hamadryad biting Tipu, strikes at the familiar flow of the plot, pushing it towards unpredictable directions, forcing it to reveal the leaps that the realities of climate change and history embed in the dynamics of real and imaginary lives.

Another distinctive feature of climate novels, the climate uncanny, is also encountered in the pages of this novel. Earlier, we made a distinction between the Freudian and the Heideggerian uncanny of cli-fi. The Heideggerian uncanny, we will recall, is an affective[18] quality joining inner and outer worlds, while the Freudian uncanny is experienced in the animation of non-human 'objects'. Often in Ghosh's novel, the uncanny is evoked and affects the character(s) and the reader in scenes where non-human agency plays an important part. We have earlier discussed in our Ockham's razor approach why these two can be contiguous.

The appearance of the brown recluse spider in Cinta's Venice home gives Deen a sort of panic attack as its unexpected presence conveys a sense of the uncanny. Tipu's delirium and his correct prediction of the beaching of dolphins are also imbued with strangeness which gives characters and readers a feeling of the uncanny as they (and we) cannot figure out how Tipu could possibly know. The appearance of the poisonous spider, which bites the gun merchant, in the strong room of Venice, is again an uncanny incident as it is considered the safest place in the city. All of these, as well as the final scene with the storm of birds funnelling down on the Blue Boat, can be put down to the Freudian sort of uncanny as they pertain to 'unnatural' behaviour which gives us an eerie feeling.

There are also scenes of unnatural weather with fist-sized hailstones, a freak tornado and the incident with the shipworms and their conceptual connection with a monster (*il monstro*) that lives in the waters of Venice. These scenes are imbued with a Freudian uncanny, especially in the description of the tornado which is almost personified:

> Glancing up I caught sight of a patch of dark cloud, heaving and shuddering, almost as though it were trying to give birth. Then all at once it split apart, like a bursting eggshell, and a thin, grey extrusion emerged from it and began to descend towards the earth, twisting like a whiplash as it grew.

> 'Oh my God!' cried Piya. 'It's a tornado!'
>
> The fear in her voice startled me, for Piya had never struck me as someone who would be quick to take fright …
>
> Every eye in the minibus was now gazing out of the window, looking leftwards, where the twisting, serpentine form was spinning and dancing above a green cornfield. For a minute its mouth hung above the ground, almost touching down but only to pull back at the last minute.
>
> (250)

Soon as this tornado passes, the characters, including Deen, Cinta and Piya on a minibus see a transformed landscape – 'the air was now so filled with dust and leaves and soil that it was as though night had descended' (251). And from this unrecognizable terrain, a 'dimly visible figure' (251), who is like 'some unearthly apparition', emerges. Here in this scene of the tornado and its aftermath, we see both a Freudian uncanny and a Heideggerian sense of it being evoked as the transformed 'unhomeliness' of the world outside affects the characters, instilling fear and connecting their inner worlds with the transformed setting.

Climate change impacts large numbers of people, while stories that drive many modern novels are propelled by individual characters and their 'moral adventure' to use a formulation of Updike.[19] There are examples in world literature, including Arabic and even American, not necessarily cli-fi, which foreground human aggregates or place their characters within large affected groups pitted against a hostile environment, as Steinbeck does in *Grapes of Wrath*.[20] In *Gun Island*, the author places some of its characters – Tipu and Rafi – within the wider group of the climate- and poverty-affected population of the vulnerable Sundarbans area, and later within the migrant community of Venice, giving a universal tinge to the suffering of their collectives as they leave their lands, and are ferried by people traffickers to distant European destinations. However, Deen and Cinta are fully developed characters with adventures of their own, albeit affected by the agency of non-humans.

Finally, the tension between aesthetics and politics, which yielded the two other major lenses, is quite evident in this novel, while Ghosh has also not lost sight of making this an entertaining read. However, this tension, as in other cli-fi, impinges upon the flow of the story, as we come across scientific facts and information about climate change and its effects. But this is not to the extent it is present in some novels, and the plot trots on at a good and entertaining pace, driven by Deen's quest.

Aesthetics is, however, not the author's foremost preoccupation here, and we rarely come across literariness or poetic use of language. The book employs a straightforward language except for certain luminous passages, for example, where he compares Venice with Varanasi, which are coded with deeper meaning. Literary language, however, plays a role in the scene with the tornado and the final scene with the 'storm' of birds and the Blue Boat, which also helps to evoke the uncanny.[21]

On the other hand, politics, especially justice issues surrounding migrant populations, constitute an important narrative thread of the story, making it possible to read the novel through that lens.[22] The politics of the novel and its transformative potential can be further gauged using the set of approaches clubbed under 'transformative potential' (Figure 2.2) and through a postcolonial reading. These will be taken up in the next two sections.

Our reading of this climate novel so far has given us a clear picture of the sense of planet woven into the story. It has also demonstrated how the author has negotiated certain creative challenges of writing climate fiction and how such challenges are negotiated with innovations in plot and setting, where the planetariness of the story, and also its politics, allow an engagement with creative-thematic features like non-human agency, nature-culture entanglements, the role of collectives and the uncanny. Alex Clark, writing for *The Guardian*, summarizes these experiments best when he says:

> Much has changed in the last three years, albeit not enough for anyone to claim that art has got a handle on how to talk about the impending disaster. And Ghosh's response in his new novel is straightforward: if realism is not a capacious enough vessel to accommodate the truth, then dispense with it. *Gun Island* brims with implausibility; outlandish coincidences and chance meetings blend with ancient myth and folklore, tales of heroism and the supernatural set in a contemporary world disrupted by the constant migrations of humans and animals.[23]

## The climate story in action

In my novel *Spellcasters*, there is a scene where the character Sujata, while escaping from a burning house, set on fire by hired henchmen, scoops up a hardback, which happens to be Amitav Ghosh's climate non-fiction, *The Great Derangement*. 'A book is always a good weapon', she tells herself, 'hardbacks are even better', as she steps out into the night.

Can books be wielded as a useful tool to change our thoughts, beliefs and ideas? Can climate novels in particular help us look forward towards a more equitable and sustainable future and prepare for climate action? Earlier, in this context, we had discussed the impact of *Uncle Tom's Cabin* on the abolitionist movement. Here we shall explore the transformative potential of climate fiction by examining *Gun Island*.

To revisit our discussion, the five approaches for examining climate novels pertain to the Application of findings of empirical ecocritical studies, Production and Consumption Flows, SDGs, SSPs and Integral Ecology (Figures 2.2 and 4.1). We will recall from that discussion that empirical ecocritical studies found that works of cli-fi indeed influence dialogue and behavioural change among a sizeable group of readers. These studies also revealed that character identification and vivid settings, which readers can personally connect with, tend to have more effect on readers and can trigger empathetic responses. The transport of the story (how it engages and transports the reader) has also been noticed in these studies as having an impact in changing beliefs and ideas. Personal stories were also found to be more effective in driving such change. Moreover, some studies noted the importance of inspirational role models who provide examples of easily imitable pro-environmental behaviour.

We will now employ these understandings gleaned from empirical ecocriticism to interrogate Ghosh's novel. Next, we will apply the three other tools to test the transformative potential of the book.[24] There is of course a need to design empirical ecocritical studies similar to the ones whose results we are using here to test the influence of particular books. However, the findings from those earlier studies are expected to provide a fair picture of the potential of new works. *Gun Island*, with its well-imagined characters and effortless facility with place (and its connection with the planetary), be it Kolkata, Venice, California or the Sundarbans can be expected to have an impact on a large swathe of readers who can associate with these settings. As we have seen earlier, Deen and Cinta's characters are well developed with interiority, and they also evolve over the arc of the story. It will be possible for many readers to associate with Deen's doubts and anxieties which gradually transform to a deeper realization about connections with non-humans. They might also be intrigued by Cinta's observations about the irrational and unseen, and inspired by Piya's connections with dolphins, all of which eventually reinforce the climate theme of the story. There is definitely a wealth of information, scientific facts and observations which can distract some readers from the story while others may be further enriched in their scientific and cultural understanding from those details.

Ghosh's novel offers evocative descriptions of Sundarbans and Venice woven into its climate plot, much of which will appeal to readers. These descriptions and their connection to climate change, as well as the enigma of the symbols on the shrine and Deen's efforts to discover their meaning, will bear the reader along through the story and are expected to leave a lasting impression on their mind. Marine biologist Piya's work for the Badabon trust, her concerns for the dolphin Rani and her pod, her effort to save Rani from a nylon net, her rushing to Gorjontola to witness the unfortunate stranding of the dolphins, in which an effluent-discharging refinery is implicated, together turn her into an imitable role model. Her dispassionate scientific research of the Irrawaddy dolphin which is coupled with empathy for these non-human beings, is expected to impress readers, as will the activist energy and effort of people like Gisa, Lubna and the others to rescue and welcome the refugees.

Finally, the admiral of the Italian navy, who takes a stand to welcome the refugees, is also a character that will leave an impression on many minds, driving home the importance of social justice with which climate change is inextricably linked. While empirical studies can help us arrive at more definite conclusions about a particular climate novel, we can say from this discussion that *Gun Island* has a lot of characteristics that can influence people. Besides, as we shall see next, it does discuss the problem of emissions and implicitly indicates what the solutions could be.

We can now take a look at some of the desirable aspects of this climate novel from the advocacy perspective using the three other approaches mentioned above. In our modified Production and Consumption flows approach to study cli-fi works, we ask what production and consumption systems *Gun Island* mentions or alludes to and whether the novel is aware of their effects, and the possible strategies and solutions. Specifically, we want to know how production and consumption flows, their contribution to climate change, and its varied manifestations as well as sustainability concepts are framed in the book.

Here it is important to uncover whether the text is conscious of the underlying production and consumption systems and flows which drive the storyworld and the climate change scenario described there. In *Gun Island*, the underlying production and consumption system often comes up in dialogue and plot, but most distinctly in

Cinta and Deen's discussion about the poisonous brown recluse spider, where they discuss how this creature has been expanding its range because of global warming. And in this context, they talk about increasing carbon emissions and how it's related to more factories, cars, aeroplanes, electric toasters and so on:

> 'Yes, I understand that', said Cinta. 'But why is the world warming? Is that natural too?'
>
> 'Yes, in a sense it is', I said. `It's happening because there's more and more carbon dioxide in the atmosphere, and other greenhouse gases too'.
>
> 'And where do these gases come from?' said Cinta. 'Do they not come from cars and planes and factories that make –' she looked around the kitchen, pointing with her forefinger 'whistling kettles and electric toasters and espresso machines? Is all this natural too that we should need these things that nobody needed a hundred years ago?'
>
> (214)

So we see the effects and causes of climate change in production and consumption systems receiving a brief but clear treatment. There are other references to displaced creatures appearing far from their habitat, like the yellow-bellied snake, which bites and kills a dog.

Elsewhere, in the historian's lecture on 'Climate and the Apocalypse in the 17th Century' delivered in the California museum while wildfires rage outside, the history of climate change is dwelt upon succinctly. The historian says, 'Couldn't it be said that it was the seventeenth century that we started down the path that has brought us to where we are now? After all. It was then that Londoners began to use coal on a large scale, for heating, which was how our dependence on fossil fuels started' (124). Here again we find a clear-eyed articulation of the historical roots of global warming. The wildfire is also commented upon in the story when the director of the museum says, 'It's something to do with the wind – wildfires are moving faster than expected' (125), thus foregrounding one of the complex processes through which climate change impacts are felt.

Ghosh also alludes to a greener economy of reduced emissions by referring to the rideshare company Uber as a mode of transport that Deen often uses. Here we note that this cli-fi text is aware of alternatives, though these are not worked out to the extent one finds in a Kim Stanley Robinson book. The plot may not lend itself to such a digression, though the politics surrounding migration and the associated justice issues are worked out in some detail, linking these to climate change.

As mentioned earlier, the migration of one of the minor characters, Bilal, is triggered (partly at least) by repeated floods in Bangladesh which can be easily linked to global warming. Bilal says, 'Every time there was a flood – which was happening more and more – they would try to move the boundaries' (192). In another plotline, we learn that the Gun Merchant was driven away from his land by a drought, presumably an effect of the LIA climatic disturbances.

Again, the incident of the beached dolphin Rani and her pod is connected to the release of effluents by a refinery, a pollution issue which has a clear link with climate change because refineries work with fossil fuels. The novel also mentions the impact of oceanic dead zones, besides making numerous references to cyclones. We know for a fact that climate change is implicated in the incidence and aggravation of oceanic dead zones and the increasing strength of cyclones.

Through this snapshot review, we can say that this novel is quite aware of the production and consumption origins, triggers, effects and some solutions of climate change and has used various devices to include these in the story. Whether they take away from the enjoyment of the novel is a different question and a problem which all cli-fi writers are negotiating and which we believe is creating a completely new idiom for the novel.

The book mentions greed as a monster which connects easily to the concept of sustainable consumption. While concepts of sustainability are not mentioned upfront, the mention of rideshares, the awareness of important characters of the ill-effects of production and consumption, all indicate a grounding of the text on the importance of sustainability.

Possible solutions, while not addressed explicitly in the plot, and the clear articulation of the problems make the solutions obvious, though not surfaced in the sense of a Kim Stanley Robinson novel like *Pacific Edge*. However, the work of environmental groups to stop a polluting refinery or the getting-together of people to help climate refugees demonstrates the author's intention to focus on the politics and organization necessary to engage with climate strife and allied issues.

We can now take a look at the UN SDG which directly addresses climate change (Goal 13), the 2015 Paris Agreement for emission reductions and other SDGs that have a bearing on the story. Goal 13 asks countries to 'Take urgent action to combat climate change and its impacts by regulating emissions and promoting developments in renewable energy.' The text of *Gun Island* is conscious about this root problem of emissions. While the plot doesn't work out the necessary action in detail, it brings up the same by referring and discussing the problems as in the historian's lecture, the brief reference to the action of environment groups, the activist involvement of Badabon Trust, the Sundarbans NGO where Piya works and elsewhere too. Besides this, the book also has a bearing on other related SDGs like SDG 12 (Responsible Consumption and Production), as evinced in some dialogues; SDG 14 (Life below Water), obvious from the important role of Rani in the text as well as from discussions about oceanic dead zones; SDG 15 (Life on land); and SDG16 (Peace, Justice, and Strong Institutions).

Finally, an integral ecology approach can be applied to test this cli-fi novel. This approach, as Barber and others explained in the context of film trailers, 'enable critical reflections on those four domains – psychological, behavioural, cultural and social/systemic – and how they might advance or impede understanding and solutions to the sustainability challenge.'[25]

This analysis, when applied to the narrative arc of cli-fi novels, can help us understand how these stories portray change in individuals as well as collectives, both internally – psychological and cultural (worldviews), and externally, that is with respect to the behavioural (practices) and social realm covering economic and political and the natural environment. Here we attempt to use this framework on *Gun Island*.

Through this exercise, we will be presenting simple snapshots of the story, briefly noting the psychological, behavioural, cultural and social changes on the path of the narrative. As noted earlier, this approach can also be presented in a four-quadrant (two-by-two matrix) form, labelling the top two quadrants as the domain of the individual and the bottom two as the social domain. The structure of the matrix is completed by noting that the psychological and the cultural worlds are 'internal' realms, while the behavioural and social worlds are 'external'.

We begin with a very short synopsis of the story: a New York-based dealer in antique books sets out on a quest to unravel the legend of a 'gun merchant' of Sundarbans and in the process is drawn into the vortex of an interconnected world affected by climate change, the strife of displaced people and other increasingly prominent effects of planetary crises.

Following this, the relevant SDGs, noted earlier, can be mentioned so that policymakers and practitioners can study changes in the storyworld using sustainable development goals and targets as a scale. Finally, for each of the four quadrants – the psychological, behavioural, cultural and social worlds of the novel, a brief presentation of the change can be outlined.

For the psychological, which is also an internal (individual) realm, initially the climate issue is not evident in the novel. It is not reflected in the principal character's (Deen's) thoughts, but through Piya, the history professor, Cinta and later in his own conversations, we find him getting more engaged and involved. Cinta's character, with her connection with non-human worlds, provides a counterpoint to

Deen's scientific rationalism, thereby providing an impetus for his gradual appreciation of humanity's involvement in the climate crisis.

At the level of culture (ideologies, worldviews), despite business as usual, we find concerned groups (environmental NGOs) engaging with climate change and allied issues. On the other hand, there are cynical characters like Tipu who are connected to people smugglers sending displaced (often climate-affected) people to the West. The world around the main characters is rife with inequity, where high-consumption lifestyles co-exist with climate-affected survivalist modes of living that we see in the present day.

In the external behavioural (practices) world of individuals in the story, it is generally business as usual, though characters like Piya and her NGO are already engaged with environmental issues, and gradually Deen also gets engaged with the strife of the displaced people (especially Tipu) as he finally joins the rescue effort to meet the refugees. The Italian Navy Admiral stands out as a positive character in the seat of power, who refuses to turn back the refugee boat, indicating that leadership from people in the seats of power can mitigate a lot of suffering.

Finally, in the external social (systemic) dimension of the story, the contrast between the high consumption life in the West and the strife of the people of the Sundarbans doesn't change over the course of the story. An important redeeming act is the involvement of people to rescue the refugees coming to Italy, but they come face to face with anti-migrant campaigners. This mirrors the present-day world where there is polarization of opinion and the strife of the displaced people (often climate affected) doesn't find all-round sympathy.

This completes a basic integral ecology approach to reading a climate novel which can be refined with relevant details from the plot that will help compare possible progress in sustainability, using parameters like SDG targets and indicators and other sustainability goals and targets, over the narrative timelines. A detailed application of this approach is beyond the scope of this book because of its elaborate nature. For the same reason, we won't replicate this approach in the readings of the two other books. But even this basic analysis can be a useful tool for policymakers, practitioners and activists, which, by focusing upon the dynamics of the individual and social worlds of a climate novel, can provide valuable insights for planning and activism around climate change. Such policy initiatives and activist engagements with a climate story will be further informed by the fact of its postcoloniality and how this resonates through the narrative. In the next section, we will attempt a postcolonial reading of *Gun Island*.

## Postcolonial planetary cli-fi

Postcolonial readings of climate fiction involve additional perspectives and nuances not fully captured by approaches like the three-pronged framework (Figure 2.2) we developed early in this book. The postcoloniality of such texts is also expected to inform and have a bearing on the categories, creative-thematic approaches and transformative potential of cli-fi in certain ways. Here we will attempt a more general survey of the postcolonial concerns of Ghosh's planetary novel.

If we read *Gun Island* using a postcolonial lens, we encounter an unexpected newness in the story. Although emerging from a postcolonial context with its themes of justice, myths and the workings of power embedded in the plot, the novel, as we have seen, also engages with climate and environmental issues, which is why a postcolonial ecocritical approach can add further value to our engagement with this climate novel.[26] Here we are not attempting a comprehensive postcolonial ecocritical reading of the story but pointing out how certain ideas and conceptualizations of postcolonial ecocriticism, discussed earlier, resonate through the text, thereby suggesting directions for more in-depth readings.

First of all, Sundarbans, where precarity and justice issues are woven into the setting, lends itself easily to a postcolonial ecocritical approach. This climate change-affected land, in which important parts of the narrative unfold, where people live precarious existences at the mercy of natural calamities and ecological degradation, demonstrates what Scott Slovic describes as the 'complex relationship between literary texts from developing regions of the world and the threatened environments'.[27] This threat, as we can see, and the injustice thereof, arises from the fact of emissions in which the rich Northern countries, rather the Global North, are clearly implicated.

The narrative of *Gun Island*, while gathering its energies from a well-defined 'place' (the Sundarbans) and its socio-environmental milieu, spins out into the wider world, like its main characters, as if in search of the stories, facts and themes that could engage the wicked and widely experienced problem of climate change. There is in fact a slippery quicksilver-like quality in the change of settings between Sundarbans, Brooklyn, California, Venice and Kolkata and the chapters, as if in concert, get names like – Visions, Tipu, Kolkata, Rani, Ghetto, Dreams, Strandings that straddle human, non-human and in-between worlds. Despite the planetarity of its settings and the underlying connections, Ghosh manages to create an active setting out of the ecology and myths of climate-affected Sundarbans, which, like a character by itself, plays a decisive role in major and minor narrative threads of the novel.

Following Tiffin and Huggan's argument to look for the underpinnings of colonialism in the text, we will note how continuing attitudes of ecological imperialism, where the natural and the non-human are considered lesser and therefore free to exploit, persist in the storyworld. This is revealed in the actions of the refinery dumping effluents in the river which affects local ecosystems, including the dolphins. Again, the transport of indentured workers in colonial times comes up in the story, which is another signifier of the text's consciousness of colonial attitudes. In the scenes above the *Lucania*, Deen notices the resemblances between the boatload of refugees seeking a home in Italy and the plight of indentured workers who were transported from the Indian subcontinent by the colonial rulers: 'There were similarities also in the circumstances under which they had travelled; like refugees, coolies too had been policed and preyed upon by "coyotes" and overseers; they too had been crammed into confined spaces' (278).

An interesting point is worth taking note of. We have seen earlier how the attitudes and sanctions for dominating the environment and the 'natural', via anthropocentrism, are closely allied to colonialism. This logic of dominating the natural, including human 'others', is visible not only in the specific instance of the transport of the indentured labourers but also in the large-scale exploitation of natural resources and land-use changes that precipitated the planetary crisis of climate change, which forms a major theme of the book.

We have also noted earlier how postcolonial ecocriticism centres an environmental justice approach by focusing on the intersection of the social and the environmental in literary texts. The activism of local environmental groups to stop the dumping of effluents into the river, which is damaging the local ecosystem of Sundarbans, points us to the environmental justice concerns of the text and the resistance and action of these groups against such neocolonial practices of exploiting 'nature', manifest as a form of a slow violence, is akin to what has been characterized as the 'environmentalism of the poor'.

Right from the climate-affected lives of the people and the non-humans (like dolphins) of Sundarbans on to the strife of the migrants looking for a better life in the West, and from there to the final scenes where right-wing groups face off with the activists aboard the *Lucania*, welcoming the Blue Boat with displaced people, all of these plot points demonstrate the strong climate justice concerns of the novel. The mechanics of justice in the story, visible through the work of activists both in the Sundarbans and Italy, are almost always ranged against what Rob Nixon has described as 'slow violence' and its impacts.

We see in this novel both the slow violence of climate change and that of toxic waste. The slow violence of climate change, a crisis unleashed by the carbon emissions of the Global North, disproportionately affects the underprivileged and the marginal of postcolonial nations like India and Bangladesh. The characters on the receiving end of this violence are the people of the Sundarbans, the dolphins exposed to toxic refinery waste and the displaced people like Lubna, Rafi or Bilal who make perilous journeys to escape the crisis. These are characters that have experienced how the floods recurred, how the cyclones grew stronger and how every time after the increasingly frequent floods, as Bilal narrates to Deen, the powerful 'tried to move the boundaries'.

Ghosh's novel neither valorizes any place as a verdant refuge nor does it dwell upon 'discourses of purity', which Rob Nixon identifies as characteristics of Western environmental writing, rather in the postcolonial mould, the book engages with themes of cross-culturation and cosmopolitanism (e.g. the Venice scenes, for example), connecting these to migration and global climate change. The novel, by engaging with myths and legends, primes the engine of the story using these as tools to scope through historical time while simultaneously engaging with the ecology and disasters of a land brought under stress by human action. This presents the reader with a postcolonial ecocritical imagination where the social and the environmental intersect.

In ways that Ghosh's postcolonial novel digs out centuries-old myths of the Gun Merchant and weaves it in with the present-day story of the exploited climate-affected migrants while undergirding these narratives with a critique of the breakdown of the relationship between nature and the human sphere also reveals a postmodern approach of this postcolonial novel. This is further visible in the narratives about non-humans intervening, informing and reconfiguring the plot through their agency, as well as in his creation of well-travelled, well-networked cosmopolitan characters and global settings, which, besides being markers of the planetariness of his novel, further demonstrate a multilayered postmodern engagement.

Recalling Dipesh Chakrabarty's assertion of the necessity to think in multiple registers as a means to engage the dual role of humans as biophysical agent driving the climate crisis as well as a bearer of rights, we notice how the novel attempts this by interweaving a planetary consciousness of humanity's role in unsustainable production and consumption with the narrative threads about activism for justice and rights. In this context, the historian's lecture about the beginnings of fossil fuel use by Londoners, the dialogues about electric toasters and high consumption, as well as the work of activists fighting a big refinery or for the refugees trying to reach Italy, are increasingly poignant.

## Planet, history and the messy present

Through this multifaceted reading of *Gun Island*, which began with a focus on the 'sense of planet' and closes with a postcolonial ecocritical survey, we have seen the gamut of concerns, interests and creative approaches used by Ghosh in his foray into climate fiction. Out of these myriad interests, the sense of planet, albeit entwined with postcolonial concerns, stood out for us as a distinctive feature of this story, warranting a detailed probe.

If we remember our triangulation method (Figure 3.4) of sniffing at cli-fi with the three major lenses, we now know how the planetary features of a climate text may exist with politics and justice issues, anchored in the present realities of the climate crisis. We also noted how, in *Gun Island*, aesthetic considerations were usually secondary except for certain memorable scenes often associated with the uncanny.

Among several other things, we found the author is focused on storytelling and narratives rather than on showing, lingering and evoking. While he attends to the interiority of characters like Deen and his 'individual moral adventure', the element of adventure often supersedes the lingering on interiority. Though the roles of individuals like Deen, Cinta, Piya and Tipu are important in this novel, we already notice here a tendency to foreground the agency and importance of collectives while placing the individual within the context of these larger groups of environment activists, refugees and sufferers.

*Gun Island* also focuses on historical contexts and scientific facts connected to climate change, besides demonstrating a clear understanding of production and consumption aspects (like emissions) and effects (displaced people) of the crisis, which are generally well-built into the plot but at times presented as facts. True for many cli-fi works, but usually absent from literary fiction, we also noticed non-human agency driving the plot as well as the evocation of the climate uncanny.

Scalar aspects, both temporal and spatial, of climate change are introduced through the story of the Gun Merchant and in the context of the LIA. Most importantly, the story travels from one continent to another, connecting narrative flows and revealing networks of global connections, thereby demonstrating a clear 'sense of planet' which is appropriate for a novel dealing with global climate crisis.

Overall, Ghosh's novel has features of a literary experiment (not in the sense of literary fiction) which, because of the mechanism of adventure and fleet-footed plotting, is highly enjoyable. In the course of this experiment, the author has employed a raft of tools and methods to engage with the climate crisis and, as Ghosh himself says in an interview, presents itself as an answer to certain questions he had posed in his climate non-fiction, *The Great Derangement*.[28]

The novel that he has written is definitely pulling away from certain established conventions of modern realist novels, including most contemporary literary fiction of which he has been a distinguished practitioner. Instead, preferring to stay with the trouble, it is leaning towards an inquiry of planetary and historical aspects of climate change and the political and economic issues that cluster around them. In the following chapters, we will be reading two other books, one of which attempts to restore, so to speak, a balance for the 'literary' in climate writing, while the other squarely engages with the politics, equity and justice issues which form the bedrock of the climate crisis.

6

# A difficult marriage

## *Climate and aesthetics*

On a chilly November day of 2023, two young people, Hanan and Harrisson, wearing identical white roundnecks and jeans, walked into London's The National Gallery and began hammering the glass case enclosing one of the most celebrated works of European art, Diego Velázquez's *The Rokeby Venus*. Having smashed the glass, the duo representing activist group Just Stop Oil put down their hammers and voiced their protest against the British government's oil and gas licensing policies.

The Rokeby Venus depicts Venus as a nude goddess reclining on a couch while looking into a mirror held by Cupid. Praised for the masterful use of colour and light, this celebrated painting, which influenced other European artists, dwells on themes of beauty and reflection. But why did it come under attack?

To look for reasons and connections, we have to turn our gaze more than a century back to the summer of 1914. That year, the suffragette Mary Richardson took a meat cleaver to Velázquez's painting and slashed it seven times. Richardson was protesting the arrest of fellow suffragette Emmeline Pankhurst, who was instrumental in helping secure women's right to vote in Britain and Ireland. In a statement afterwards, Richardson said, 'I have tried to destroy the picture of the most beautiful woman in mythological history as a protest against the government for destroying Mrs Pankhurst, who is the most beautiful character in modern history.'[1]

In a video posted on Twitter by Just Stop Oil after the hammer attack on the Rokeby Venus, we can see Hanan speaking to the audience, 'Women did not get the vote by voting',[2] she says calmly, while Harrisson joins in 'Politics is failing us, it failed us in 1914', thereby justifying their methods and then calling for stopping oil. Their statements clearly forge a connection between the suffragettes' protest for women's rights and that of the climate activists' demand for a better future.[3]

But why is art coming under attack from activists? Part of the answer is already provided in Mary Richardson's statement, but the larger logic is about engagement and course correction. As Shayok Mukhopadhyay, who represents climate activist group Extinction Rebellion, explained to National Geographic magazine:

> The function of art is for people to be able to understand the world that they live in and reflect on the human condition, but big art isn't fulfilling that function. That's the reason for us to be in museums: to tell people that we are in the middle of an emergency, and it is the time now for you to face that emergency.[4]

Others advocating such tactics, in one of which activists threw tomato soup (Figure 6.1) at one of Vincent Van Gogh's *Sunflowers* series of pictures, want museums and galleries to engage with the climate crisis and the underlying issues of justice, accept their dark legacy of colonialism which added to their collections, and stop taking funds from oil companies. Clearly the relationship between climate and art is fraught in our times.

As a creative writer and activist, this fraught relation naturally encompasses personal dimensions. Why is it that acts of art vandalism throughout history have often been connected to political causes or mental illness? In a Foucauldian vein, I have often wondered whether it is only the mentally ill and the politically aware activist who can see through the illusions and violence of modern civilization, one of whose signifiers is great art? On the other hand, what about those

**Figure 6.1** Just Stop Oil activists throwing soup at Vincent Van Gogh's 'Sunflowers' (27 September 2024). Source: Just Stop Oil. Image credit: Jamie Lowe.

works that engage climate change and planetary crisis while still succeeding as works that enthral with their artistry? It is perhaps this train of thought which leads me on to a deeper analysis of Itäranta's novel. But first, let me digress with my own story to address the personal dimensions of the contradictions between climate change activism and a writer's vocation, where the aesthetic impulse is held in high accord.

Before I tried my hand at writing stories, I used to review books for newspapers and magazines. This was perhaps one of the more responsible of my reckless manoeuvres in seeking out a profession, the prospects of which, at that point, swung between discount-card salesperson and talent spotter for a shady modelling agency. But the freelance work for the media introduced me to activism, and the spirit imbibed there has lingered on to this day.

But my point here is about reviewing books, and what I mean to say is that before I published any fiction, I delved into their mechanics and the art. The effect is not always salutary, and as a writer friend who also teaches creative writing in a British university warned, 'knowing the mechanics too well can be damaging for the art'. Which could be true, but because there's a hornet's nest somewhere down that alley of logic, I won't step further in that direction.

I think reviewing books followed by writing them must have been the trajectory of many of my community, my situation being slightly qualified by the fact that I was also running campaigns for the climate and environment. But, in those early days, my activism was still not reconciled with my creative interests, and the two were often pulling me in different directions. I had been smitten by the printed word.

The joy of receiving freshly printed volumes from editors, getting introduced to new ways of telling, the fascinating experiments with form, the felicity of prose, the poetic beauty of language, the unplumbed depths of characters and the fireworks of a hundred emotions issuing forth from the tortuous darkness of inscapes and, most of all, the heady grip of well-told stories, like gin and tonic after a long abstinence, and the challenge of conveying what I enjoyed in those books to the readers of my reviews was extremely rewarding, and so, over those years, I had watched my bookshelves filling up with the work of artists of the written word.

In this journey of a reviewer, I worked with various book review editors who, with their insights and indulgence, enriched my chosen trade of interpreting stories for readers. Among them was the elderly editor of a respected Asian journal who taught me the importance of understatement and the need to communicate the strengths rather than focusing only on the weaknesses of a novel. Then there was the book editor of a newspaper who rarely spoke but schooled me through his edits to forsake certain quirks of style, while another senior shared instructive stories about books and life, pointing out how great works are born.

It is in this phase of reviewing books that I must have developed an interest in literary fiction with its focus on language, characters, imagery and depth of emotions. My reading otherwise had been eclectic, where Alan Poe's gothic rubbed shoulders with Herman

Hesse's bildungsromans, and Kafka played mind games with writers of Bangla speculative fiction, not to mention the growing piles of American hard-boiled and Russian masters jostling for space on my bookshelves. There was really no rhyme or reason in my reading, but my review work had been unconsciously pushing me towards literary fiction, maybe because it was more of those stories that landed on my reviewer's desk.

This bent towards the literary has never really faded, and I believe my own stories continue to be a battleground where the literary tussles with the improbable, and there is seldom any peace. This is a difficult marriage, no doubt. How I arrived at this juncture in my writing and how it informs storytelling and plot is a more complex question with no easy answers, but I believe my engagement with climate change has had as much contribution in my journey as my eclectic reading and the job of a reviewer of mainly literary fiction.

My first novel, *Amber Dusk*, was strongly rooted in the tradition of literary fiction; even there, in hindsight, I can discern the incipient presence of themes of darkness and the improbable. With the unfolding climate crisis and personal experience of disasters like cyclones and flooding, to which our part of the world is no stranger, I have increasingly felt the need to build the themes of the improbable and the uncanny into my stories. Be it in the tale of a phantom lover in my book *Hotel Calcutta* or the story of the slow sinking of a city amidst a raging pandemic in *The Butterfly Effect*, these themes, driven by an interest in the unimaginable – which has been gradually turning into our lived experience – have continued to inform my creative efforts.

Because of all such reasons, Emmi Itäranta's novel, which we are going to discuss now, held a special appeal for me in its blending of the literary art with the unimaginable aspects of climate change. Like the other climate novels examined in this book, Emmi Itäranta's *Memory of Water* also arrived as a review copy. As before, and also in acknowledgement of my book reviewer persona, I will begin my examination of this novel with an extended story summary which incorporates parts of the review that appeared in the pages of Scroll magazine.[5] This time around there will be spoilers.

## Poetry of a Scandinavian dystopia – reading *Memory of Water*

According to the author's website, *Memory of Water* has been translated into twenty languages besides being shortlisted for the Philip K. Dick Award, the Arthur C. Clarke Award and the Golden Tentacle Award. The book, I am told, is being made into a movie. It was also a finalist for Premio Salerno Libro d'Europa. What might also be of interest to readers is that this climate fiction was written by the author both in Finnish and English.

The novel begins with a prologue and ends with an epilogue. The story is divided into three parts named Watchers of Water, The Silent Space and The Blue Circle. The first and second parts are each eight chapters long, while part three has three chapters.

Stories are at the centre of Emmi Itäranta's novel – hidden stories, lost stories and the most striking feature here is the poetic beauty with which they are narrated. While sharing many characteristics of climate novels, this post-apocalyptic tale of a world that has almost run out of water stands apart for its literary flavour. We will examine this in detail later, but first let us concentrate on the story.

The teenage protagonist Noria Kaitio, in a water-scarce future Scandinavian Union, standing by the dry bed of a river, muses about people from past times:

> I imagine one of them standing by the river that is now a dry scar in our landscape, a woman who is not young or old, or perhaps a man, it doesn't matter. Her hair is pale brown and she is looking into the water that rushes by, muddy perhaps, perhaps clear, and something that has not yet been is bleeding into her thoughts.

> I would like to think she turns around and goes home and does one thing differently that day because of what she has imagined.
> (25)

But Noria is not too sure if those visions bleeding into her mind, perhaps of an imagined future, dark and fearsome, would really have moved the stranger on that riverbank of the past to act differently. However, by the end of this finely woven tale that grows upon us like an incessant whisper, Noria, the young daughter of a tea master, would put her faith in the need to tell stories for 'there will be others who will carry the story forward. Perhaps some small stretch of the world will be more whole after them' (259).

*Memory of Water* is set in a post-oil climate dystopia, mostly around a small village of the Scandinavian Union which, along with large parts of Asia, has been occupied by the New Qian. Noria lives with her father and her scientist mother at the edge of the village. Water scarcity is rampant in the region, and many past world technologies have been lost. In this world of water quotas, water crimes and ruthless blue-uniformed water guards, the introspective teenager and her industrious friend Sanja chance upon a carefully hidden secret which could change the stories of the past as much as it could change the future.

Told in the first-person narrative of Noria, this coming-of-age story is about choices in the face of utter hardship, questions of environmental ethics and the role of an ancient tea masters' tradition as a lodestone of meaning and a compass to navigate the darkness of the world.

'The distance from dreams to words is long and so is the way from words to deeds' (172), Noria says, bringing us back again to the theme of the importance of the imagination in fashioning the world, albeit slowly – the world will always be an image of what we dream. The power of the author's own imagination, vivid yet measured, rendered in poetic prose which is melancholic in a myriad of monochrome shades, makes this a very different climate novel in a genre whose early years, as pointed out by Axel Goodbody, are crowded with thrillers.

As we have already noted, the poetic beauty of its prose is what sets this novel apart. This is not to deny the so-called functional aspects of this cli-fi novel. In this context, we will remember Gregers Andersen's views about how cli-fi allows us to feel and comprehend climate-altered worlds and Sophia David's argument about cli-fi's role in engaging readers and making climate change 'meaningful' to non-scientific people. Itäranta's novel, with its close attention to setting and story as well as a finely honed aesthetic sense, accomplishes these tasks, transporting us to this possible future of terrible water scarcities, distant wars and a life of untold hardship that looks increasingly real in our times.

While the altered future is revealed to the reader with starkly drawn images of uncommon beauty, the author also devotes pages to look back at the widespread impact of climate change in the 'past-world era' when things began to fall apart: 'On the old map North and South Poles were shown in white. I knew this stood for the ice that had sometimes been called eternal ice, until it became clear that it wasn't eternal after all. Near the end of the past-world era the globe had warmed and seas had risen faster than anyone could have anticipated' (64).

Not far from the village where Noria lives is the Dead Forest. In evoking the past and the present of that vanished wilderness and all through the story, the author, through carefully chosen words and the felicity of her style, plants poignant images in our minds:

> The Dead Forest had once been called Mosswood, a name that recalled deep-green leaves moving in the wind and verdancy so lush and moist that you could feel it on your skin. Even longer ago, when words for such greenness were not needed yet, because it was a given in these lands, the forest had not had a name at all ... now it's bare trunks and branches twisted towards the sky sand-dry and colourless like a cobweb woven across the landscape, or the empty husks of insects caught in it. Life no longer circulated in them, their

> veins were brittled and broken, their skins frozen into letters of a forgotten language, near-incomprehensible marks of what had once been.
>
> (203)

It will be no exaggeration to say that this novel easily convinces us about the dangers that tomorrow might bring with its use of evocative prose and carefully calibrated storytelling in a way scientific papers or sensational media bytes about the climate crisis may not. It is the magic of her prose style that is the beating heart of this book, alongside the setting, which coupled with deft characterization, adds persuasiveness to this story.

*Memory of Water* is also about contrasts. There is an enduring quality, a kind of changeless essence, in the centuries-old tradition of a long line of tea masters who had lived in the same house as Noria, and there is also the transience of the world around them that is slowly unravelling – things turning from bad to worse, scarcities multiplying, wars raging endlessly, the military water guards getting more and more ruthless towards those illegally tapping into water pipes.

In this backdrop of a gathering darkness, Noria's mother, who is a scientist, plans to travel to a distant city called Xinjing to pursue her research. Meanwhile, her father introduces her to a generations-old secret, hidden inside a cave of the Alvinvaara fell: A secret spring watched over by tea masters over the centuries: 'You're seventeen, and of age now, and therefore old enough to understand what I'm going to tell you', my father said. 'This place doesn't exist. The spring dried a long time ago. So the stories tell, and so believe even those who know other stories' (203).

This very secret, as Noria soon realizes, will draw her family into trouble as the local Qianese administrator Commander Taro suspects they have access to a hidden source of water, and to investigate this, he digs up their garden and wrecks the tea house. Noria is well aware of the weight of the secret she is entrusted with when she promises to her father not to divulge it, '"I'll remember," I told him, but didn't realise until later what kind of a promise I had made. Silence is not empty or immaterial, and it is not needed to chain tame things. It often guards powers strong enough to shatter everything' (12).

There is a strand of philosophizing woven into the narrative, in the thoughts and reflections of Noria, which complements the subdued brilliance of the prose. This was the author's debut novel, and already at that time, critics had compared her writing to that of Ursula K. Le Guin. We also find good reasons to seek parallels between the spare but lyrical quality of her writing and the language employed by Cormac McCarthy in *The Road*. In both these books, style and voice, and in McCarthy's case even the vocabulary, go beyond the needs of the narrative, entering into a fascinating symbiosis with the story to evoke the denudations of a ravaged planet.

The world where Noria's tale unfolds is meticulously crafted, down to the use of blazefly lanterns to light up houses, beeping message-pods, slow-moving solar-powered (supplemented by human-powered pedals) helicycles and helicarriages, plastic waterskins for carrying water, heavily guarded desalination plants for urban water supply, ubiquitous seagrass bags and a sprawling plastic grave which hides another secret that drives the plot. Rummaging through the plastic grave for past-world tech, Noria and her dear friend Sanja chance upon compact-disc voice recordings from the Twilight Century, which was when the world ran out of oil.

This recording by explorers of the Jansson expedition and another chance discovery seem to indicate that fresh water may be available in the earlier contaminated forbidden region of the Lost Lands, but sinister powers may be withholding this secret. The log from the Jansson expedition reveals that the explorers were preparing to plant purifying bacteria in those waters.

On returning home with the excitement of these discoveries, Noria finds soldiers led by Commander Taro searching through their premises with machines to find if there was any secret source of water that they haven't informed the authorities about. While they don't find anything significant, and the secret of the spring from which a hidden water pipe leads to their house still remains a secret, the tension of the narrative, however, rises a few notches. Having found nothing, the soldiers take away the books containing details of tea masters' ceremonies to examine them for any possible clues.

Meanwhile, the tension between Noria's father and mother increases. Noria's mother has been offered a post at the distant University of Xinjing, and concerned about her daughter's safety, she asks Noria if she would like to accompany her. But Noria chooses to stay back, and she and her father accompany her mother to see her off at the train station in the city of Kuoloyarvi. The train will be travelling via New Piterburg to Ural and then on through New Qian to Xinjing.

After her mother's departure, Noria's father begins preparations for the Moonfeast while also restoring his house. As Noria's graduation ceremony as a tea master is imminent, he takes her again to the secret spring and tells her that from ancient times, tea masters have been watchers of water, and long ago, each tea master had a spring they took care of. Eventually, nearly all springs dried up and the remaining ones were taken over by the military. In these conversations between father and daughter, past stories of tea masters and their connection with water are revealed, and the agency of water is strongly evoked:

> 'Past-world tea masters knew stories that have mostly been forgotten,' he said quietly. 'But one is recorded in every tea master's book we kept in our house. The story tells that water has a consciousness, that it carries in its memory everything that's ever happened in this world, from the time before humans until this moment, which draws itself in its memory even as it passes. Water understands the movements of the world, it knows when it is sought and where it is needed. Sometimes a spring or a well dries for no reason, without explanation. It's as if the water escapes of its own will.'
>
> (90)

Noria's graduation ceremony gets over with some hitches, and she and Sanja visit the central square of the village to take part in the

Moonfeast celebrations, where they see Ocean-Dragons made of junk plastic, watch the fishfires (Aurora Borealis) and have the intoxicating blue lotus cakes that give a 'drifting feeling of languor' (108). On her way back, she notices a figure spying on their house and then finds her father lying on the ground; he had suffered a stroke.

Part two of the novel, The Silent Space, begins with the death of Noria's father and the funeral service that follows. The guests include Major Bolin, who used to be her father's friend, the plasticsmith Jukara with his wife and sister, Sanja with her father, some tea masters and three lament-women, whose singing is 'beautiful and ugly at once' (117). At this gathering, Noria and Sanja see a blond-haired stranger whom they cannot recognize and suspect that he is a soldier in civilian clothes. An uprising had taken place somewhere during the Moonfeast, and so the authorities, it is learned, are keeping a close watch on people. After the ceremony, Major Bolin warns Noria to be careful because Taro will be in charge from then on. Bolin also returns the tea masters' books that Taro had carried away.

As the news of arson by unionists spreads, the occupation force of New Qian becomes even more ruthless, arresting commoners and imposing stronger water rations till all water supplies to homes are stopped, and people of Noria's village have to collect water by queuing up at the central square. While the water rationing becomes stricter, people are found to be begging for water. The authorities begin to punish people for water crimes by marking their houses with a blue circle and isolating them from society. Later, it will be learned that these people are finally executed.

Meanwhile, Noria begins to study the old tea masters' books, and within these, in the accounts of a past tea master named Miro, she finds more evidence of the Jansson expedition and proof that there could be pure water available in the Lost Lands. In fact, two men and a woman from the expedition had visited Miro, and he had given them shelter.

Moved by her friend's need for water and worried upon discovering that she was building an illegal water pipe, Noria begins to supply more and more water to Sanja till one day she reveals to her the secret of the spring. Inside the cave, they discover more CDs from the Janssen expedition.

Now Noria receives a message from her mother on a hacked message-pod asking her to take Bolin's help and leave for Xinjing because she was no longer safe where she was. This puts Noria in a quandary. She thinks, 'I could follow my mother's wishes and travel to Xinjing, or my father's and stay here to guard the spring. Or I could do as I wanted, and choose an unfamiliar path that was not dictated by either one of them' (177).

Finally, she and Sanja will choose this unfamiliar path by planning to set out in search of fresh water in the Lost Lands. But before they begin to plan, the two of them are discovered by Jukara while they are coming out of the cave leading to the secret spring. The news spreads through the village, and soon Noria is supplying water to many, when one day a subordinate of Taro comes to investigate, pretending to have mixed up the date of a tea ceremony. Luckily, the subordinate fails to discover the illegal sharing of water.

Now, Bolin arranges a solar-powered helicarriage when Noria tells him that she plans to go selling chattels. But the plan is exposed and the helicarriage with all the provisions for their trip vanishes from its hiding place. As Noria returns, she sees soldiers outside Sanja's house and the next morning, a blue circle appears on Noria's door.

Part three of the novel is mostly about Noria's memories as she decides to record all her experiences in the tradition of tea masters. Noria remains under house arrest till the end, recording her story, as soldiers provide her with meals to keep her alive till her execution. In between, Commander Taro makes a visit, offering her and Sanja's freedom if they agree to spy on people on behalf of the military and hand over the rights of the secret spring to them. Taro tells Noria that Sanja had asked her to accept the offer, adding that she had approached them with information. However, Noria flatly refuses.

The novel ends with Noria recording her story in the tea masters' book while facing imminent execution. In the epilogue, we find

Sanja in Xinjing meeting Noria's mother, sharing everything that had happened and giving her the discs of the Jansson expedition. It is apparent from Sanja's story that Taro had lied, and Sanja was never captured and had hidden in the forest with the helicarriage for weeks while unsuccessfully trying to contact Noria.

With Noria Kaitio, Itäranta has created a character who is a spring of humanity amidst a world starved of water. In his essay on climate novels, Axel Goodbody, writing about this book's 'sensuous evocation of the sight, sounds, smell and taste of water' comments on its 'use of the element as a multidimensional symbol, linking climate change with an exploration of personal development and issues of gender and sexuality, and beyond these with reflection on the meaning of life and the ability of art and writing to provide a permanence which human life does not afford'.[6] Even on the first reading, *Memory of Water* stands out as a cli-fi work where the literary meets a purposeful engagement with planetary crises that are engulfing us all.

In an activist pamphlet about water written years ago, we had focused on citizens' rights.[7] After reading Itäranta's novel and following years of tracking the climate crisis, I now realize that the question is not only about rights but also of duties. The duty to share, the duty to acknowledge nature's gifts, the duty not to hoard and the imperative as stewards of the planet to protect scarce resources like water. Like the tea master of this book, whose allegiance to tradition is like a conceptual bulwark against the disruptions of the climate crisis, we have to say in one voice, 'Not everything in the world belongs to people … We are the watchers of water but first and foremost we are its servants' (91).

In the next section, we will be focusing on definitions and characteristics of literariness and the literary which constitutes our second major lens of aesthetics we had discussed earlier.[8] After that, we will examine how the aesthetic values of this novel can be explored primarily by employing the concept of literariness. Finally, we will study the novel using the other major and minor lenses and normative approaches (Figure 2.2) outlined earlier.

## Cycling through the unfamiliar – *Ostranenie* and literariness

Imagine a cyclist passing through a new country which she has never visited. She hasn't researched or read anything about this nation but had been looking forward to this experience. As she rides through towns and villages, she is pleasantly surprised to find small tables laid out for her on the way by the authority. Each such table has a flask containing a drink or a plate with some other refreshment. But none of these drinks or refreshments is familiar to her. As she picks up a flask here, a sweet or baked treat there, and sips or munches on that particular offering, she lingers on their unfamiliar tastes, trying to connect them with her past experience of refreshments, drinks and cross-country cycling. While continuing on her way, she arrives at new conclusions about her experience of the food and drink (culinary culture of the country) in particular and the cycling expedition in general.

Now think of another cyclist passing through the same unfamiliar country. As she pedals across the miles, she also comes across these little tables set out by the authority. However, in her case, the refreshments served, standard cans of Coke and boiled toffees, are quite familiar to her. In this case, the ride would not have any unique interpretative significance for the cyclist, besides the experience of the road which we assume is more or less the same for both. We will shortly see how the experience of the two cyclists can approximate the idea of 'literariness' that we experience while reading *Memory of Water*.

The concept of 'literariness' appears in the work of Russian Formalists, an influential school of literary critics who, early in the last century, had developed a scientific approach to analyse and read texts.[9] Among them, the Russian-American linguist and literary theorist Roman Jakobson had defined 'literariness' which can be described as 'a quality that makes a verbal message a work of art'.[10] In other words, literariness is 'the sum of special linguistic and formal properties that distinguish literary texts from non-literary texts'.[11] The mechanics of literariness had been further elaborated in the work of the great Russian literary theorist and fiction writer Viktor Shklovsky, who, in his classic work *Theory of Prose*,[12] introduced the concept of *ostranenie*.

*Ostranenie* (translated both as defamiliarization and enstrangement[13]) is a technique that allows the reader to perceive the text over an extended period of time. Thus, defamiliarization gives value to the act of perceiving, and through it, the process of creativity. This technique or device is a prominent feature of literariness. In Shklovsky's words, 'By "enstranging" objects and complicating form, the device of art makes perception long and "laborious." The perceptual process in art has a purpose all its own and ought to be extended to the fullest. Art is a means of experiencing the process of creativity. The artifact itself is quite unimportant.'[14]

But there is more to literariness than defamiliarization, as David Miall and Don Kuiken of the University of Alberta have pointed out.[15] While the concept of 'literariness' has come under fire from postmodern theorists and has been subsumed under other explanatory frameworks, Miall and Kuiken have shown through their empirical work that these contesting theories don't explain it fully. According to them, the phenomenon of 'literariness' is a dynamic process, where the reader's involvement is as important as the text's narrative features and style. Literariness entails the device of 'foregrounding' which draws attention to certain features of the text (like metaphor, imagery, symbol, among others) which are different from the ordinary which then leads to defamiliarization. Defamiliarization consequently brings about a 'reinterpretative effort' on the part of the reader, thus making readers respond differently to a text. Miall and Kuiken have argued how foregrounding evokes a feeling which provides a 'route to the self' that then through defamiliarization leads on to new ways of interpretation.

Let us now redirect our attention back to the two cross-country cyclists to complete our thought experiment about literariness. Their experience of cycling is a metaphor for the act of reading a text, say a novel. Here, the reader is the cyclist, traversing the length of the text. The first cyclist's experience approximates the response of a reader to a literary text where 'literariness' is the dynamics of her interaction with the unfamiliar drinks and refreshments presented before her ('foregrounding') on the tables, her realization of their unfamiliar nature ('defamiliarization') and her reinterpretation ('reinterpretative effort') of the tastes and their connection with her past experience of refreshments and of cycling too. For the second cyclist, served Coke and toffees, and so also for readers of texts lacking in literariness, none of the dynamics of foregrounding, defamiliarization and reinterpretative effort would come into play. Her ride would be lacking in the unique experience of the first cyclist.

Shklovsky's conceptualization of defamiliarization as an apt method that fulfils what he believed is the purpose of art, which is to engage perception (rather than knowing) and the lengthening of perception, has also received scientific backing. Arguing about Shklovsky's aesthetic and defamiliarization, critic Nancy Easterlin, in her innovative biocultural approach to literary theory, points out that current research in neuroscience has shown that familiar forms allow processing at low levels of consciousness, which is not good for art.[16] Thus, a possibility arises that more conscious processing of a work, which is granted by a technique like defamiliarization, may be the route to engage its ideological content.[17]

The reader would have noted that while sharpening the lens of aesthetics (and its tension with politics, another major lens), we primarily employed the concept of 'literariness'. But alongside it, we have also mentioned the broader term 'literary' as a marker of aesthetics in the novel. This is based on common perception wherein the literary, or more specifically literary fiction, is considered to be a vessel for aesthetics. By bringing together (Figure 3.4) both the formalist device of 'literariness' and the general category of 'literary fiction', we are therefore trying to sharpen our lens of 'aesthetics'.

Let us examine if literary fiction is indeed a bearer of aesthetics and how this relates to 'literariness' of a text. We can begin by visiting some defining features of 'literary fiction' while asking the question, whether there is any discernible category that can be labelled as such. Literary fiction is a characterization that is encountered more in everyday language and genre-focused book marketing plans, and to a lesser extent in academic texts. Its meanings are many and diverse.[18] The spectrum of its, sometimes overlapping and contested, meanings can cover anything that is not clearly commercial fiction, through many kinds of modern realist storytelling right up to the mansions of 'serious fiction'. Critics like Jeremy Rosen have also noted the tendency of literary fiction writers to venture into so-called genre fiction, thus blurring the lines, while trying to maintain a kind of purity by refusing genre labels.[19]

To avoid the quagmire of mixed genres and blurred borders, let us focus on the characteristics of literary fiction and where aesthetics might reside therein. In the words of Frederic Jameson, all genres are, 'contracts between a writer and his reader'[20] which means they entail certain expectations. This is equally true for literary fiction. Such expectations, among other things, also constitute the tropes of a particular genre. Joyce G. Saricks has listed a number of such genre expectations from literary fiction as characteristic of the genre. Among these are characters exploring philosophical questions, a focus on character over plot, an attention to style, slower pacing, complex structure and importantly, poetic language.[21] To this we can add interiority (psychological explorations), use of universal themes and exploration of serious issues, evocative use of language, use of imagery, emotional depth and nuance, while also noting how elements of the lists bleed into each other.

Now poetic language,[22] as a characteristic of literary fiction, is also closely associated with the formalist concept of literariness which is our marker for aesthetics. Thus, in our examination of literariness in cli-fi, we will automatically be searching for a characteristic which is also present in literary fiction. Besides this, it will also be worth our while to examine if some of the other features of literary fiction mentioned above also occur in cli-fi. If so, this will allow us to argue that certain works of climate fiction, besides demonstrating literariness as a marker of formal beauty (aesthetics), also reveal other features of literary fiction, thereby bringing the two genres[23] even closer (Figures 3.2 and 6.2).

Before we analyse *Memory of Water* with the lens of aesthetics, embodied in literariness, while also probing the novel for other signals

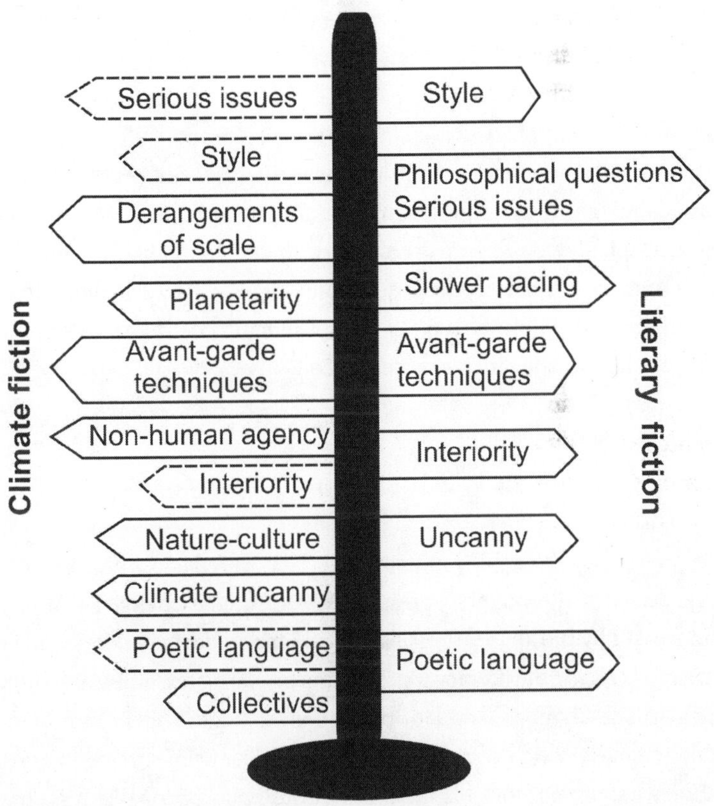


**Figure 6.2** Climate fiction and literary fiction.

of the literary, a few more words about the relationship between genres and movements are in order. Saricks, in characterizing literary fiction, further noticed an intellectual approach or an avant-garde style,[24] which is usually associated with Modernist innovations in literature, thus forging a link between the two. In this context, we can recall Kerridge's assertion of how certain techniques developed by the Modernist movement in literature can provide representational advantages to the ecological imagination. This is another means by which climate fiction, in its use of avant-garde techniques, can move closer (Figure 6.2) to literary fiction and modernist writing.[25]

On the other hand, Saricks' assertions that in literary fiction characters explore philosophical questions and that the genre's focus is on character over plot seem to be of a piece with the 'individual moral adventure' of characters in the contemporary novel, which was critiqued by Amitav Ghosh.[26] Ghosh argued that this resulted in the contemporary novel's turning away from collectives (and the non-human), thereby putting these works at a representational disadvantage in communicating the climate emergency. Insofar as writers of literary fiction are taken with the individual characters' exploration of philosophical questions, they will find it difficult to engage one of the important creative-thematic challenges of climate fiction, that is, the representation of collectives.

## Climate and aesthetics in *Memory of Water*

In *Memory of Water*, Emmi Itäranta has employed a technique where resistance of the material presented by a climate-changed world is addressed by the application of a formal literary device often found in poetry. It is as if the literary writer, being forced by the improbabilities of a climate-changed world to abandon the use of the fillers of modern realist novels which concealed the improbable turns of narrative, yet somewhat uncomfortable in their 'primitive' improbableness, has fired up the old lantern of defamiliarization borrowed from Russian Formalists to signal those turns.

The effort is no doubt commendable, as evinced by critics and reviewers who have endorsed the aesthetic value of this novel. Reviewers writing for *The Guardian*, *Washington Post* and *Library Journal*, respectively, used expressions like 'poetic', 'beautiful' and 'gorgeous' in describing Memory of Water. Meanwhile, a critic like Katarina Leppänen has marked the 'uncanny (un)familiarity of the made-up world'.[27]

Throughout the book, we find foregrounding of features that are out of the ordinary, which then leads to defamiliarization and then an effort from the reader to reinterpret what was presented. It needs to be repeated that many climate novels, because of their focus on the uncanny (or rather the climate uncanny), are thematically imbued with this possibility of defamiliarization. By exploring this possibility to its fullest, Itäranta has successfully overcome the resistance that the improbable and the uncanny present to the form of many contemporary novels where fillers tend to conceal improbable events.

However, the thematic possibility of climate novels for such defamiliarizing interventions, as we shall shortly see, flows from the settings and story, and may not automatically guarantee the 'literariness' which, as we discussed, is dependent on the foregrounding of a wider set of stylistic and narrative variations that constitute defamiliarization. Therefore, the uncanny imparts in the climate novel the possibility of defamiliarization, which in itself may not guarantee literariness which will be dependent on the author's craft, style and representational goals. In *Memory of Water*, the author has successfully employed these possibilities of defamiliarization to represent the improbable and the uncanny of her climate story, thus imbuing the novel with literariness and a general literary flavour which we will call the 'climate literary'.

In the prologue of the book we find the young Noria, trying to get a few drops of water out from the tap in their house and she 'speaks' to the water which does not flow: 'I spoke to it in pretty words and ugly words, and I may have even screamed and wept, but water doesn't care for human sorrows' (1). This act of 'speaking' to water is not only foregrounded, but it also defamiliarizes because communication is not something we usually attempt with water.

Then in the first chapter, the first-person narrator Noria says, 'Water walks with the moon and embraces the earth, and it isn't afraid to die in fire or live in air' (5). A few paragraphs later. 'Death is water's close companion. The two cannot be separated ... Water has no beginning and no end, but death has both. Death is both. Sometimes death travels hidden in water' (5).

In all these three quoted instances, we find something unusual or striking in the way the author presents the character's thoughts to us. Phrases like 'I spoke to it (water) in pretty words', 'water walks with the moon' and 'Death is water's close companion' or 'water has no beginning and no end' are not only striking, they tend to stand out from the surface of the prose, waving the lantern of defamiliarization at the reader. We are not familiar with speaking with water, nor do we immediately grasp the meaning of water walking with the moon or water having no beginning and no end.

As this defamiliarization affects us, we try to impart new meaning and interpretations based on past experience. To one reader, speaking to water might imply speaking to something that is ever flowing, hard to grasp, so speaking to nothing at all, essentially a futile exercise. Again, 'water walks with the moon and embraces the earth' strikes us as an unusual imagery which can evoke different kinds of interpretation, including the imagery of tides which rise and fall with the moon's journey around the planet. One may also think of water being omnipresent, everywhere, flowing through the night and touching all regions of the planet. Walks with the moon can also be interpreted as flowing in secret when the sun is not in sight. Finally, 'death is water's close companion' may evoke thoughts of journeying from one life to another, the immutable soul and how the unchanging flow of water evokes this journey.

So we can see how the foregrounded features of the text first lead the reader to react with a defamiliarizing response where she marks the phrase as out of the ordinary or unusual followed by an interpretive effort on her part where she tries to impart meaning and significance to what she has read. As Miall and Kuiken have demonstrated through similar analysis of other texts, we find all three components (foregrounding, defamiliarization and reinterpretative effort) of literariness present in Itäranta's prose.

If we read more closely, we will notice something even more interesting happening here. The foregrounded features of the text tend to cluster in certain sections of the book.

For example, the section from where the two quotations from Noria's monologue are taken ('Water walks with the moon …', 'Death is water's close companion') repeats such foregrounded descriptions that are defamiliarizing, that is, they make the ordinary unfamiliar. Such descriptions, in this case, also evoke the uncanny, a feeling of strangeness or eeriness in relation to the very familiar object of water. This then gradually focuses the reader on the uncanny nature of water in the water-scarce climate crisis-affected setting of the novel. More such sentences recur in that monologue – Noria says about water, 'When you step into it, it will be as close as your own skin, but if you hit it too hard, it will shatter you' (5) and a little while later, 'sometimes water will chase death away, but they go together always, in the world and in us' (5).

This clustering of defamiliarized descriptions, besides imparting literariness to the text of the novel, also strengthens the uncanny aspects of the setting – a severely water-starved post-disaster rural area of the Scandinavian Union ruled by an oppressive occupying power. The uncanny that we encounter in this example, and many similar descriptions throughout the book, is primarily the Heideggerian uncanny which connects the transformed outer world with inner feelings. However, the Freudian uncanny is also and often parallelly evoked when the author suggests water's agency, that it can 'walk with the moon' or 'shatter you'. This is how climate uncanny, through the dynamics of literariness and a clustering of foregrounded elements, comes into play in Itäranta's novel.

It is important to mention that such foregrounding, which leads to defamiliarization and reinterpretation, recurs throughout the book and is an immediately noticeable feature of the prose. Which is why we argue that *Memory of Water* is a climate novel marked by its literariness.

Let us look at a few more examples: When Noria's father dies, three lament-women arrive at the funeral. The author writes, 'They spoke little and followed death wherever it went, and when they lamented, stones seemed to ache around them' (116). Then again, when the water guards search Noria's home, expecting to find some secret source of water that they haven't declared, Noria says about her parents:

> In those days a silence wavered between my parents, dense with stirring, well-hidden fear and nameless, unspoken things. It was like a calm surface of water … a single word dropped on it, a single shifting stone at the bottom would change it, create a circle and another circle, until the reflection was warped.
>
> (62)

The reader will be curious to know how the single stone or the single word dropped into that silence can create warped reflections.

Again, while describing the trees of the Dead Forest, the narrator says, 'Life no longer circulated in them, their veins were brittled and broken, their skins frozen into letters of a forgotten language' (203). What does 'skins frozen into letters' of a 'forgotten language' signify? Is it only a surface description, we ask.

In all these instances and elsewhere, we find the consistent application of foregrounding (followed by the dynamics of defamiliarization and the reader's reinterpretative effort) through striking descriptions, elaborate metaphors and other features which support our contention about the literariness of the text in both its specialized formalist and more general sense.

In the above description of the Dead Forest and Noria's risky journey into it to find the hidden helicarriage, we again notice a clustering of foregrounded images and descriptions. Noria says, 'A smoke-dark haze of insects hovered in the air like clusters of abandoned shadows' (203). They fall apart as she walks through them, 'and clench again into swarming statues dimming the landscape like ancient spirits risen from under stones or buried memories made visible'. This clustering of defamiliarized descriptions once again helps to evoke the element of uncanny around the forest, which is the site for a dangerous secret (the hidden solar-powered helicarriage) as well as a signifier of the climate crisis.

To return to the example of our first cyclist in the unfamiliar country, the experience of reading *Memory of Water* is akin to a long ride where time and again you are drawn to appealing but unfamiliar refreshments set out along the way, which makes you curious as you stop and savour their taste, while your mind works at forming new connections and cultural meaning from what is served. This no doubt makes it a pleasurable and unique sport. And then again, there is suddenly a large cluster, a table full of the unfamiliar potions and savouries, which you try, and these secret brews begin to work on your mind, and suddenly you are held in the thrall of the eerie and the uncanny, and the stark dystopian reality of a water-scarce future takes hold of your mind. You stand face to face with the climate uncanny.

This, of course, brings us in conflict with aesthetes like Théophile Gautier, who believed everything that is useful is ugly. The *Memory of Water*, despite its evident literariness, that bestows a poetic quality to its prose, also serves the oft-noted functions of the climate novel, which is to help us imagine possible futures, prepare for the same and maybe also take necessary action. We will discuss these functions and the potential use of the book as an activist tool a little later, but before we do that, let us also ask a question whose answer is somewhat obvious by now – does *Memory of Water* demonstrate some of the other characteristics of literary fiction, discussed earlier, that Saricks, among others, has pointed out?

We begin by reaffirming that elements like evocative and poetic language as well as imagery, which are included in our first characterization of literary fiction, have kinship with the elements and techniques that impart 'literariness' to a text like *Memory of Water*. As we noted earlier, reviewers have employed expressions like 'poetic', 'beautiful' and 'gorgeous' in describing Memory of Water. Other reviews of the novel acknowledged its well-crafted language and nuance that we expect in literary fiction. So we find words and expressions like 'lyrically rendered', 'gorgeous and delicate writing', 'poetic', 'language is carefully crafted', 'beautifully written' and 'emotionally nuanced' employed to describe the novel in popular and specialist media like *Kirkus Reviews*, *Library Journal*, *The Guardian*, *Voima*, *Me Naiset* and *Helsingin Sanomat*, respectively.[28] These demonstrate that this cli-fi novel had been accepted in the popular review and book critics' community as one with a flavour of literary fiction.

We can take a deeper look at the element of character development which is important in literary fiction. We would remember Saricks specifically mentioning a focus on character over plot and characters exploring philosophical questions. In *Memory of Water*, we find Noria's transformation important to the story, and this often gets precedence over the plot of the novel. However, while exploring ethical dilemmas and answering philosophical questions, Noria's character, true to the nature of cli-fi, does not get totally separated from the collective of the village in which she is rooted.

There are a number of major conflicts or turning points that change Noria as the story progresses. First of all, when she decides to stay back and pursue the traditional profession of tea masters instead of following her scientist mother to Xinjing, we find her character getting grounded in the dystopian theme of water scarcity that is central to the book. Another plot point which transforms her as a person is when she reveals the secret of the spring to her friend Sanja, thus helping their family in the face of serious scarcity. Then, when the secret of the spring becomes public knowledge, Noria begins to help other villagers by providing them with scarce water at great personal risk, redeeming her as a fearless person whose humanity shines through the darkness of the story world. Finally, her decision, in the face of great risks, to prepare for the journey into the Lost Lands, where fresh water may be available, presents her as a courageous person to the reader.

The element of interiority is also strong in Noria's character, which is another feature of literary fiction. Much of her story is told through interior monologues, and she comes out as a person steeped in reflections and contemplation which adds further meaning to her journey through the book. Then again, in the attention to style and the slow meditative pacing, especially in the first and last parts of the book, we notice important markers of literary fiction. Though the novel doesn't have a complex structure sometimes encountered in literary fiction, Noria's emotional depth does bear the hallmarks of the genre. Finally, the book does engage universal themes of ethics and existential choice through the character of Noria, which is also a preoccupation of literary fiction but can also be present in environmental fiction.

All things considered, including the absence of any discernible or consistent effort to prioritize plot above character, the focus on well-crafted language, universal themes and dilemmas, character development, interiority, slow pacing, attention to style and most of all in its 'literariness' and the clustering of foregrounded features, we find good reasons to suggest that this novel is a work of climate fiction strong on its aesthetics and possessing a literary core. Therefore, we can choose to label *Memory of Water* as a work of 'literary climate fiction' and its style and technique as 'climate literary'. It is, in fact, one of those climate novels which stand as the advance guard of a new wave of climate writing, marking an inflection point in literature's encounter with climate change, which in certain ways parallels the New Wave movement of science fiction that began around the middle of the last century.

## Where to place this story?

On which climate fiction shelf do we place *Memory of Water*? Does the aesthetic focus of a novel automatically allow an easy categorization? From our discussion of categories, we can say this is not the case. As we are attempting various means of reading and analysing cli-fi, we will next examine this novel using the organizing principles we have discussed in the first part of this book.

Before examining Itäranta's novel using the organizing principles of cli-fi, let us begin by saying that the work, with its consciousness of anthropogenic emissions as the driver of climate crisis, fits with the definitions of climate fiction mentioned earlier. The novel also satisfies the Climate Reality Check, as climate change is a reality of the story (historical and present), and at least one character (Noria) is aware of it.

Without repeating the names of organizing principles (Figure 2.2) developed earlier, let's begin with the first which is about climate imaginaries. Very clearly, the book with the story of severe water scarcities, an autocratic government, distant wars and growing suffering belongs to the Social Breakdown imaginary of climate fiction. But within this scenario of breakdown, there are elements of hope in the use of solar-powered vehicles, the extensive presence of sustainable material (seagrass) and the simple and possibly sustainable diets in the world of the story. These sustainable choices, however, may partly be influenced by scarcity and social breakdown rather than conscious care for the environment.

Looking at the second perspective based on the Costanza Framework matrix, we will place the novel in the techno-pessimist box, where a strong and autocratic occupying force exercises absolute power (for water rationing, among other things) and employs only a few technologies (e.g. desalination plants and solar panels) to adapt to and mitigate climate change while ruling over occupied lands. The indicators of sustainable living that we notice in the text are most probably driven by scarcities and the actions of the occupying power.

Applying the third set of classifiers, this book comes out as a cautionary tale, where the worst effects of climate change (water scarcities and rising temperatures) have been extrapolated to a not-so-distant future. There are also clear indications and warnings about the climate crisis in names like 'Twilight Century' which precede the timeline of the book, in the descriptions of old maps of the polar ice caps which have consequently disappeared, and in the mention of violent storms and migration. There are, however, hints of resistance in Noria's helping other characters with supplies of water, her decision with Sanja to go to the Lost Lands in search of uncontaminated water, the risks taken by the Jansson expedition to explore the Lost Lands and in the stories of unionists and other revolutionaries fighting against the forces of the new Qian.

The division between realist and futurist stories constitutes the fourth classification. *Memory of Water* is clearly set in the near future when the polar ice caps have melted, the world has run out of oil, an occupying power rules over the 'Scandinavian Union', and large landmasses have been flooded. However, the water scarcities that the story depicts are quickly becoming a reality in parts of the world, which is another way the imagined realities of climate futures are seeping into the lived realities of the present.

The fifth classification examines the tension between sci-fi and cli-fi. This story is not science fiction in the sense that there are no scientific discoveries influencing plot or setting, and in fact, there has been an erasure of technologies connected to fossil fuels. There is no extrapolation of existing science into the future, and all changes we notice are the results of human action in the past. If, however, we agree with the contention of certain scholars and consider the climate-changed world of the book as a 'novum' which creates 'cognitive estrangement' brought into being by catastrophic climate crisis and water scarcities, then this could still be slotted as science fiction.[29]

Here, it is interesting to note the kinship of the concept of 'cognitive estrangement' used by Suvin for science fiction and 'ostranenie' of Russian Formalism, which, as we mentioned, can be translated both as defamiliarization and estrangement. In fact, Suvin arrived at the concept of cognitive estrangement from the Russian Formalists, whose conceptual insights we have used to test the dynamics of 'literariness' in *Memory of Water*. This kinship and the obvious use of defamiliarization throughout the novel, among other things, seem to push it towards the genre of science fiction, and in fact, reviewers have called this novel 'soft sci-fi'.[30] However, one can argue that the defamiliarization or estrangement that operates here is at the level of language and it imparts literariness to the text. When it clusters together, it does evoke the uncanny, but the uncanny or eeriness that is evoked is a climate uncanny and not necessarily the effect of a science fiction novum.

Applying the sixth classification, we ask whether the novel is dystopian or utopian. *Memory of Water* is evidently a dystopian story of the future, where things go from bad to worse. The book is dystopian in setting with water scarcity, totalitarian rule, wars and so on, but in contrast, we also find a narrative strand of hope when Noria's character evolves to the point where she takes great personal risk to provide water to her friend and then the villagers and also plans the expedition to the Lost Lands, where fresh water may be available. The young Noria is also anchored to the centuries-old tea masters' tradition connected with water, which affords her moments of strength and repose in the face of harsh circumstances and grave dangers.

The final classification looks at mitigative and adaptive narratives. *Memory of Water* is mostly a narrative of adaptation where people adapt to the crisis and somehow carry on with their lives. For example, we find adaptive technologies like desalination plants mentioned in the story. However, in the use of solar-powered transport like helicycles and helicarriages and the use of sustainable materials like seaweed, there are hints of mitigative efforts. The question remains whether these mitigative efforts are matters of choice or circumstance because oil has run out and much of past-world technologies have been lost.

## Climate and the imagination in *Memory of Water*

Earlier in this chapter, we have seen how a climate novel can convey an aesthetic experience through its use of language and the associated literariness of the text. In doing this, does the author lose out on the other representational goals of cli-fi? How does the 'climate literary' engage with the creative challenges posed by the unimaginable, probability-laden, nature-culture entanglements of climate change? Is it up to this task, or does it lose its way in the play of language and form, missing out on its important role of imagining and interpreting the crisis for readers?

We have already studied Itäranta's climate novel under the lens of aesthetics, wherein we also discovered how literariness can be employed in evoking the climate uncanny. Let us now take a look at some of the creative-thematic challenges of climate fiction and how the author has imaginatively addressed these. This will, among other things, help us get a better idea about how a work of literary climate fiction can handle creative-thematic challenges and if its focus on aesthetics affords it any advantages or disadvantages in representing climate change in fiction. As before, we examine the novel using all the creative-thematic features (except aesthetics) listed in Figure 2.2, which between them constitute the minor lenses and the two remaining major lenses of our study.

In *Memory of Water*, the natural world is portrayed through contrasts and denudation. The major setting of the book is a water-scarce dystopic Scandinavian Union, but alongside this, there are images of contrast which portray how it used to be earlier. For example, in describing Mosswood which has now turned into the Dead Forest, the author writes:

> The Dead Forest had once been called Mosswood, a name that recalled deep-green leaves moving in the wind and verdancy so lush and moist that you could feel it on your skin. Even longer ago, when words for such greenness were not needed yet, because it was a given in these lands, the forest had not had a name at all, so my father had told me.
>
> (203)

Here in these contrasts, the author evokes the entanglement of the natural with human life, words and language, foregrounding expressions like 'forgotten language' when describing the present state of the trees of these woods. Once more, this entanglement is noted when she writes, 'Life no longer circulated in them, their veins were brittled and broken, their skins frozen into letters of a forgotten language, near-incomprehensible marks of what had once been' (203).

Noria uses maps to contrast the old fossil-fuel-driven world and the one she inhabits, and in her interior monologues, we encounter the effects of climate change through rising sea levels and the triggering of wars and large-scale migration:

> The lakes and rivers in the Scandinavian Union had merged into wider waters, and the old coastlines were long gone.
>
> That was not all.
>
> Drowned islands, coastal plains, river deltas turned salt-bitten; and large cities, now silent ghosts of lives past in their shroud of sea, everywhere, everywhere.
>
> On the old map North and South Poles were shown in white. I knew this stood for the ice that had sometimes been called eternal ice, until it became clear that it wasn't eternal after all. Near the end of the past-world era the globe had warmed and seas had risen faster than anyone could have anticipated. Tempests tore the continents and people fled their homes to where there was still space and dry

> land. During the final oil wars a large accident contaminated most of the freshwater reserves of former Norway and Sweden, leaving the areas uninhabitable!
>
> (64)

In such descriptions, as in many other parts of the story, the nature-culture connection is starkly presented, demonstrating how systemic connections impact all beings and the 'inanimate' world.

As in many other climate novels, a scientist is an important character here, but instead of a male scientist, we have Noria's mother playing quite an important part in the drift of the narrative and in framing the story. We will remember Caren Irr noticing how the role of the male scientist is being disrupted in a certain kind of cli-fi, and in both Itäranta, and Ghosh earlier, we have seen how the male scientist has been replaced by a woman. Also, the presence of the scientist mother as well as someone like Sanja, who is good with gadgets and technology, alongside Noria with her rich interiority, further reaffirms the fusing of the natural (scientific) and the cultural in this novel.

Issues of temporal scales and associated climatic change are also addressed in this book as it traverses at least three distinct periods or ages, namely the dystopic present of the book, the Twilight Century that preceded it when the world ran out of oil, and the 'past-world' (approximating our present) when with growing emissions the climate situation began to get worse, the polar ice melted, many lands were submerged, there were large-scale migrations and oil wars were triggered.

While the focus of the book is on the dystopic future of water scarcities, there are plot points connecting this setting with the Twilight Century and the time ('past world') before that, through narratives involving past world technologies (CD players) and forgotten expeditions undertaken in search of fresh water. This engagement with long temporal scales and the geographical awareness of planetary effects of climate change allows, following Timothy

Clark, a multi-scalar reading of the text, thus adding an extra layer of meaning to the timeline of the major incidents of the novel.

Coming to the challenge of imaginatively depicting non-human agency, we immediately notice the remarkable engagement with water. Passage after passage talks of water in memorable prose till it becomes a sentient, all-knowing being, twined with life, death and destiny. For example, Noria's father tells her a past-world tea master's story about water having consciousness and how it can comprehend the movements of the world. Water's non-human agency in this novel is further supported by Fatma Aykanat, who contends, '*Memory of Water*, treats water as an agential nonhuman element with the capacity to change the morphology of its surroundings as well as having a consciousness enabling water to store "in its memory everything that's ever happened in this world", both literally and metaphorically'.[31]

The agency, myth-making and evocation of water as a character is arguably the most visible involvement of the story with non-human agency besides references to phenomena like fish-fires (aurora borealis) which also resonate with meaning and agency in the story. How this quality of water is evoked again and again throughout the book can be encapsulated in two short quotes.

The author writes about turning on the tap and trying to speak with water, 'I spoke to it in pretty words and ugly words, and I may have even screamed and wept, but water doesn't care for human sorrows. It flows without slowing or quickening its pace in the darkness of the earth, where only stones will hear' (1). Then again, through the foregrounding of a word like 'shatter', the author hints at the agency of water, 'Water walks with the moon and embraces the earth, and it isn't afraid to die in fire or live in air. When you step into it, it will be as close as your own skin, but if you hit it too hard, it will shatter you' (5). There is a definite sense in all this that water has an agent-like expression in the story and is not inert matter. If we recall the foundational concept of Actor-Network theory, we can see how water, in this novel, connects with other actants through networks of dependencies where no one is independent of each other.

We have already dwelt at length on how the novel evokes the uncanny in certain scenes through a clustering of the tools and dynamics of literariness. Otherwise also in various scenes involving the Dead Forest, Noria's secretive journey to check the helicarriage, in certain descriptions of the secret spring, in the scenes preceding the death of her father and in the narratives of the days of her final incarceration, we can find evocations of the uncanny in the novel, almost always helped by the poetic quality of her prose.

Climate change affects large collectives of people and other beings which is why collectives are important in climate stories, becoming an active backdrop from which a number of individual protagonists may stand out. Nick Admussen writes, 'Most stories specifically identify individuals who profit from narratives of progress, whether intellectually or materially … The triumphal feeling of these stories comes from their selective attention to just a tiny part of the relationships that enfolds their characters.'[32]

*Memory of Water*, though driven by the conflicts faced by its main character Noria, never loses sight of the larger collectives of people in the background. Right from the other villagers and neighbours of the protagonist to people in far-off places affected by a war or taking part in an uprising, the collective keeps returning in the narrative, strengthening the plot and providing it more meaning and context in the backdrop of a dystopian climate-affected future. In one of the poignant scenes of water scarcity, Noria finds the people of the village, 'were trying to fill waterskins, and buckets from the shallow, murky-watered brook that ran near the edge of the grave. My parents had always warned me to never drink from it' (134). Then again, when the secret of her access to the spring water becomes common knowledge, we find her helping villagers with water at great personal risk. So the community and the collective are there in the backdrop, sometimes informing and determining the main character's actions. However, this climate novel invests a lot in characterization and literariness, and so the individual character's (Noria) journey gets precedence while being underpinned by the trials and tribulations of the larger collective.

The sense of planet, as a distinctive feature of literature's encounter with climate change can also be noticed in this novel as the story telescopes back and forth from the small village where Noria lives, to the world beyond, to far-off cities like Xinjing where her mother shifts, to the recordings of the expeditions to the Lost Lands which were forbidden and inaccessible, where the water was contaminated by wars and places further afield. In fact, the setting of the story is often deterritorialized, as a shimmering nameless world where Scandinavian people and place names coexist with those that sound Chinese, Korean, Japanese and Russian, where East Asian tea ceremonies happen under a sky painted by Northern Lights. Axel Goodbody, drawing attention to the real-world settings of some climate novels, writes, 'Noria's village is in the "Scandinavian Union", a land of white nights, where the sun does not set in midsummer, and there are "fishfires" in the sky in winter reminiscent of the Aurora Borealis', while also noticing how Itäranta 'estranges and universalises' the setting by 'introducing elements from other places and times.'[33]

Katarina Leppänen has probed Itäranta's novel using the concept of 'eco-cosmopolitanism', also developed by Ursula Heise. Heise, we will remember, has stressed on the importance of a sense of planet and the appreciation of global networks of beings, human and non-human, in a highly interconnected world affected by overlapping crises. Leppänen has argued that the storyworld of *Memory of Water* does not support an eco-cosmopolitan outlook which would also imply the impossibility of a sense of planet in its literary imaginary. She writes, 'If, for example as in the *Memory of Water*, electronic communication by message pods, as they are called in the book, breaks down and if there is hardly any infrastructure or fuel for physical travel, then the whole idea of planetary eco-cosmopolitanism stands on shaky ground.'[34]

Thereon, she argues that an eco-cosmopolitan imagination requires a substrate of ecomodernist principles and economic growth to work. This, while valid, does not consider the possibility of individual imagination, at the level of a character, expanding to assimilate a wider temporal and geographical collective and concerns in the present moment, as well as in the past. Noria's solitary journeys to past worlds of growing climate crises and migration through maps, her realization that fresh water is to be found in the Lost Lands and her determination to seek it out are all indicative of a lurking sense and realization of bigger planetary forces and global networks at play, an appreciation of distant temporal and spatial connections, which act as a scaffolding for the story. Noria says, 'In my dreams I was with them, in this strange landscape, where the voice of water was ever-present. Yet I couldn't see their faces or talk to them … The distance from dreams to words is long, and so is the way from words to deeds. Yet the more I listened, the shorter it grew' (171). Refracted through the activist imagination of the reader, this eco-cosmopolitan imagination can, in fact, have powerful resonance.

Earlier, we have seen how Itäranta's novel invests most in its aesthetics,[35] by which we meant literariness of text, poetic language, character development and some other features of literary fiction. However, politics and issues of justice are also present in the background and surface at various moments of the story. There are indications that the Scandinavian Union is under occupation (possibly Chinese), and away from the main setting of the story, there are stirrings of a revolution. Justice concerns also come to the fore when the author tells us that the cities are supplied by desalination plants while the villagers struggle with meagre water resources. We also realize how the occupying power imposes its will on the villagers by its control over water and how, finally Noria and her friend Sanja try to seek a way out of this oppression but fail.

This underlying framework of politics, wherein a teenage character (and her friend), anchored to a centuries-old tradition of tea masters, rebels and acts decisively, affirms personal freedom and greater common good (sharing the spring water and then researching and planning to seek out the fresh water reserves in the forbidden lands), imparting added meaning and direction to the plot of the novel. Though it is not known how and if Noria could have helped her community if she had successfully made the journey to the Lost Lands and discovered clean water there, the decision itself and her meticulous planning for it is in itself a political act – an act of rebellion. This reaffirms the fact that *Memory of Water*, while strong in its aesthetics, doesn't fail to engage politics and the quest for justice that is rooted in the scarcities, sharing and search for water.

To summarize the imaginative engagement of this climate novel, we can say that while it wears its aesthetics on its sleeve, it also engages with the creative challenges arising out of literature's encounter with climate change. The literariness of the text, which we discussed at length, has, among other things, a bearing on the evocation of the uncanny while the poetic language and lyrical passages also help the portrayal of the non-human agency of water, and to an extent, nature-culture entanglements. However, literariness and the literary do not seem to serve the purpose of negotiating other creative-thematic challenges like the depiction of a planetary sense, the role of collectives and derangements of scale. That Itäranta's novel still enters into a spirited engagement with these other challenges is because of a wider awareness of the author about the science, the future pathways and the complexities of nature-culture that climate change has revealed to humanity. Somewhat more obviously, and here we can also remind ourselves of the arguments of Adorno and Lukacs about the political novel, the politics of this novel is perceived in its undercurrents, while the aesthetics is what leaves the deepest impression. Still, there remains the possibility that this climate story, through its characterization, settings and transport, besides other embedded elements, can have an influence on the reader's mind. This we explore in the next section which probes the transformative potential (Figure 2.2) of this climate novel.

## The climate story in action

We can once again recall Théophile Gautier's assertions about beauty and usefulness. The French novelist had said, 'Nothing is really beautiful but that which cannot be made use of; everything that is useful is ugly.' How far is this true for cli-fi? Is it possible that such a novel while focusing on aesthetics can also be a useful tool for climate action? We have already noted this aesthetic quality of Itäranta's novel. Now we can get down to exploring its usefulness by examining its transformative potential.

As explained earlier, we will be looking at three out of the five possible ways to test the normative machinery of this cli-fi. These pertain to the Application of findings of empirical ecocritical studies, Production and Consumption Flows and Sustainable Development Goals (SDGs). To keep this analysis concise while providing a fair portrayal of the transformative potential of the book, we are dropping the Integral Ecology and SSPs-based analyses which have been explained earlier in the book.

Empirical ecocritical studies, we will remember, noted the importance of character identification, vivid settings and the transport of the story (how it engages and transports the reader) in communicating climate change. Among other things, these studies also noted the importance of emulatable role models and the influence of solution-focused stories.

Noria's character is carefully developed with a lot of interiority. Her negotiation of the challenges of the climate dystopia, the ethical position she takes while refusing Commander Taro's offer to become a spy, the way she helps her friend with water and her general nature as a compassionate human being are expected to impress readers, thereby deepening their awareness about climate change. Noria's caring father is also a character who will leave a similar impression.

The accomplished evocation of dystopia, while impressive, can turn off some readers from engaging with climate change and taking action. While this may be true for a sizeable number of readers, the darkness of dystopia, as we have said earlier, can also redeem and provide the spiritual grounding for taking action. Then there are also those readers who, while enjoying the tropes of the dystopian genre, can still absorb its inherent warnings.

Furthermore, the aesthetic strategies of the novel involve the reader in a reinterpretative effort, thereby connecting her intimately to the world of the story. This, besides the surface beauty of the prose and the vivid descriptions, can be expected to facilitate communication of the underlying cautionary messages of the novel. Carefully designed empirical studies involving readers can help to decipher the real influence of literary cli-fi novels like this one.

Finally, Noria and her friend Sanja are inspirational characters at two levels. First of all, they both practice sustainable living. Noria's family uses Sanja's repairing services; they use sustainable materials like seaweed and generally seem not to cherish a consumerist lifestyle. However, the point here is that this sustainability is mostly induced by scarcities of the storyworld. Still in the use of renewables and frugal living coupled with Noria's ethical stand in sharing the secret of the spring with her friend, her decision to stay back and her final conversations with Commander Taro paint her as a courageous person and an emulatable role model with a strong sense of ethics.

We can now apply the two remaining approaches of Production and Consumption flows and SDGs to study the advocacy potential of this novel. On the surface, the book is set in a dystopian future of water scarcities when the world has warmed further. However, there are intermittent references to how we ended up here, mainly in the conversations between Noria and her friend Sanja, and also Noria's own thoughts. A major plot point revolves around the Jansson expedition to the Lost Lands, involving a group of people setting out in search of fresh water. The Jansson expedition, we come to know, from an old recording, happened in the Twilight Century when the world ran out of oil and wars followed. Here, the book implicitly acknowledges the centrality of fossil fuels in pushing the world to where we find it at the beginning of the story.

There are also repeated references to the 'plastic grave' where past-world technology, including a whole automobile, is buried. By weaving the plastic grave – 'past world plastic took centuries to degrade' (20) – including the automobile into an important strand of narrative, the author makes an implicit connection between the polluting and unsustainable habits of the past and the dystopic present of the book.

The dystopia of *Memory of Water* is, however, not all-round darkness. People use helicycles and helicarriages powered by sunlight; there is a ubiquitous use of seagrass in bags, awnings and elsewhere; two important characters (Sanja and Jukara) run repair shops; and there is no mention of meat-eating which, as we know, is one of the great drivers of the climate crisis. There is also an important scene where people barter goods in the absence of money.

However, as we keep pointing out, many of these changes may have been affected because of scarcity, the need to stay alive, the rules imposed by an authoritarian government and the lack of alternatives following the wars, and not as a conscious switchover to sustainable lifestyles. The role of the occupying power in steering the world of this novel towards a semblance of subsistence-level 'sustainability' is ambivalent, but this is still not an imaginary of complete social breakdown, and that is why it also fits with the Costanza matrix box where a strong government and not high-technology defines the contours of, in this case, a scarcity-ridden world. Still, the mention of sustainable materials and frugal habits signal the author's intent to flag these alternatives.

In one important scene of the book, the young Noria asks her mother about ice which is no more to be found; in fact, the polar icecaps have all but disappeared. 'When I'd been six years old, I had read in a past-world book about snow and ice, and asked my mother what they were' (39). When she asks her mother why there was no snow and ice anymore, her mother somewhat cryptically says 'the world changed' (39). She goes on to add, 'Most believe that it changed on its own, simply claimed its due … and there are those who think that people changed the world, unintentionally or on purpose' (39). On further prodding from her daughter, she unambiguously says, 'I believe the world wouldn't be what it is today if it wasn't for people' (40). So here again, we find the author making a connection between people and the state of the planet.

Also in one of the poignant moments of the book, which we keep returning to, Noria is standing on the banks of a dry river thinking of someone from the past world: 'looking into the water that rushes by, muddy perhaps, perhaps clear, and something that has not yet been is bleeding into her thoughts. I would like to think she turns around and goes home and does one thing differently that day because of what she has imagined' (25). Here again, we find a consciousness about the possibility of change, the possibility that individual actions can help to deal with the crisis of climate change.

Finally, if we take a look at solutions, the book doesn't explicitly mention any, except for Noria's rebellious act in planning to set off on a dangerous expedition in search of fresh water. However, as we mentioned before, many habits of sustainable living, from the use of sustainable materials to solar-powered transport, are woven into the plot of the novel.

The book also engages many issues addressed by the SDGs, like clean water and sanitation (SDG 6), affordable and clean energy (SDG 7), responsible consumption and production (SDG 12), climate action (SDG 13), among others. However, as we have seen from the preceding discussion, none of these are explicitly addressed as points of action; rather, they are elements that inform the world building and character conflicts of this novel.

Though we do not use the Integral Ecology and SSPs approaches to probe this novel, we can conclude this analysis with one final observation. The fact that the author has dwelt briefly on the systems and trajectories of past worlds, and because there is a marked worsening in social cohesion and power relations over the arc of the story, provides ample opportunity to use those two approaches and gather lessons from the dynamics of change. Such lessons, along with other insights, could be useful for policymakers, activists and in fact for every reader who wants to engage meaningfully with the worsening climate crisis.

## Art for planet's sake

We have now arrived at the end of our reading of Itäranta's novel which stood out as a work of literary climate fiction. To consolidate our analysis, we can say this is a dystopian climate novel of social breakdown with elements of hope embedded within. This element of hope, in the form of sustainable technologies and material may, however, not be a conscious societal choice but rather a forced adaptation born out of crisis and its attendant scarcities.

A significant feature of this work is the author's use of foregrounding which, through the associated dynamics of defamiliarization, imparts literariness and aesthetic appeal to the text. This, combined with deft character development, interiority and certain other features of literary fiction, albeit placed within the improbabilities and uncanny settings of a climate ravaged near future, caused by human action, places this book in a space that we can call the 'climate literary' where climate fiction melds with literary fiction while not losing its major goal of representing the unthinkable aspects of the crisis.

We also observed how defamiliarization clusters around certain poignant settings and scenes of the book, thereby evoking the uncanny as well as depicting nature-culture entanglements, which are distinctive features of literature's engagement with climate change. Other features of this engagement, like the representation of non-human agency, often aided by literariness, are also well woven into the plot of the book, most significantly in the depiction of water and its agency and the connection of water with the tea master's traditions.

The sense of planet, while evinced in the thoughts about the past world and its gradual breakdown, does not carry through to the central storyline of the book, where, because of lost technologies and conflict, the interconnections between distant places are broken, though not completely.

Long temporal scales of the climate crisis are also taken up in the novel through the stories of past worlds and how human action gradually led to devastating changes that led to wars and occupation. The tea master's tradition plays an important role throughout the book as a locus of immutability, fixity and a possible source of hope and resistance against the onslaught of disaster, denudation and the workings of the occupying power. The tea master's historical records and the records of the plastic grave yield possibilities and hope that could have led on to more desirable outcomes, but perhaps in keeping with the requirements of the dystopian trope, the story ends in darkness, at least for the main character.

The politics of Itäranta's novel is not overt and can be noticed in individual action and acts of rebellion as well as distant echoes of revolution and collective resistance, but it is always the aesthetic values that leave an impression. Could we expect more collective effort in changing the status quo as a possible plot strand of such books, and if so, how would such a storyline affect their aesthetic core? This is a question the activist-minded reader of cli-fi may well ask. In the third and final climate novel we are now going to read, we will find that the political and the collective get further precedence. The political agency of that work, shot through with justice and equity issues, will acquaint us with another necessary and important intervention in literature's ongoing encounter with climate change.

7

# Heart of darkness

## *Climate and justice*

When Cyclone Amphan had struck eastern India and Bangladesh, I had been involved with the work of some NGOs that were doing relief work as well as supporting those affected by the pandemic. These were trying times, as we were in the midst of a Covid-19 wave with lockdowns affecting incomes, and adding to collective suffering was the cyclone which had cut a swathe of devastation through eastern India and parts of our neighbouring country. More than 120 people had died from the storm, and total damages were estimated at US$ 14 billion.

Donning N95 masks and armed with hand sanitizers, we had set out early that morning with a truckload of relief supplies for isolated villages bordering the Sundarbans. The roads were mostly deserted, and Park Street, which is the most happening part of town, had turned into a stretch of desolation with uprooted trees blocking the road and not a soul in sight. Stretches of road had become so unrecognizable with hundreds of fallen trees[1] with their giant canopies blocking the view, it would seem that a sorcerer, practiced in the dark arts, had twisted the dimensions and made familiar places totally unfamiliar. It reminded me of Woland, in Bulgakov's novel,[2] who could manipulate reality as he pleased, but the feeling that this devastation communicated is best described as what we have come to know as the climate uncanny.

The journey to the village was slow, and we reached the area around midday. People had already gathered because we had earlier communicated our intention. The distribution of medicines, dry food, sanitary supplies, clothes and other necessities among a large number of affected people from neighbouring villages took the better part of the day.

On our way back, as we were crossing the outskirts of the last village in that area, a few women and children with empty eyes, visibly malnourished and weak, came out of their damaged huts. They had not received any of the material we had distributed because no one had told them about the relief effort. But our supplies were exhausted by then.

With a heavy heart, we left the place, promising to be more careful next time so that no one is left out. And surely not the weakest and the most underprivileged, who suffer the most from natural disasters and overlapping crises[3] that are becoming increasingly frequent because of the climate emergency.

But I knew right then, as I do now, that this will not be easy. Because, tangled with the effects of an overheating planet, a host of political, economic and other factors overlap and militate against underprivileged people the world over, aggravating their suffering and perpetuating inequality. This is the real murky core of the climate crisis, and if we are to win this battle one day against the forces of greed and indifference, then this is the space that has to be lit up first. This, as we shall see from our in-depth reading of Anita Agnihotri's *The Sickle*, is the challenge of climate justice.

## Barren fields and bitter-sweet harvests: Reading *The Sickle*

One of the abiding functions of the novel is that it can hold up a mirror to society. Besides being a crucible for individual characters, this narrative form can paint telling portraits of collectives, and indeed of a time, with all its complexities and concatenations, in ways dreary official reports cannot. Anita Agnihotri's novel, in Arunava

Sinha's elegant translation, does all of this and more. It turns the focus away from the big city and gets down to telling the half-heard, often-misrepresented accounts from a region of western India – the state of Maharashtra and its vast hinterland.

Like the two other novels discussed before, *The Sickle* too was sent to me as a review copy from a newspaper. The novel being written originally in Bangla (titled *Kaste*, meaning sickle), my mother tongue, I used both the original (Figure 7.1) and the translation when writing the review and also for this extended analysis. Parts of this section, where I summarize the story, are from my review of the book which appeared in the *New Indian Express*.[4]

*The Sickle* is divided into three parts that bring together a large canvas of characters whose paths gradually connect till, in the final chapter, the author portrays a long march of farmers, Indigenous people and activists heading for the Azad Maidan of Mumbai (the capital city of the state of Maharashtra and India's financial capital) to demand their rights. The three parts of the book are titled Sickle, It's Best to Stage a Turnaround and The Long March. The first part has eight named chapters, the second has four and the final part is one chapter long.

The first part of the book has three important characters, all women, namely Terna, Minu (Nakoshi) and Daya. Terna, named after a river, is a migrant sugarcane labourer from Chhindwari village at the edge of Latur town, who, like hundreds of others, has to travel with her family, every year from the drought-ridden Latur to the sugarcane fields of Satara, to work for months under unsafe and exploitative conditions.

Terna, who belongs to a denotified tribal group still marked with the colonial prejudice of crime, the Banjaris, has to undertake this journey because there is sparse rainfall and no irrigation in her village which would allow round-the-year farming. Meanwhile, thousands upon thousands of acres of thirsty sugarcane crop deplete the dwindling groundwater reserves of another district of Maharashtra. While the climate connection to this drought is not explicit at the

**Figure 7.1** The cover of *Kaste*, the Bangla original of Anita Agnihotri's *The Sickle*. Cover illustrator, Debabrata Ghosh. Courtesy: Publisher of the Bangla novel *Kaste*, Dey's Publishing, Kolkata.

beginning, later on the book reveals how global warming is implicated in the droughts here and in other parts of the country. Thus, Ranjan, an agricultural researcher who appears in the second part of the novel while studying a satellite map of the country, discovers that

> The extent of districts prone to drought and those affected by it regularly have kept rising over the past four decades. In the 1960s, sixty-six districts in five states were considered prone to drought, but by the beginning of the twenty-first century this had increased to 40 districts across twenty-three states, with the declaration sometimes coming as early as the middle of the year. It isn't as though the rains are less copious, but global warming is changing the cycle of the monsoon and the rhythm of its movements.
>
> (186)

Other studies[5] have also implicated climate change as a factor in the droughts of Maharashtra, driving the migration of sugarcane labourers like Terna that we find in this story.

The narrative strand centred on Terna's life in the sugarcane *toli* (temporary row of labour shelters) – where labour contractors (*mukaddams*) and their accomplices violate women at their will and run operations with an iron hand – is portrayed with empathy and a meticulous attention to detail only possible from someone who knows this land like the back of her hand. Agnihotri writes, 'Humans were "sickles" here, they had no names but numbers … A sickle is released only after enough sugarcane is harvested to recover the advance payment. Had the labourers here been thought of as humans, it wouldn't have been possible to make them work twenty to twenty-two hours a day' (13–14).

The sugarcane factories, we learn, are run as 'cooperatives' of farmers and factory owners. However, unlike the apparent inclusiveness hinted at by a cooperative structure, the sugarcane industry has become a locus for the concentration of power in which political forces, labour contractors, farmers and owners are deeply enmeshed. Migrant labourers like Terna and her family, who come to harvest the sugarcane, work on a system of advances which they have to win back with their punishing labour that continues in shifts through day and night.

The *toli* where Terna lives for eight months a year with her husband, Datu, and two children, has no electricity, just one tap, basic shared toilets and their individual dwellings don't even have doors, and Terna is soon violated by one of the mukaddams who have unhindered access to these dwellings.

The next chapter introduces the feisty lawyer Daya, from the sugarcane-growing Satara district, who runs a campaign for women's rights with a focus on female foeticide which is rampant in the district of Beed which is more than 300 kilometres from where she lives. She has gathered a dedicated team of men and women around her, among whom is Yashwant, who runs a *dhaba* on the road to Shirur-Kasar, a hotbed of the female foeticide racket of Beed. Yashwant turns into an informer for Daya, passing on news about people from near and far who visit for clandestine gender testing and foeticide conducted in the mushrooming diagnostic clinics of the area. The lucrative business of gender testing and female foeticide is well entrenched in this area, involving doctors, the police, politicians among others, and by running her campaign, Daya soon steps on many toes. Right at the beginning of Daya's story, there is a bomb attack in the district court targeting her daughter, but this does not weaken her resolve.

We are next introduced to the story of Minu (or Nakoshi) and her husband Sagar from Sangebari village of Beed district, who are also migrant sugarcane labourers. Minu is the mother of three children, the youngest an eight-month-old daughter, whom she brings along with her to the sugarcane fields of Satara. The author writes, 'Among families of small farmers whose land receives neither rainfall nor irrigation, who live their bruised, barren fields behind to harvest sugarcane in Satara every year, the birth of a daughter means '*ek kaita kami*, one sickle less' (53). In fact, Minu's given name, Nakoshi (*Nako* meaning 'no more'), suggests that her parents want no more daughters. We see how drought, migration, exploitative labour and female foeticide are entwined through the plot that the author weaves.

Daya's awareness campaigns bring her to Minu's village, Sangebari, where she organizes awareness meetings. Daya tells them about the falling sex ratio, and soon Minu's husband Sagar also joins her campaign, working as an informer for Yashwant, passing on news about the clandestine activities of the clinics of Shirur Kasar. Meanwhile, Daya's awareness efforts have also led to a change in Minu's attitudes as she gradually becomes more aware of her rights.

The story now centres on Daya's tireless efforts to fight the clandestine gender-testing and female foeticide racket as she gradually focuses on a notorious couple (Manju Patil and Dr Vrindaban Patil) who run an operation from a clinic in Shirur Kasar. Throughout the novel, the author employs social realism which blends storytelling with reportage and analysis of socio-economic realities of the lives of the people, the systems and rules of the sugarcane trade, the workings of the clandestine foeticide business, the lives of the migrants and the local economy of the region. While carrying on with her efforts to expose the female foeticide business, Daya also involves herself with other kinds of activism, travelling hundreds of miles to visit villages like the drought-affected Sangebari, where she organizes piped water supply besides creating awareness among women about their rights. As the years pass, she organizes more people, and her small movement grows bigger.

There is, however, a strand of despair that now begins to surface, as Daya faces intransigence and the lack of motivation from villagers and town folk to better their lot. She discovers how the villagers of Sangebari do not have the slightest motivation to replace a stolen tap for the water supply she had organized, or how for months upon months, people in the towns do not pay electricity bills, resulting in extended power cuts in places like Shirur Kasar.

While Daya's weariness grows, she is not prepared to give up and soon devises a plan to send decoys to Manju Patil's clinic. Although earlier efforts to send decoys, of which Minu and Sagar had been part, had not always been successful because the chain of corruption ran deep and far, she is determined to expose Patil. This time, she sends Sagar and a pregnant activist, Kausalya, to the clinic, and despite great personal danger, they manage to sneak out with photos of the goings-on inside the notorious clinic where hungry dogs are fed the illegally removed foetuses.

Daya achieves success and manages to get the clinic closed and the two perpetrators jailed, but the complex socio-economic situation and mindsets that lead to the rampant practice of female foeticide in this region are hard to change. In the final chapter of this part of the novel, we are introduced to the backstory of Daya's trusted informer Yashwant and his relationship with a young woman Rupali whom he cannot marry because of constraints imposed by the caste system.

Rupali gets married to a grocer who tries to kill their newborn daughter, Durga, by throwing the child out of the hospital window and is caught red-handed by Yashwant. This story ends with the marriage of Durga; Durga, who in Hindu mythology is symbolic of feminine power. Meanwhile, Daya discovers she had struck a hornet's nest by challenging the clandestine female foeticide racket, and soon enough there is an attempt on her life in Delhi, where she is invited to collect a prize, the Nari Shakti (Women's Power) Award. By now, it is obvious that a politician at the highest level is involved in this attempt on her life.

The second part of the novel, 'It's Best to Stage a Turnaround', begins with the story of the cotton farmer Umesh and his wife Vaishali of Kajli village in the Marathwada region in the same state of Maharashtra. This part of the novel focuses on the plight of debt-stricken cotton farmers of Vidharba (northeastern Maharashtra) and Marathwada (eastern Maharashtra) where lack of irrigation, debt and drought militate to a situation where farmer suicides are common. 'With every passing day', the author writes, 'the monsoon in Marathwada and Vidarbha is getting more and more erratic; even long-standing farmers cannot tell when the rains will come and when they will leave' (168–9).

The story delves into the details of how cotton farmer Umesh sinks into debt because of a combination of factors. When his wife is humiliated by debt repayment agents and a bank official makes sexual advances towards her, promising a *quid pro quo* debt relief, Umesh hangs himself from the rafters.

Written with meticulous detail, entwining the cultural (like bull worship) with socio-economic commentary, the narrative now examines the overlapping and intersecting reasons of climate change, drought, lack of irrigation, agricultural input prices, debt and corruption in irrigation projects to present a comprehensive portrayal of the plight of cotton farmers in the Marathwada and Vidarbha regions of Maharashtra. Presenting a stark account of the seriousness of the issues and the attendant human cost in lives lost, the author writes, 'There was nothing new about a cotton farmer dying by suicide; if calculations were to be made, 300 or 400 farmers took their own lives every year in each district of Vidarbha. One farmer dies every hour' (168).

In the course of the story, we are introduced to the intrepid Ranjan Patil, a farmer's son who is a mechanical engineer with an MTech but with close connections to the land. Ranjan is pursuing a PhD on the utilization and management of water resources, and while doing this work, he develops a deep understanding of the socio-politics, agro-climatic regions and farmer indebtedness in the state of Maharashtra. Soon enough, Ranjan and Vaishali's paths cross. Ranjan collects all details of the death of Vaishali's husband, her humiliation by the bank officials and insists she file a report at the police station. Over time, Ranjan develops a romantic attraction for Vaishali, and in one of the memorable scenes of the novel, set on the banks of a millennia-old crater lake, he proposes marriage to Vaishali, but she refuses. 'No, Ranju dada, don't ask to marry me to save me from humiliation', she tells him (218).

The festering corruption in the allotment and implementation of irrigation projects, which aggravates the plight of the farmers in this drought-stricken land, now takes centre-stage of the story through the character of the irrigation contractor Amresh, owner of the 'Water Solutions' company. Because of an honest and courageous police officer, the net around Amresh closes fast, and he kills himself with a bullet to his head. It is as if Amresh's death serves as retributive justice for Vaishali's husband Umesh's death and the numerous other farmer suicides that are linked to irrigation scams, droughts and other factors leading to farmer indebtedness of this benighted land.

By the end of this part of the novel, Ranjan gets introduced to Sachin Chavan, the secretary of the All India Kisan Sabha (farmers' wing of Communist Party of India and a countrywide farmers' movement), who is planning a farmers' march to the state capital, Mumbai. Ranjan's mentor believes that his involvement with organizing this long march will help channel his agitation about the sorry state of affairs and the attendant plight of farmers.

In the third and final part of the novel, titled 'The Long March', all these strands of the narrative come together in the flow of thousands upon thousands of farmers marching on the commercial capital Mumbai to demand their rights. While characters like Terna, Daya, Ranjan and scores of activists are all part of this flow, the main protagonist here is the elderly Rukma Bai, a small farmer from an Indigenous peoples (Adivasi) group who cultivates a hilly tract of land surrounded by forests. Rukma Bai, who has to take care of a differently abled son, is marching for recognition of her rights over the forest-adjoining land, while others march for access to irrigation, loan waivers and a host of other issues. In these final scenes, the power of community organization, manifested in the long march for rights and justice, challenges entrenched corruption, policy paralysis and systemic ills, the impacts of which have been complicated and aggravated by climate change.

Here, Agnihotri goes into great detail about the plight of Adivasi forest dwellers, who, despite the passing of a law, haven't received formal acknowledgement of ownership or tenancy of the land, while their fields remain unirrigated and they have to depend on erratic rains. Joining them are people like Terna, who have to migrate every year to work in the sugarcane fields of Satara because of droughts and meagre rainfall in their villages. Also in this endless sea of humanity are farmers from other regions coming together for the common cause of rights, and much of the story here goes on to describe the hardships on the long march to Mumbai.

The Kisan Sabha, which is leading these protests, is however present everywhere in facilitating this flow. The author writes, 'The Kisan Sabha is a formidable organisation, each and every village is allotted to a leader or to their deputy, all the way down the ranks. They are like an army without a uniform, no deviation is permitted' (235). As this endless procession, bearing red hammer and sickle flags, converges upon the commercial capital, Rukma Bai feels exhausted and sick. In the end, she does manage to reach her destination, but she will die a few days later, unable to recover from the tortures of the journey on her frail body.

The farmers' procession is successful in that politicians meet the farmer leaders and accept all their demands. But even after six months, not a single file moves, and there is no progress. While the rains are kind that year, the battle for rights and justice is far from over. In the symbolic promise of carrying on the struggle, the book ends with the hope that community and comradeship have been built. Vaishali doesn't marry Ranjan, but the long march has brought them closer as comrades.

*The Sickle* ends with these poignant lines:

> Ranjan had looked after her during the entire journey, and she him. They had taken care of each other's meals, water for bathing, sleeping arrangements; sometimes, out of earshot of the others, they had taken their lips close to each other's ears to whisper, comrade. All of this was as true as daylight.

> Vaishali would stay alive with the details of that journey in her heart, till it was dawn again.
>
> (259–60)

Throughout this novel, as we read about the plight of the sugarcane labourers, the indebtedness of cotton farmers, the implementation bottlenecks that withhold forest rights from Indigenous people and how climate change, irrigation scams and misdirected policies play in concert to affect human lives, one is reminded of *Grapes of Wrath*, John Steinbeck's timeless classic about migrants in the backdrop of the Great Depression. The American author was writing about drought and dust storms long before global warming entered public discourse. *The Sickle*, which addresses climate justice and its complex interplay with economics and politics, shares its humanism and the ability to tell stories about collectives of people in the face of great adversity.

Agnihotri, whose important works include the great river novel, *Mahanadi*, has fashioned this book like a network of streams, one flowing into another in a mesh of narratives, painting a stark and memorable portrait of deprivation and suffering in the backdrop of a scorched and denuded earth. Still, there is the tinkle of cowbells in these pages, as there are vignettes of festivity, and in the end, a glimmer of hope.

The book is also a bold experiment with form, where the story is interspersed with facts, figures and even names of real organizations, like the All India Kisan Sabha. Here precise analysis follows illuminating anthropological enquiry while never missing the timeless and the profound, as in the magical scene on the banks of a crater lake where Ranjan proposes unsuccessfully to Vaishali.

Some years ago (2018), Indian farmers congregated in Mumbai's Azad Maidan. Then again, they held year-long protests (2020–1) at the gates of India's shiny capital. All these will remind us of the importance of Agnihotri's capacious novel as an important commentary on socio-economic injustices and the devious effects of climate change and weather patterns on the lives of the underprivileged sections of society.

Having surveyed the story, we can now explore the connections between climate change and justice. In the next section, we will present the theories and activist framings of the idea of climate justice, thereby sharpening the lens of justice (Figures 2.2 and 3.4) which we shall use to read Agnihotri's novel. In the course of this presentation, we will see why climate justice happens to be the bedrock of the climate crisis, demanding our undivided focus and attention, as we go about framing policy and channelling activism to deal with the existential crisis of climate change that humanity faces today.

## Meat-eaters, Mandarins and the shapes of climate justice

Imagine two side-by-side panels on a computer screen. On the left, we find a well-groomed Westerner with a neatly trimmed beard wearing an expensive-looking jacket. He is confident, slightly overweight and is sitting at an ornate wooden table laden with platefuls of meat and other delicacies. He is eating. Our man is single-mindedly attacking the food, slicing chunks of meat with a shiny silver knife, spearing the pieces with his fork, transferring it to his mouth, chomping noisily then going on to the next. In between, he washes down the animal flesh with sparkling wine. Till now the right panel is hazy.

Gradually, the right panel clears up and we see a long row of trees at the edge of a forest. A bright sun is shining in the sky. In the foreground is a small plot of land where we see a man, a woman and a little child. The man is tilling the land, the woman thrashing grain and the child playing with a goat tethered to a post. To their right is a small thatched hut. The man and woman are dark-skinned, of short height and they are sweating profusely in the heat.

Now something strange begins to happen. As the man on the left panel transfers a chunk of meat to his mouth, right that very moment, a tree on the right panel bursts into flames. With each chunk he devours, another tree of the forest catches fire. The farmer couple despairs, the woman runs to fetch water from a pond nearby, but it has run dry and dead fish lie scattered in the mud. By and by as the forest lights up, panic-stricken animals come rushing out seeking shelter: wild boars, spotted deer, snakes and a band of screeching monkeys. On the left panel, the man continues to eat nonchalantly.

Nuremberg sausages on a pewter plate, a pile of fried salami, a fully loaded burger and a well-done steak are cleared one after another. As he reaches out for another plate heaped with food, a giant wave comes crashing at the farmer couple in the right panel. They are not far from the sea. The man is washed away. Another wave lashes at the woman. She falls while crying out his name. The water creeps closer. The glutton in the left panel continues nonchalantly with his gargantuan meal, apparently oblivious of the fact that with each bite of his, the world in the right panel is coming to an end.

This visualization is a basic representation of what we mean by climate justice, with climate impacts and connections simplified for the purpose of exposition. It can help us comprehend that the concept of climate justice tries to capture how disparities in production and consumption lead to disproportionate impacts on the less privileged while deepening inequality in the world. In other words, the study of climate justice is both a political and scientific engagement with the causes and effects of anthropogenic climate change in an attempt to expose the inequities in production, consumption, distribution, access to resources and political power which lie at the root of the climate crisis and which in turn lead to unequal impacts on the less privileged. In simpler terms, climate justice examines how the effects of climate change and the burden of adaptation are experienced by those who are least responsible for the crisis. In its broadest interpretation and scope, climate justice is intersectional and interdisciplinary, consisting of an overlap of production and consumption flows, science, economics, women's rights and the rights of underprivileged humans in general and that of other beings.

Let us now revisit our example to see how climate justice is embedded in our visualization of the farmer couple and the meat-eater. The meat-eater on the left panel very clearly represents the resource-intensive consumption habits of the Global North (rich and privileged people of advanced industrialized countries and everywhere else) which is largely responsible for historical and present emissions, precipitating the climate crisis. On the right panel are the sufferers of the Global South (poor and underprivileged people of developing nations and everywhere else) who, despite low levels of consumption, because of their economic condition and lesser political power, suffer disproportionately from the effects of climate change. Climate justice attempts to expose this injustice by calling for common but differentiated responsibilities, better representation of the underprivileged in decision-making and compensation for bearing the maximum loss and damage from climate change.

Let us attempt another thought experiment. Suppose you are a European who has the power to kill someone by merely wishing his end. Now you come to know of a mandarin[6] in far-away China, whom you can thus kill (with minimum or no consequences to you) and thereby inherit all his wealth in Europe without anyone finding out. Will you go ahead and wish so? This ethical dilemma has come to be known as the Mandarin Paradox, and it examines the problem of the operation of ethics at a distance, in the absence of the possibility of punishment, and especially when separated by geographical, cultural and other factors. In our previous visualization, the meat-eater, even if he is aware of the damage he is causing to the distant sufferers through climate-mediated effects, may well continue with his overconsumption.

Here the meat-eater is not inheriting a fortune, but he is anyway able to carry on with his consumption habits while affecting the quality of life of vulnerable people at a distance, mainly because the sufferers are out of his sight. In the case of climate change, however, there is hardly any guarantee that the meat-eater will remain unaffected for long because of the increasing global manifestations of the crisis. However, because of his privilege, he may be better able to weather those storms.

Kantian ethics[7] which is based on universal moral laws and independent of consequences would stop the European in the example to wish the Chinese mandarin's death. Such a position is quite similar to thinking I wouldn't do something (harm) to someone which I wouldn't have done to me. This therefore creates a basis for justice in general and climate justice in particular where the mere fact of knowing that emissions of the Global North are disproportionately affecting the vulnerable of the Global South should be reason enough to take responsibility and follow a sustainable path.

John Rawls's theory of justice[8] which begins with the well-known 'veil of ignorance' thought experiment can provide better structure for addressing inequalities and fairness which are also central to climate justice issues. The 'veil of ignorance' imagines individuals behind a veil asked to determine principles for a just society. At this point ('the Original Position'), these individuals have no knowledge of their individual, social and historical circumstances (gender, race, age, power, wealth and so on). Rawls argues that given such an initial situation of equality, humans will conceptualize an equitable and just society. It has been shown in experiments that the veil of ignorance framework can be very effective in inducing decision-making agents to come together and follow a sustainable intergenerational path.[9] However, voluntary compliance to international agreements on climate action remains the Achilles Heel which can break down the stability of this process. With these philosophical formulations of justice, we will now move on to activist framings of environmental justice followed by critical, legal, spiritual and policy engagements with the issue.

Climate and environmental issues are closely interlinked. Therefore, the history of climate justice movements needs to be traced through movements for environmental justice. The beginnings of environmental justice activism can be located within various independent movements that have been going on for many decades. Among these, the Chipko movement of India against deforestation that we mentioned in an earlier chapter and the movement of the Ogoni people of Nigeria against oil drilling are two well-known examples. According to the *Environmental Justice Reader*, the first concerted global movement for environmental justice was seen in the 1999 protests in Seattle against 'World Trade Organization's support of multinational corporate objectives and trade agreements that contribute to the building of a global economy where control over local environments, communities, cultures, education, and health care is no longer in the hands of the people but in the hands of big business'.[10]

The above volume, published in 2002, defined environmental justice as 'the right of all people to share equally in the benefits bestowed by a healthy environment' while by environment it meant 'the places in which we live, work, play, and worship' (4). The editors of this book also noted how movements by marginalized communities have helped to focus on the 'crucial intersections between ecological and social justice concerns' (4).

Pointing to this fact of intersectionality of issues, the editors of the above book also noted how various civil rights, antiwar, antinuclear, women's and grassroots movements coalesced in the environmental justice movements (4). They pointed out how issues of race, class, gender, social justice and ecological integrity have been centred in the early days of this movement, where environmental racism, which (as we know) connects to the history of colonialism and continues in neocolonial manifestations of power, has also received due focus (5). Stressing this last point, the *Reader* notes how the role played by colonization had been flagged in the seventeen Principles of

Environmental Justice drawn up by First National People of Color Environmental Leadership Summit (1992) which, committed to work from the grassroots, 'to secure [our] political, economic, and cultural liberation that has been denied for over 500 years of colonization and oppression' (5). Many of these principles, directions and mandates have been later replicated in other civil society principles of climate justice.

The issue of environmental justice is again closely engaged in *Sharing the Earth*, which is another environmental justice reader published in 2015. There it is argued that overconsumption of resources by the Global North has led to a disproportionate burden of the impacts of ecological devastation on the world's poor, while the fruits of consumption are enjoyed by the rich.[11]

This volume describes environmental justice as a concept and a movement with both aesthetic and activist expression which 'yokes concern for the environment, including all life on the planet, to commitment to social justice' (1). By social justice the editors of the volume mean 'human equity in terms of race, gender, religion, nationality, and class' (1).

The uniqueness of this second volume is that it addresses a host of environmental impacts like toxic waste, nuclear radiation, climate change, hazardous chemicals, species extinction, resource depletion and more through the justice lens, thereby presenting a number of representational forms which include literary as well as activist texts. From executed Nigerian activist Ken Saro Wiwa's last communication with the outside world to Rabindranath Tagore's short story 'Bolai', and from a traditional Lakota story about the importance of sharing with neighbours to excerpts from *Das Kapital*, and much more in between, this volume covers extensive ground, stressing on the importance of political engagement, international coalitions and the role of literature in the continuing struggle for environmental justice (2, 4).

While noting the obvious implications and overlaps between environmental justice and climate justice from these foundational texts and documents, we can now shift our focus to critical and activist texts focused specifically on climate justice, thereby sharpening the political lens we will be using to read Anita Agnihotri's novel.

Many commentators have observed that the underlying story of injustice and inequality is often missed when proposing solutions to the climate problem. Apparently well-meaning engagements with climate change in theory, policy or fiction (because we are discussing novels) tend to focus on scientific, technological and economic solutions while formulating the emissions problem as a techno-scientific problem, which can be managed with appropriate technical and economic instruments.

Ecofeminist author and critic Greta Gaard, in her analysis of competing narratives of climate change, brings up these issues while writing about climate change narratives from the United States. Gaard argues, 'by shaping their narratives primarily with techno-science analyses and solutions, these narrative genres have not inclusively portrayed the additional facts of climate change – namely, the underpinnings of colonialism, neoliberalism, speciesism, and gendered fundamentalisms – and thus the activist and systemic solutions they present are partial and ineffective'.[12]

Without examining speciesist imperialism, colonialism and its neocolonial avatar, which in conjunction with capitalist accumulation and modes of production and consumption, globalization and the logic of the market, resulted in the creation and persistence of inequalities, besides harming the planet with emissions and overlapping crises, it will not be possible to deal with the climate crises or dream of justice and equality. Only such an approach and its practice in policy, activism and the imagination can attempt to close the gap between climate science and people (and other beings), or more generally, in Greta Gaard's words, 'between the environmental sciences and environmental humanities'.[13]

Right from the days of the early imperialists to our present times, the exploitation of people, other beings and ecologies has been possible using the logic of othering and a denial of agency. For example, the overconsumption of meat in the Global North is only possible because of industrial-scale livestock farming practices that are enabled by exploitative use of land resources, cheap labour and clearing of trees, primarily in developing and also developed nations. According to the Food and Agriculture Organization of the United Nations, 14.5 per cent of all anthropogenic emissions come from livestock farming.[14] This gives us an indication on how overconsumption, made possible through exploitation of land and people, drives a planetary crisis.

During the pandemic years, some of us got together to edit an anthology of solarpunk stories from around the world. Solarpunk, as a fiction genre and movement, besides advocating for sustainable living, has been attempting to focus on the injustices and inequality. In the introduction to that volume, we had written:

> The reasons that have been historically used to justify exploiting nature and people are eerily similar. Be it skin colour, culture, religion and beliefs, consciousness, brain complexity, mobility, the ability to feel pain, or indeed being alive distinguishing someone or something as different, other, and often somehow less, is to this day used to perpetuate injustice. To decide who may be controlled. One of the deepest lines in the sand among these is the question of agency: whose actions shape our world?[15]

Covertly or overtly, justifications for the exploitation of people and ecologies are still being employed to drive the planet-damaging engine of resource-intensive high-emissions growth.

While these connections are being exposed persistently, there is still not enough movement in policy circles to comprehensively address climate change through an engagement with justice issues. This is also true for literary texts, the book we are about to discuss being one of the exceptions.

Within activist circles and movements, the importance of climate change as an issue of justice is however being flagged for quite some time now. One of the earliest documents to lay stress on the issue of justice in the climate context is The Bali Principles of Climate Justice (2002) which, released the same year as the Seattle WTO protests, was endorsed by a number of international activist groups.

Right from its preamble, the Bali Principles are very clear about the disproportionate burden of climate change on local communities, women, youth, Indigenous people and the poor. Thereon, the twenty-one principles present a vision for climate justice that affirms ecological unity and the interdependence of species and calls for reduction and elimination of greenhouse gas emissions, protection of biodiversity, providing a leading role for affected communities in decision making, representation and voice for Indigenous peoples among other action points.[16]

The Bali Principles also focus on the concept of ecological debt and hold transnational corporations and industrial countries responsible for emissions and call for compensation, restoration and reparation. The rights of access to sustainable and affordable energy for the poor, women and rural and Indigenous peoples are also affirmed in the principles with a stress on clean, renewable and locally controlled energy. The Bali Principles further affirm that technological and market-based solutions to climate change should be 'subject to principles of democratic accountability, ecological sustainability and social justice'. Besides laying a stress on the protection of culture and biodiversity, and the prevention of externalization of environmental costs, the principles also flag the need for socio-economic models that 'safeguard the fundamental rights to clean air, land, water, food and healthy ecosystems'.

The Bali Principles further stress on community rights over the sustainable management of natural resources on which they depend. This extends to the right to self-determination of Indigenous peoples and the control they exercise on their lands. The document repeatedly mentions the local community and Indigenous people's role in decision-making, planning, enforcement and evaluation, as well as the need for solutions that address women's rights. Besides emphasizing the rights of future generations and sustainable consumer choices, a number of these principles also engage with the role of the fossil fuel industry.

In the context of a recent judgement in a Swiss court[17] where climate change has been addressed as a human rights issue, it is also important to note that the preamble to the Bali Principles mentions that 'the perpetration of climate change violates the Universal Declaration on Human Rights, and the United Nations Convention on Genocide'. Incidentally, the Indian Supreme Court has recently delivered a judgement on a case relating to climate change, invoking the right to life and liberty and equal protection before the law.[18]

Before we move on to unravelling the idea of climate justice as it might apply to policy, it is also pertinent to note that the Encyclical (Laudato Si') of Pope Francis, which is an influential document that took up the issue of climate change and ecological crisis, mentions justice in several places. Among various other assertions, it notes, 'we have to realize that a true ecological approach always becomes a social approach; it must integrate questions of justice in debates on the environment, so as to hear both the cry of the earth and the cry of the poor'.[19] Such statements tying together the social and the environmental sphere can be noted in many world religions as well as in belief systems of Indigenous peoples.

It is clear from the discussion so far that climate justice is the scaffolding on which any programme of climate action has to be built if we are serious about change. Because the novel we are going to discuss engages deeply with policy paralysis and systemic fault lines in the context of aggravating climate and environment effects, it is pertinent to ask the question: How can the concept of climate justice be transformed into policy? What are the focal points through which climate justice can be understood, discussed and implemented?

Paul Cairney and others, in their systematic review of literature addressing climate justice policy, while acknowledging how the definitions of justice and equity are contested, find three focal points for social justice addressed in most climate justice studies.

These are recognitional, procedural and distributional justice, where 'Recognitional, (is) to challenge the privileging of some voices and marginalisation of others; Procedural, (is) to ensure fair ways to participate, deliberate, inform and make choices; Distributional, (is) to ensure fair ways to pay for, and minimize inequalities associated with, climate change mitigation and adaptation'.[20] This three-tiered approach to climate justice will be useful in our context when we examine Anita Agnihotri's novel, as it will allow us to analyse how the story addresses one or more of these aspects.

It is obvious by now that the climate justice approach, contrary to market-based (like carbon trading) and technological approaches (like geo-engineering), is more people focused and hence environmental humanist.[21] Because it addresses inequalities and disproportionate burdens, it is naturally more political and contested, with neoliberal approaches[22] trying to monopolize the policy space, which is why climate justice is often driven and goes hand in hand with the work of activists who believe in its underlying principles.

The Indian environmental activist and ecofeminist Vandana Shiva is an important voice in these debates. Shiva's concept of 'Earth Democracy' speaks clearly to the idea of climate justice. In her essay 'Soil not Oil', Shiva holds that the climate crisis is 'at its roots a consequence of human beings having gone astray from the ecological path of living with justice and sustainability'.[23] Her approach, right from the beginning of this document, is a justice-oriented engagement with the crisis, which goes on to examine systemic issues and ruptures that have led to the situation we find ourselves in today. 'The real problem', Shiva writes, 'is the conflict between the economic laws that have reduced the planet and society to a supermarket where everything is for sale and the ecological laws that maintain the planet's ecological functions and social laws that distribute nature's goods and services equitably. The real problem is a global economy that has created a planetary ecological imbalance.'[24]

Justice and equity are closely woven into the solutions that Shiva suggests in her essay. While expanding on the concept of Earth

Democracy, she stresses on the need for the rich to reduce resource consumption and energy use so that everyone can have equality of access to 'land and water, food and fiber, air and energy'. Bringing up the idea of Gaia, she further says that whatever harms Gaia, harms the poor, and vice versa. More significantly, and relevant in the context of the plot of the novel that we are about to analyse, she argues for grounding the idea of equity in the earth and in people's struggles and movements against displacement, because displacement and uprooting militate against rights and freedom to work the land and gather from the forest and affect the spiritual connection that communities have with place.

In my own engagement with these issues, I had written in my column for the *New Indian Express* that in our present times, 'one can sense three growing and often overlapping estrangements (or ruptures). This dark triad of ruptures is between groups of people, between people and technology and people and planet.'[25] As we can see, the context of justice is implicitly embedded in the first and second ruptures, the first signifying growing inequalities and disproportionate burdens, and the second focusing on application of technological fixes which are not human-centric and equity conscious. The third rupture of course broadens the scope of examination to include sustainability and equity for all species.

Some years ago, I had the good fortune to listen to my co-lecturer, the Nigerian professor of global climate and environmental governance Chukwumerije Okereke, speak about climate justice for a lecture series.[26] In his analysis, Okereke framed the issue of climate justice on the basis of three asymmetries, those of contribution, impact and voice. In other words, he is looking at how disproportionately countries contribute to emissions and global warming, how the skewed distribution of impacts of climate change affect the less privileged of the planet, and finally how the most affected have the weakest voice and participation in negotiations and decision making about climate change. Okereke goes further by analysing climate justice on the temporal and spatial axes (international, national and intergenerational) besides focusing on the gender dimension of climate justice which has been increasingly recognized[27] as an inalienable part of these debates.

However, and what is quite obvious today, the struggle for equity and climate justice is far from over. Okereke notes in a paper that despite the recognition of justice issues in the climate regime, this 'has not provided a basis to sufficiently upset the underlying forces and abiding structures of global inequality'.[28] One of these underlying forces is the insidious and ever-present working of power.

Right from the times of colonial expansion to the intransigence of current socio-economic structures and the international regimes of globalization that continue to affect equity and justice, there still remains a long road ahead. By examining the facts and impacts of climate change through the lens of social inequities and distributive justice, the climate justice approach makes an important intervention in humanity's efforts to deal with many of these obstacles on the road to better futures.

Elsewhere, in his 'Six Proposals', Nick Admussen had drawn our attention to the importance of the literature of climate change to address climate justice, implicitly, when he writes, 'full partnership for everyone in a global ecosystem means redistributing the rewards that the developed world has already incurred by harming it'. He went on to suggest that we should be reading 'the contemporary art and speech of the global underclass: the voices of the poor telling us not what we want to hear, but what is actually happening', which is essentially calling attention to the resistance to and representation of what Rob Nixon calls 'slow violence'.

The stress on reduced resource consumption of the rich that we find in Vandana Shiva, or the call for redistributing the rewards we notice in Admussen, is again echoed in Greta Gaard's writing about climate justice narratives which we quoted at the beginning of this discussion on climate justice. Throughout her essay, Gaard weaves in the argument that most climate fiction has tended to portray climate change as a failure of technology and science, missing the real picture of intersectionalities, systemic connections and most importantly overconsumption by the Global North that results in the persistence and aggravation of the fault lines of species, gender and environmental justice. These inequalities of gender, race and species according to Gaard lie at the bottom of narrative hierarchies about climate change.

In her work, Gaard uses an ecofeminist approach to dig out such neglected narratives in cinema, music videos and stories that address this important climate justice perspective. Now, we will examine how Anita Agnihotri's *The Sickle* presents such neglected narratives and how her climate novel engages with various perspectives on climate justice that we have outlined here.

## Climate and justice in *The Sickle*

Agnihotri's book deals with a number of issues that are closely linked to or propelled by climate justice considerations. Among these are droughts, migration, corruption in irrigation works, female foeticide, farmer indebtedness, activism and community action. The climate connection with many of these issues, that intersect and overlap with each other throughout the story, is hard to miss. As we have noted earlier, the author mentions that global warming is responsible for the unpredictable weather and droughts in the region of Maharashtra, where the story unfolds. The drought inevitably leads to the annual migration of people like Terna to the sugarcane fields of Satara where they toil under exploitative conditions to grow the water-thirsty sugarcane for the market. The inevitability of this migration is further ensured by the fact that the region where Terna comes from is a rain shadow area.

According to the Internal Displacement Monitoring Centre, India experienced 5.4 million internal displacements in 2024 due to natural disasters.[29] If we look at annual migrations necessitated by livelihood and weather which often has a climate component, an Oxfam study found that nearly 500,000 migrate from the Beed district every year to work in the sugarcane fields of Maharashtra.[30] The same study points out that the tents for these labourers are small and lack basic amenities like water, electricity and toilets. *The Sickle*, which is set in the region of Beed, among others, portrays a similar picture (Figure 7.2) of the sugarcane labourers' *toli*, where the book mentions communal toilets and the lack of indoor lighting with the occasional electric post to light a large area. The Oxfam report goes on to state, 'Women and girls, who migrate for work, face added hardships. They have to fetch water from a public water supply for the entire family, and have no option but to bathe in the open.'[31]

In the year 2022, India emerged as the largest producer and consumer of sugar in the world as well as the second-largest exporter of this commodity.[32] While part of the sugarcane produce is used to manufacture ethanol, which mixed with petrol[33] can allow a modest reduction in emissions, thereby having an impact on climate change,

**Figure 7.2** A migrant sugarcane labourer of Maharashtra. *c.*2018. Photograph by Anita Agnihotri.

the social and environmental costs and the entwined justice issues of sugarcane production are too large to ignore.

Despite the fact that sugarcane is a water-thirsty crop which depletes the groundwater level, farmers in Satara continue to cultivate it instead of switching to other alternatives because of the support price provided by the government. Meanwhile, the western Marathwada region which covers the districts of Latur and Beed, among others, suffers from scanty rainfall, droughts and irrigation scams.

In one of the poignant scenes of the novel, we see Terna and her family returning home to their village after the annual harvesting of sugarcane, when they stop at a railway crossing to see a water train headed for the town of Latur. While the whole of Latur district is drought-stricken because of local politics, this train carrying 500,000 litres of water from the Krishna River journeys 350 kilometres to deliver it only to the district town (also named Latur) as the ones in power want to score a point with an opposition leader. This is clearly a failure of what Cairney and others call distributional aspects of climate justice policy or what Okereke would frame as equity across regions or national equity. Distributional climate justice policies, we would recall, ensure 'fair ways to pay for, and minimize inequalities associated with, climate change mitigation and adaptation'.

Evoking the irony of this misdistribution, Agnihotri writes, 'The sun-scorched farmland and dried trees along the way observed with melancholy and envious yellowed eyes the passing of the train with long whistles and no stops anywhere, their thirst increasing while they watched. So much water, and yet the train wouldn't offer a drop to any of them. The calculations of politics were different' (30).

So we see how climate change and droughts, along with corruption and other political and economic factors, intersect and aggravate a situation leading to migration, exploitative labour and lack of basic needs and safety for people like Terna. Etienne Piguet and others, in their paper on climate change and migration, address such a possibility by pointing out how climate change tends to exacerbate existing issues. Proposing a solution, they suggest, 'policies that focus on the climate change-migration nexus must be accompanied by renewed efforts to combat the very context that make people vulnerable in the first place'.[34]

In carefully portraying the life of Terna and her family, the author engages the justice issue head-on. As the water train chugs away, Terna's young son asks:

> 'What's in the round compartments, ma?'
>
> His eyes are wide with surprise.
>
> 'Water, baba, it's water', Terna was about to say, before she clamped her lips shut. They had no water to drink on the way. They had stopped once for a drink at a tap, along with tea and pao-bhaji. What if the boy felt thirsty if he was told the train was carrying water, what if he wanted some?
>
> After all, there was an entire river within Terna once. Where had it vaporized?
>
> (31–2)

The story of Terna is indeed a classic case where climate intersects with market economics and misdirected policies and systemic corruption to aggravate the hardships of thousands. The drought, in which climate change among other factors is implicated, not only drives the annual migration, it also impinges on climate justice issues like women's rights and voice, flagged by Okereke among others. These twin justice issues of voice and women's rights gradually assume greater importance in the novel as we move on to the story of the rights activist Daya Joshi.

We have seen how Daya's activism is directed against illegal gender testing of foetuses and female foeticide. She also creates awareness about water, fights against child marriage, closes illegal breweries and takes up issues of women's rights in general. Based in the sugarcane-growing region of Satara, Daya travels hundreds of kilometres to the drought-affected Marathwada which is home to important women characters like Minu (Nakoshi), Terna and Vaishali. It is important to note how women's rights are entwined with climate change and justice in the narrative around Daya and Nakoshi. Just as Terna's character, named after a river, flags the issue of water and the lack of it in the earlier part of the novel, Nakoshi, who is also a migrant sugarcane labourer, gets her name from the attitudes towards a girl child that we find among the people of this region. Agnihotri writes, 'When girls were born in succession to a couple, it was customary to name the last one Nakoshi. Nako, meaning no more' (51).

But what are the underlying causes for this attitude towards a girl child? Among the social evils of dowry and violence against women which perversely influence this attitude, there is also the consideration among small migrant farmers that a girl child means 'one sickle less' (53). For the drought-affected villagers of Beed who migrate annually to work in the sugarcane fields of Satara (where each labour couple is counted as one sickle, or unit of labour, by the advance-paying contractors), having a girl child means a reduction in their future income, as the girl will be married away to another family.

This is how climate, droughts, lack of irrigation, along with exploitative practices, are implicated in the attitude towards women and the social evil of female foeticide. The enormity of the problem is portrayed by the author through cold statistics, 'figures for Marathwada showed that the proportion of women had kept decreasing over the past 100 years, and was at its lowest in these districts. Beed was the worst off – there were only 796 girls for every 1,000 boys at birth' (80).

Minu (Nakoshi) too has to deal with this evil when her in-laws press her to get the foetus of her girl child aborted, but her husband, Sagar, stands by her with all his strength. Gradually, both Minu and Sagar are drawn into Daya's movement against gender testing of foetuses and female foeticide, besides other issues. Daya, with comrades like Minu, Sagar, Yashwant and many others, not only put up a brave fight against gender testing and female foeticide, but she also achieves occasional success, like when she manages to close down the notorious clinic run by the Patil couple. We also find Daya, who stands out as a champion for intersectional issues connected to justice, creating awareness in villages, motivating them to repair water taps, fighting against underage marriages and illegal breweries which drain the migrant labourers' meagre income.

Nakoshi, among other women, is strongly influenced by Daya's awareness efforts. This also foregrounds women's improper burden of household work besides their task of fetching water and kindling: 'The women had tied the dried greenish leaves in bundles and taken them back to the village for use as kindling' (62). The increasing burden, as a result of climate change, of collecting fuel and water which falls on women, is well recognized in studies. So this is one more way Daya's activism touches climate justice issues pertaining to women. In this context, we are reminded of the Bali Principles which, recognizing the disproportionate burden of climate change on women, states, 'Climate Justice affirms the need for solutions that address women's rights.'

Agnihotri writes, 'Nakoshi aka Minu didn't understand these things initially, but listening to Daya *tai* over the years had changed her. What seemed acceptable once was unacceptable now. It hurt her, made her angry too. She no longer listened in silence, she talked back straight away' (67).

While generally not addressing climate change impacts at their source, as in the above example, Daya's actions and activism help women to adapt to and ameliorate their suffering and engage with the injustices that persist and grow because of a host of factors, including the climate. In her activism and collective action, Daya emerges as a model character for a climate change novel which has a clear focus on justice issues.

Nick Admussen's 'Six Proposals' call for retiring the portrait of the single soul in climate stories. He writes, 'In the stories we need, though, nobody exists outside of some reference to social and physical contexts. Life touches at life from all points on the globe at all times.' Daya's character, though important in herself, gets her narrative momentum and turns into an important voice for gender justice through her work within a collective of men and women, demonstrating the importance of social and physical context and that of being a part of a collective and being together that Admussen hints at in his proposals. The Satara area, where Daya lives, does not suffer visibly from climate effects and social evils, but she travels hundreds of miles to fight against these, and so her character motivations encompass a holistic and intersectional appreciation of justice that is often lacking in hero-driven narratives.

The Bali Principles, as well as Okereke's work, lay stress on justice for women and future generations. Similarly, the environmental justice principles and concepts discussed earlier lay an emphasis on social justice in terms of equity with respect to gender, race, class, as well as the activist role of grassroots movements. We see how Daya's activism in Marathwada, which grows stronger as the plot progresses, addresses women's rights and the rights of future generations (to be born) through a movement which engages with social evils that are born out of a concatenation of factors, among which drought and climate change play important roles. The power of collective action and activism that we find in Daya, and its inalienable connection with justice-based movements, are echoed and amplified once again in the last part of the book, where the farmers and Indigenous peoples march on Mumbai demanding their rights.

But before we get there, we will examine the story of another important woman character, Vaishali, her cotton-farmer husband, Umesh and the researcher, Ranjan. Here, through the character of irrigation contractor Amresh, we will find a direct connection between climate change and irrigation scams which has strong justice implications for characters like Vaishali and Umesh, the migrant sugarcane labourers Terna and Nakoshi, besides broader impacts in perpetuating social evils like female foeticide in the Beed region.

Cotton farmer Umesh commits suicide, unable to pay back his farming loan to the bank officials, one of whom misbehaves with Vaishali. Umesh's death, like that of many other farmers from the region, is the result of a mix of factors which include climate change-related erratic weather, increasing input costs, and in Umesh's case, an additional burden of home improvement that he takes upon himself.

The connection between farmer suicides and climate change has been revealed by a number of studies.[35] It has also been established that 'In states reporting the highest suicide rates, farmers are more heavily engaged in cotton cultivation.'[36] Agnihotri writes, 'With every passing day the monsoon in Marathwada and Vidarbha is getting more and more erratic; even long-standing farmers cannot tell when the rains will come and when they will leave. With no irrigation, their only hope lies in borewells or rain. The earth has dried up, while the costs of farming cotton and soybean keep rising' (168–9).

The impact of climate change on the production of cotton in Maharashtra has been well researched. According to a report of the Institute of Sustainable Communities, 'Rainfall makes up the largest share of the climatic challenges currently faced by cotton. Large amounts of intense rainfall have caused a lot of damage to cotton plants.'[37] Further complicating this situation is the use of genetically modified cotton seeds which the farmer has to buy and which needs irrigation. The same report goes on to state that, 'High yielding Bt cotton varieties require irrigation and ample inputs for best performance, but most farmers cultivating it in Maharashtra do not have access to irrigation, which may be a factor in the low yields seen across the state.'

We will remember that the skewed distribution of impacts of climate change affecting the less privileged of the planet has been addressed by Okereke while discussing the three asymmetries of climate justice. The farmer indebtedness and suicides like Umesh's, in which climate change has a clear role to play, squarely address this asymmetry, to be taken up again in the narrative impetus behind the farmers' march at the end of the novel.

Vaishali, in the course of the story, meets other women whose farmer husbands had also committed suicide. Among them is Radha, who eventually helps her with advice for the paperwork needed to get government aid. The author delves into detail about the hardships of these farmers and the socio-economic causes and bottlenecks driving their indebtedness. While the climate connection with farmer suicides is clear, the situation is further worsened by irrigation scams which result in public money being siphoned off and much-needed water not reaching the fields.

The story of Amresh, the irrigation contractor, portrays the depth, extent and *modus operandi* of corruption that ultimately affects cotton farmers like Umesh or migrant labourers like Terna and Nakoshi, who have to migrate annually for working in the sugarcane fields because their parched lands will not yield enough produce. While irrigation contractor Amresh's suicide, when he shoots himself, is a kind of symbolic justice for all these affected characters of the story, this only offers a closure for the reader, following certain conventions of storytelling. Neither Terna nor Nakoshi, who have to leave their parched villages every year for work, come to know of it. However, the researcher Ranjan, who helps Vaishali in filing a police report, is aware of Amresh's death, and in this context remembers cotton farmer Umesh's death – 'Ranjan remembers that Umesh had also been dead on arrival ... I have no sympathy for such criminals [like Amresh]' (207), he tells himself. In the real world, which this novel closely represents, one contractor's death does not amount to much and can hardly guarantee that the evil of corruption gnawing away at lives will vanish.

Ranjan, the agricultural researcher, performs two important functions for the novel. Critics like Trexler[38] have noted the presence of scientists and similar characters with technical expertise in many cli-fi works. Ranjan is such a character, who, noticing the growing shadow of droughts in the country, helps to stitch together the scientific basis of climate change with the socio-economic and cultural layer of the novel, thereby affording them completeness as climate texts.[39] In this novel, Ranjan, by helping Vaishali, also performs the role of ameliorating the injustice and hardship faced by those affected by climate change and a host of other intersecting factors. Daya Joshi, as we have also noticed, serves a similar role through her movement, fighting social evils and exposing the layer of festering corruption and crime that aggravates the sufferings of the affected.

The final part of the novel, through the character of Rukma Bai and the narrative thread of the long march of farmers (including Indigenous people) to Mumbai, channels all the conflicts of the novel, arising from injustice and hardships into a coordinated demand for rights under the leadership of the All India Kisan Sabha. In this, the small farmer Rukma Bai, who belongs to an Indigenous peoples (Adivasi) group, with her demand for rights of ownership of the forest land she cultivates, stands out as a symbolic representative of oppressed peoples suffering the impacts of multiple overlapping and connected injustices. Here it is also important to note that the book, in the final groundswell of action, does not project an individual saviour[40] of the Indigenous people, the poor migrants and other aggrieved, instead highlighting the importance of collective action.

We have already noted how climate change is insidiously present as one of the underlying causes that feed, foster and aggravate these myriad issues. In the long march to Mumbai, which covers the final part of the book, we find most of the important characters taking part. Terna, Nakoshi and others march for the right to irrigated land so that they don't have to migrate annually to the sugarcane growing region of Satara, characters like Ranjan and Vaishali are also marching for similar causes. Others we find hit the road for a fair price for crops, leases on forest land, potable water, toilets, security of women, among a host of other demands and issues. Among these characters, and the unnamed multitudes, Ranjan, who has the best appreciation of the systemic issues and fault lines, gets closely involved with the organizers of the march, thus welding the scientific and the activist layers of the novel.

It is important to note here how the organization of the three parts of the novel (Sickle, It's Best to Stage a Turnaround and finally The Long March) echoes the gathering weight of injustice flowing from an interlinkage of climate and other factors into an activist groundswell of farmers marching for their rights. We will remember how Vandana Shiva, while expanding on her concept of Earth Democracy, mentions the need to ground 'the idea of equity in the earth', thereby laying stress on 'peoples struggles and movements' for causes like displacement and the right to gather from the forest. In the character of Rukma Bai and other Indigenous people and small farmers who are marching for rights to their forest land, we find an echo of what Shiva says about rights, equity and justice.

If we look back at the Bali Principles of Climate Justice, we will find that both the preamble and the principles discuss the impact of climate change on Indigenous people and their rights. These rights cover the right to representation, voice, self-determination, access to sustainable energy, among others. Other affected groups like women, elderly, poor are also mentioned in the affirmations of the Bali Principles. The stories of affected women like Terna, Nakoshi and Vaishali and Indigenous people like Rukma Bai and others, not only address such impacts but also their joining the long march is symbolic of their efforts to win these rights mentioned in the Bali Principles. While Ranjan may be only among a few persons among the marchers who are aware of the role of climate change in aggravating these justice and equity issues, it is obvious from the thousands joining the march that climate change and its impacts are intersectional in nature, where multiple issues overlap and intersect in complex systems, affecting each other.

While the book doesn't delve specifically into the causes of climate change, we have seen how closely it engages with intersectional issues of justice where global warming and attendant climate change play an important role. In this context, we will remember how climate justice policy can be distributive, procedural and representation. The novel addresses these three features of justice not only through the story but also in the background commentary that stitches together various elements of the narrative.

Agnihotri writes, 'Exploiting the drought in the afflicted areas of Marathwada for business gains leads to an incessant cycle of moneymaking here. The representatives of the people, even entire governments, are controlled by the people who are grabbing profits with both hands – contractors and industrialists' (186–7). This is clearly an issue of the lack of procedural justice because the affected people lack voice and there are no 'fair ways to participate, deliberate, inform and make choices'.[41] The issue of distributive justice is present all through the story, beginning with the improper distribution of water resources, the meagre payments made to the sugarcane workers and the bottlenecks in the provision of loans to cotton farmers. The question of representational climate justice policy comes up again in the commentary surrounding the farmers' march at the end of the book, where the author points out how policy is skewed to benefit the corporate houses and the rich. Agnihotri writes, 'Despite a multilevel election process, the government was the representative of the wealthy and of corporate houses, since its policies were formulated keeping their interests in mind' (245).

This brings us to the end of our reading of *The Sickle* from the perspective of climate justice and the intersectional issues that cluster around it. We have seen how through the stories of characters like Terna, Nakoshi, Daya, Vaishali, Ranjan, Amresh and several others, the author has woven a yarn that welds together the social and the environmental in a story that speaks to various aspects of climate justice and equity, aggravated by corruption, scams, policy failures and policy paralysis and manifest through forced migrations, farmer indebtedness, declining sex ratio, exploitation of women, lack of Indigenous people rights, farmer suicides and much more. We have also seen how, in the workings of the plot, her various commentaries and asides, the author has addressed various elements of climate justice policy, like procedural and distributional, as well as the important questions of the voice of the affected and equity across regions and generations.

In a further imaginative leap, Agnihotri has gathered it all together by channelling the affected people's demands for justice, equity and rights in the form of movements championed, on a smaller scale by a character like Daya, and on a wider and more inclusive scale by the national farmers' body with which the agricultural researcher Ranjan joins forces. The stress on political engagement and activism that we noted in our discussion of environmental justice concepts finds powerful representation in several instances, most significantly in the closing scenes of the book with the long march of the affected people.

With this canvas of concerns, this climate novel manages to address what Greta Gaard in her paper calls the 'bottom narrative of hierarchies of climate change' that 'covers inequalities of gender, race and species', instead of dwelling only on the economic and the technological. As we mentioned earlier, Gaard writes that the earlier narratives had not inclusively portrayed 'the additional facts of climate change' by which she meant 'the underpinnings of "colonialism, neoliberalism, speciesism and gendered fundamentalisms"'. By addressing how women, Indigenous people, small farmers and migrants from the disadvantaged sections are caught in the tangled web of factors that in concert with climate change considerably affect justice and equity, this novel makes an inclusive and wide-ranging intervention in the growing field of climate fiction.

In his Encyclical about climate change, Pope Francis wrote, 'a true ecological approach always becomes a social approach'. Novels like *The Sickle*, of which there are still very few, are an imaginative response to that assertion. It is, as the letter from Pope Francis goes on to say about the true ecological approach, a work that listens to and represents 'both the cry of the earth and the cry of the poor'.

## Where to place this story?

How does this novel of climate justice speak to the different attempts of categorizing (Figure 2.2) cli-fi? Does the focus on justice and politics allow an easier slotting into any of the taxonomic categories that we discussed in detail earlier? In fact, it does. The focus on justice will automatically label the work as a novel of Resistance, and also in the Costanza framework sub-category where community action is important. Furthermore, climate justice themes can also speak to mitigative or adaptive frames of our climate fiction categories.

Having studied *The Sickle* from a climate justice perspective, we will now attempt a more general survey of the work using the classifications of cli-fi. But first of all, it would be worthwhile to check whether this postcolonial climate novel satisfies some of the definitions of climate novels we discussed before. The book does indeed satisfy the Climate Reality Check because one character (Ranjan) is aware of climate change and the effects of climate change and droughts are all over the story. *The Sickle* does not engage global warming as a narrative element and so may not satisfy the definition of climate fiction proposed by Gregers Andersen. However, the definition proposed by Goodbody and Putra, with its acknowledgement of stories that engage social issues and its 'open border' to related work, suits Agnihotri's novel.

That Andersen's definition may not work for this novel should be understood in the context of our earlier argument that the concerns of postcolonial climate fiction writers can often be different (from Western authors) as they would tend to focus on issues of justice and the workings of power while still being aware of the climate effects operating in the background. In fact, Agnihotri's novel very much engages these climate effects, most visible through droughts and erratic rains, but by concentrating more on justice while keeping the emissions angle generally invisible in the text, it stands out as an exemplar of postcolonial climate fiction.

Let us now get down to the taxonomies of cli-fi listed in Figure 2.2. We begin with the set of classifiers, constituted by the five imaginaries proposed by Gregers Andersen. The world presented in *The Sickle* clearly does not fit the Conspiracy or Sphere imaginaries, nor is it talking mainly about Loss of Wilderness, though drying rivers and clearing of forests do appear in commentaries and settings of the story. The novel is also not really a story of Judgement where nature strikes back; rather, it is an imaginative record of growing ruptures and faults in the socio-economic fabric arising out of exploitation, injustice and policy paralysis among other factors. As we have seen earlier, climate change does have a role to play in the persistence and aggravation of injustices, but society does not completely break down in the book. Instead, the affected people get together and march for their rights, thereby presenting us with a glimmer of hope. So we can say that *The Sickle* hovers close to the 'social breakdown' imaginary, but being a work of realist fiction, it engages in describing the fault lines and suggesting ways out of the overlapping crises.

The second classification is derived from the Costanza framework for science fiction which had a futurist vision. As this is a realist novel set in the present, it may not be appropriate to employ our modified Costanza framework. However, being a novel of climate justice and therefore engaging with the power of community action (with its failures and successes), the story seems to tilt slightly towards a vision of social cooperation (or community action) and not a techno-optimist vision of high-tech fixes. This aversion to hi-tech, though not directly connected to climate change mitigation or adaptation, is to be found in a scene with Nakoshi and her family when a young boy comes to inform them that the sugarcane farmer has employed a mechanized harvester. The author writes, '

A little boy ran towards them, his arms up in the air, shouting, "rangada ala," the tank is here.

Rangada meaning battle tank … It was the sugarcane harvesting machine, resembling a tank in some ways' (55)

Naturally the symbolism of the battle tank and death is not lost on the reader. The scene continues:

> The gigantic machine was devouring the sugarcane on a field of the same size in just two hours. Its constant roar was deafening … With more machines at work, they would have no more work in a few years, or perhaps the contractors would force down their wages and advances. What would they do then?
>
> The migrant workers would wither away in their own homes and die.
>
> (57)

Looking at the third set of classifiers, we can straightaway say this is neither a cautionary tale in the sense of *The Road*, nor is it one dealing with Denial, Acceptance or Avoidance. The characters are not really blind to their plight, and they do not finally accept their situation and come out to protest and demand rights. This climate justice novel is, at least in the final pages and because of the presence of strong characters like Daya and Ranjan and actants[42] in the form of the farmers' protest, which is in direct opposition to the overlapping factors of corruption, injustice and policy paralysis, very much a novel of resistance, symbolized by the sickle in its title, which is a signifier both of the sugarcane labourers exploitative labour and that of collective action of the farmers, many of who carry the red flag with sickle and hammer during the long march.

The fourth classification divides cli-fi on the basis of realist and futurist narratives. Clearly, *The Sickle* is set in the present with a strong connection to the real world. Agnihotri rarely employs satire in this work; neither do we find the employment of myths to drive the plot (the bull worship and crater lake scenes being exceptions), nor do we come across apocalyptic scenes or climate catachronism. So we cannot call this work a 'realist-hybrid', unlike Ghosh's *Gun Island*. We would rather describe this novel as a work of social realism with a strong theme of climate justice.

In a review for a newspaper, the writer, Swati Bhattacharya described the novel as 'political literature'.[43] We will recall in this context Trexler's scepticism about realism because of its commitment to a 'desultory status quo' which makes it 'unlikely to imagine novel political affiliations'. However, as we have seen, a novel like *The Sickle* can still gather political agency because of, among other things, its representation of real and close-to-real political assemblages across a variety of intersectional issues connected to climate change.

The fifth set of classifiers foregrounds the genre tensions of climate fiction. We can easily see that the novel is not science fiction. It is a work of cli-fi, more specifically climate justice, that fits into other genres of realist fiction like the socio-political novel, thus again tilting the balance towards the argument that cli-fi is actually a supergenre absorbing various kinds of writing. It would not be out of place to suggest the possibility that the author may not have started out to write a climate novel but one about social justice issues set in the present, but as we have seen, it is impossible to ignore the underpinning fact of climate change in the themes and plotlines she engages. Which is another way to say, turning around the words from Pope Francis' Encyclical, that a true social approach will always become an ecological approach and vice versa because the two are intertwined.

Using the sixth classification, we ask the question whether *The Sickle* is dystopian or utopian fiction. It is quite obvious that the book is in no way utopian in the sense that society has been already transformed into a better place where all beings live in harmony with each other and the planet. On the contrary, the novel presents itself as a meticulous examination of the fault lines of justice that persist and widen because of the impact of climate change and other overlapping and intersecting factors. In fact, some of the precarious settings and lived realities of the novel can be considered dystopian which should be read with the complicated dystopian experience of the Adivasi characters.

*The Sickle* is, in fact, a realist novel with features of docu-fiction, and it is not trying to depict a future utopia or dystopia but is telling the story of injustice, inequity and decay set in the present. It is a story of how the world of the characters is falling apart in the present, and the setting and storyline are firmly anchored in current incidents (like the farmers' march) and realities (of droughts and migration) in Marathwada and Vidarbha of Maharashtra. This is not to say that climate novels of justice cannot do otherwise, Octavia E. Butler's post-apocalyptic *Parable of the Sower* being one good example. Perhaps reasons for setting the novel in the present can be located in the fact that the author has worked in the regions portrayed as a civil service official, and also her declared affinity to be among people and away from the city.[44] While on the surface much of the scenes and settings can be easily read as dystopian, we need to stress that this is not an imagined future climate dystopia stemming from climate and other impacts. As much of the background stories, data and information, from the farmers' marches to the data on suicides, is true (and not imagined), this is a work of realist fiction with a strong political focus.

Finally, the seventh set of classifiers examines whether the novel tells a story of mitigation or adaptation to climate change. *The Sickle* is definitely not a story of climate mitigation, as most of the plot is busy with the stories of people adapting and carrying on with their lives in the face of punishing environmental, social and economic factors. But as they adapt, they also protest and demand justice. The core of justice and politics, therefore, places this story in the category of adaptive narratives with a strong political voice. How well the characters manage to adapt in this case, however, remains an open question.

## Creative representations of crisis in *The Sickle*

How does a climate novel which centres the issues of justice and politics engage with the other representational challenges of climate fiction? We had earlier noted the contrary pulls between politics and aesthetics in fiction. We have also seen from our reading of *Memory of Water* how cli-fi focused on aesthetics can still address political concerns to an extent if the author intends. Here, we will again address this question while flipping the positions between aesthetics and politics. We will also examine how the author of *The Sickle* negotiates the other creative-thematic challenges (Figure 2.2) which together constitute the two remaining major lenses (planetarity and aesthetics) and all the minor lenses for our study of climate fiction.

We have noted how climate novels can yoke Nature and Culture (the human sphere) together in their narrative flow, and *The Sickle* is no exception to that. As the author tells the story of drought-stricken Vidharba and Marathwada areas of Maharashtra, human life and the suffering of characters like Terna, Vaishali, Nakoshi and others are well embedded in this setting. But twined always with this human sphere are the facts of drought, erratic rains, affected crops and much more, which all pertain to natural and the non-human. A reviewer of the book, writing for *Parabaas* magazine, notes, 'The author first sets down the broad context (including nature, deprivation and struggle) and then shows the meetings of Krishak sabha (farmers' group) in twenty-four districts in 2015, the farmers' satyagraha at Nasik in 2016.'[45]

In this novel, we perceive an attempt to present a narrative coordination of the natural, depicted mostly through climate impacts like droughts; scarcities, with some associated statistics; and the sphere of human action and reaction in building, living and fighting for a better and dignified life. This is done through scenes where the human bleeds into the natural and vice versa, and also through devices like vignettes, authorial asides and a documentary approach to storytelling in certain cases. While the documentary approach sometimes slows down the story, the human agents who are both sufferers (Terna, Nakoshi) and instigators (Amresh) play their parts well, till in the final pages we find the activist agency of the affected people grow in importance. True to the nature of much of climate fiction, there is occasionally this sense that the reader gets of observing the unfolding of an experiment, where the art of the novel tests ways of engaging with the agency of weather, droughts and other actants as they shape and mould and in turn get moulded by human action.

Two of the chapters are titled Drought and Crater Lake, one at the beginning of the book and another at the end, just before the protest march begins. It is as if the author has consciously framed the human story with these two chapters to remind us that we cannot think of nature and the human sphere separately. Similarly, in naming one of the main characters, Terna, after a river, the author reminds us about the inextricable links between the human and the non-human. Agnihotri directs our attention to these links, as well as how one (river) affects the other (human) through its absence when she writes, 'After all, there was an entire river within Terna once. Where had it vapourised?' (32). Elsewhere, in the scene where the marchers are forced to sleep on a river bed, we find this description: 'Her eyes still shut, Rukma bai could hear the heart of the dead river pulsing again to the beat of human footsteps' (230).

While reading the book, the reader experiences this intertwining of the natural and the social (cultural) as the narrative shifts from descriptions of human suffering to portrayals of changes in the natural surroundings and back. We see this again when, the water train driven by political machinations rushes through the scorched region of Latur, the denuded land all around becomes personified in this description, 'The sun-scorched farmland and dried trees along the way had observed with melancholy and envious yellowed eyes the passing of the train with long whistles and no stops anywhere, their thirst increasing while they watched. So much water, and yet the train wouldn't offer a drop to any of them. The calculations of politics were different' (30).

Descriptions of weather patterns and nature are interspersed throughout the text, often to create the context for the human stories. Besides the mention of global warming, the author also focuses on weather patterns and the monsoon. Agnihotri writes:

> The monsoon winds that carry the rains across the country take till the beginning of July to reach Marathwada. The south-west monsoon brings rain to the Malabar coast around the middle of June, after which the monsoon reaches the entire west coast of India, along the Arabian Sea. When Mumbai's roads are flooded with water, when torrential rain makes rows of cars stall on waterlogged streets, pre-monsoon showers begin in western Maharashtra too. The skies are overcast, and it rains across the districts of Pune, Satara and Kolhapur; the Sahyadri ranges get rain too. But the rain-bearing clouds cannot clamber quickly over the Western Ghats and into Marathwada; nor does the south-west monsoon arrive by then.
>
> (76)

With the above description, she creates the context for the unbearable weather through which Daya Joshi travels for her activist work.

The novel is replete with descriptions of trees, rivers, lakes, mountains, parched land and animals, just as it paints vignettes of rituals like bull worship, where mutuality and kinship between humans and animals are refracted through a ritual:

> The bulls had to be invited formally on the day before the rituals. With an offering of paddy, tender grass and vermilion, they would be told, come tomorrow, I will bathe you, put ornaments on you, give you food to eat. And let you rest.
>
> For two days the bulls would be allowed to rest, they would neither have to work in the fields with the heavy yokes on their shoulders, nor draw the carts weighed down with crops. The domesticated animal stood shoulder to shoulder with humans, toiling on the land under the scorching sun and pouring rain, withstanding the long drought together. Sometimes food became scarce, sometimes the sheer effort in turning over the moistureless clods of dry earth made it close to death, it even sensed the deep sighs of the suffering peasant being humiliated by banks and moneylenders feel – it was just that it couldn't express itself.
>
> (164)

We will now examine the issue of time scales. Though not a major plot driver, geological time scales come to the fore in the chapter where Ranjan and Vaishali meet at the crater lake. In one long and memorable description of the crater lake (Lonar Lake) where Ranjan proposes to Vaishali, the author invokes geological time, describing the arrival of the meteorite and its choosing this particular spot in the Buldhana region of Maharashtra to enter the planet's bosom. In the imagining and description of this millennia-old event, the text imparts agency to the non-human planet and the meteor while also twining the story of Vaishali, Ranjan and others around this. Agnihotri writes:

> The meteorite had hurtled towards the earth at an acute angle, raising a storm of wind and dust on impact as it scoured the surface with great force. There also rose from the bowels of the earth, expelled like flattened lava, countless sorrows, spreading into the distance, even leaping into the sky, and then, finally, when everything became calm again, the earth and rocks that had emerged from the crust of the planet lined the edges of a gigantic crater …
>
> All this happened 60,000 years ago. Where were Vaishali and Umesh, Ranjan and Amresh then? Mere particles floating in the wind. Now, two of them were here, waiting to see the sun set …
>
> Halfway between the orbits of Mars and Jupiter lies the asteroid belt, covering an enormous span as it circles the sun. Many of these meteors are their skin and dust, some of them burning to ashes once they enter the atmosphere, others evading the gravitational pull of the earth to go deeper into the void of space. And some embed themselves in the green soil of our planet teeming with colours and diversity.
>
> Was this meteorite arcing downwards 60,000 years ago smitten? Was it drawn irresistibly to the spread-out wings of the Buldhana range of hills, harbouring hopes of a safe sanctuary, generated by the contrast between the green vegetation and the black soil?
>
> (215–17)

The author further reveals a mythic-cultural layer to this story of the lake, by narrating the Puranic myth of Lavanasur, who took refuge in Lonar after Vishnu killed two other asuras and how the asura's blood was converted into medicated saline water, while also connecting that story to the persecution of a tribal (Indigenous people) leader by an Aryan god. Interestingly, this telling is also interspersed with scientific detail as the author explains how the salt in the meteorite has resulted in the alkaline taste of the water of the lake.

We will remember Timothy Clarke's insights about the scalar subjectivity of literary works and the example where he reads

Raymond Carver's short story through the lens of different time scales. It is as if this particular chapter of *The Sickle* is conscious of such a possible reading as it layers together geological time, ancient history, mythical time, recent history, as well as the climate-changed present where Vaishali, bearing the burden of loss of her cotton farmer husband, meets the agricultural researcher Ranjan on the banks of the crater lake. In doing this, the author seems to acknowledge the vast time scales through which the history of the planet unfolds while gradually getting entwined with human history.

Another creative-thematic feature of climate change novels that we are analysing throughout this work pertains to non-human agency which is closely allied to the story's awareness of nature-culture entanglements. As far as non-human agency is concerned, it is the agency of weather, the truant rainfall, the punishing summers that have the maximum impact on the storyworld and the characters' lives, manifest in migration, exploitative work, gender inequality and other effects.

If we revisit our discussion of actor-network theory, we will remember that agents are not independent and are connected through dependencies. We have already seen how the characters get affected and driven by the non-human agency of climate effects, which work through a complex network of overlapping socio-economic and political factors or dependencies, thereby aggravating the situation till the farmers are driven to march for their rights. Also, in certain vignettes and descriptions of the novel, we perceive non-human agency, for example, in the agency of machines, like the sugarcane crushers, and their possible impact on employment of the climate migrant labourers, and in a fallen tree that blocks Daya's path, triggering an uncanny experience and some others.

The uncanny, which is another creative-thematic feature of climate novels, is, however, not easily encountered here. There are certain scenes, however, like the one mentioned above, or in the description of the sugarcane crushers at work and in the personification of nature that we noted when the water train rushes past, that are tinged with the uncanny. The water train scene, in particular, where the description of the parched landscape affects the reader and the characters, evokes the uncanny, both in its Heideggerian and Freudian senses.

Among the three novels we have discussed in this book, *The Sickle* demonstrates maximum engagement with the role of collectives in shaping the world and fighting the manifest injustices of the plot. Though individuals like Ranjan, Daya, Nakoshi and Terna do demonstrate agency with their own character arcs (most prominent for Daya and Ranjan), it is in their actions through collectives (Ranjan gets involved with the farmers' movement later) that their efforts achieve significance, meaning and some amount of success. This follows from the fact that *The Sickle* is a political novel with its ear to the ground, ever aware of atomic as well as wide-ranging occurrences of injustice in its storyworld, which in all practical terms needs the concerted action of many interconnected co-sufferers, and not a single Campbellian hero.[46]

Finally, we address aesthetics and planetarity which are the two remaining major lenses (Figures 2.2 and 3.4) of our analysis. In sharpening the aesthetic lens, we had depended primarily on the definition of literariness while also listing certain features of literary fiction. Similar to Amitav Ghosh's *Gun Island*, here too we rarely encounter foregrounding, defamiliarization, reinterpretation and the associated literariness. However, in the interiority of characters like Daya, the well-developed character arcs of Daya and Ranjan, and the occasional scenes of stylized writing, we find traces of literary fiction. Also, Modernist influences as in the use of collages, cut-aways and interspersed forms (narration with meteorology, socio-economics and more) appear in the story which, remembering Kerridge's arguments, often serve the climate and ecocentric approach of this work.

This book does not experiment consistently with language in the sense of Cormac McCarthy in *The Road* or Emmi Itäranta in *Memory of Water*, to reflect the suffering and transformations on the ground and in the lives of the characters as a result of climate and overlapping factors. This is perhaps due to the fact that the author generally adopts a docu-fiction approach where 'fiction meets fact'[47] taking us, in the words of critic Somak Ghosal, 'closer to realities that are beyond the scope of journalism',[48] which is not to disregard the fact that there are passages, as in the chapter set around the crater lake, and descriptions, which foreground the author's powers as a prose stylist, often illuminating her engagement with injustice in a new light. The reviewer for *Parabaas* has noted these specialities of her language (in the original Bangla) with examples, commending her use of wonderful similes and an eclectic vocabulary which, in certain scenes, imparts a literary flavour to this political text.[49]

The sense of planet, or planetarity, is the final major lens that we use to briefly examine this work. We have extensively discussed planetarity in the climate novel in the context of Amitav Ghosh's *Gun Island*. Agnihotri's novel, with its focus on justice in a specific geographic context, does not invest its energies on planetary connections to the extent that Ghosh does, but there is the acknowledgement that the warming which is impacting the setting and her characters is 'global' and that the drought is not local; rather, its footprints are spreading across the nation.

While not being planetary in scope, the novel does connect people from different regions of Maharashtra through the stories of hardship and suffering in much of which climate change is implicated. In that sense, Maharashtra, with all the political, social, economic and environmental forces and networks, acting in tandem, becomes a microcosm of the planet in this novel. However, leaning more towards the unmasking of hegemony and power, the author of this postcolonial text brings a surgeon's scalpel and a microscope to the material of suffering, exploitation and social evils, while the implicit awareness of bigger forces and networks, both human (corruption, politics) and non-human (weather, climate) at play, is always there in the background.

Like the other novels discussed in this book, *The Sickle* also demonstrates a tension between the aesthetic, the entertaining and the political. While being intellectually stimulating and engaging, it will be clear to most readers that this novel doesn't aim to 'entertain' in the sense a climate thriller may do. It is clearly a political novel that centres justice while not abandoning the aesthetic quest of the literary writer altogether. Because of its formal experiments, where vignettes coexist with documentary information and a stream of activism (Daya, Ranjan and the farmers' organization) runs all through the book, the text leans clearly towards the political where the politics is both 'emitted' in the Lukacs' sense through portrayals of life and society but is also manifest in the data and information on deprivation, suffering and injustice presented in the course of telling the tale. The climate justice lens we have used to study this work has clearly demonstrated the political core and activist direction of *The Sickle*, and this we believe is a useful way to engage with Agnihotri's work, which brings us to the end of our discussion of creative representations of climate change and intersectional issues in this novel, propelling us on to its activist core. This we shall now examine with the tools we had defined for the purpose.

## The climate story in action

Can Daya, Ranjan, Terna and Vaishali's stories help us better understand intersecting crises and perhaps influence climate action? Can the act of reading political cli-fi motivate readers to seek justice and an equitable solution to the climate crisis? Do climate fiction works carry in their core a mantra that can influence the human mind and help us understand and engage with the complex realities of climate change? These are questions we will try to address here by exploring the transformative potential of Agnihotri's work.

Following the approach and reasoning outlined in the previous chapter, we will be looking at three out of the five possible ways (Figure 4.1) to test the transformative potential of this cli-fi. These pertain to the application of findings of empirical ecocritical studies,

Production and Consumption Flows and Sustainable Development Goals (SDGs).

We will remember that the presence of role models, good characterization as well as solutions have been shown to influence beliefs and behaviour of climate fiction readers. *The Sickle* is driven by well-evolved characters like Daya Joshi and Ranjan, whose struggles and motivations are not difficult to relate to. While it might be problematic for the urban reader to identify with characters like Terna or Nakoshi, their suffering is narrated with empathy that will move the reader. The collectives of the novel (farmers' organization) and their joint action are also quite inspiring, not the least for their real-world correlates, and can leave a strong impression on the reader.

Both Daya and Ranjan, in their activism, bravery and empathy, together stand as a bulwark against gender and environmental injustice, and the role played by patriarchy. They are characters who can serve as role models for readers. The author also points to solutions through detailed socio-economic analysis while foregrounding the role that collective political action can play in dealing with justice issues, thus presenting a useful template for change.

The settings of the novel, like barren villages, the sugarcane labourers camps, the benighted town of Shirur Kasar – centre of the female foeticide business, hills, rivers and the drought-stricken land are evoked with great felicity and purpose, as is the crater lake where an important scene is set, which true to the nature of cli-fi, begins to impact plot and character.[50] This attention to setting will no doubt have an influence on the reader's mind. However, such descriptions, following the style of this novel, are often interspersed with socio-economic and ethnographic background which might distract from the enjoyment of the story, bringing us back to the fact that the representation of climate change in literature is an ongoing experiment.

Because of these particularities, it is difficult to say without designing empirical studies whether the story will 'transport' readers, thereby influencing them, but the intellectual and politically minded reader will definitely have much to take home. It should also be noted that the narrative around the long march of the farmers, and the female foeticide racket, is based on real incidents and so is an accumulation of easily relatable personal stories of thousands of affected individuals. Such personal stories tend to leave a strong impression on the reader and help in the easier dissemination of the embedded messages of a fictional work.

We can now delve deeper to examine how an understanding of climate change, its solutions and sustainability issues is woven into the plot. We do this using the two other approaches, focusing on Production and Consumption Flows and SDGs. First, we probe the work about its awareness of production and consumption flows as they relate to climate change as well as its awareness of possible strategies and solutions. We do this by asking how production and consumption flows, their contribution to climate change and its several manifestations, as well as sustainability concepts, are framed in the narrative.

The story demonstrates awareness about the unsustainable use of resources like water.[51] It comments on the harvesting of the water-thirsty sugarcane when large parts of the state of Maharashtra suffer from droughts. After commenting on the impact of global warming on rain patterns, the author goes on to say, 'Why does Marathwada, with no irrigation facilities, have to grow so much sugarcane?' (186).

Because the stories of the book are largely woven around drought and water scarcities among other issues, the concepts of production, consumption and sustainability are all refracted through the issue of water shortages, its unsustainable use, corruption and profiteering. Connecting droughts and the unsustainable use of water with issues of climate justice, whereby women have to bear the brunt of scarcities, the author writes:

> The profiteering ring around potable water is even more sinister. The wells in Marathwada and Vidarbha begin to dry up after winter every year. … The enormous tanks wait for the monsoon rains with wide-open jaws, displaying the bony staircases leading down to where the

> water collects. Enterprising housewives and their daughters go all the way down those stairs, digging beneath the soil and shifting the rocks in the hope of finding some water. Often, they return home with empty pitchers on their heads under a blazing sun.
>
> This is when the water entrepreneurs wake up, collecting thousands and lakhs of litres of water, as if by magic, and distributing them by tankers among the residents of small towns and villages. Even where there are arrangements for piped water, it's available only two times a month.
>
> (187)

The other resource-consumption issue that the novel deals with at length is the unsustainable use of forest produce. The march of Adivasis (Indigenous people) like Rukma Bai is propelled by their demand for the right to cultivate forest adjoining lands and use forest produce.

Echoing Ramachandra Guha's and J Martinez-Alier's insights about the environmentalism of the poor[52] which explain how the poor protect and use resources sustainably, the author points out that Adivasis in fact protect the forest while only using it for their basic needs. She writes, 'The area used to be full of high-quality teak and rosewood trees. But contractors appointed by the Forest Development Corporation, a government department, began to clear out the forests. City dwellers say adivasis cut down forests, but the truth is just the opposite – forests survive only where adivasis live' (224). This is another means by which the book engages unsustainable resource use and the sustainable habit of the poor, thereon connecting it to the march for justice. In the *Scroll* interview quoted earlier, Agnihotri said:

> I saw signs of these extinct forests where they farm now. The land had not been measured, nor had leases been given, although all of this should have been done under the Forest Rights Act. The farmers were worried that the government land would be taken away under

the pretext of creating land banks for industrial houses, that tribal farmers would lose their land as well as their livelihood.[53]

So we see that the book is aware of the unsustainable use of natural resources like water, land and forest and how these connect to issues of justice in which climate change also plays an important role. While possible solutions to these problems of unsustainable use, corruption and policy paralysis are not worked out in detail, the author uses her administrator's[54] understanding to explain the roots of many of these issues (e.g. the business of drought) through the story as well as in the authorial commentaries. Finally, as a possible solution and a signal of hope, Agnihotri points to the importance of collective action and political activism demonstrated through the farmers' march.

Now we can examine the book in the context of related institutional tools like the SDGs and the Paris Agreement for emission reductions. The SDGs Goal 13 calls for 'urgent action to combat climate change and its impacts by regulating emissions and promoting developments in renewable energy'. *The Sickle* as a text focused on the manifestations of climate injustice engages with intersectionalities and embedded justice issues. The story does not directly address climate action, emissions or mitigation measures. However, as we have seen earlier, injustice remains inextricably linked with climate change, both in its causes and impacts, in its origins, in the procedures, processes and systems that are created to deal with it, and in the unequal distribution of resources and entitlements that perpetuate and aggravate it. *The Sickle*, as a text of climate justice, engages more with these nodes of injustice (like poverty, exploitation, inequality, forced migration, deprivation of rights) and the fault lines of policy and corruption.

The author repeatedly stresses upon this fact of intersectionalities and interconnections. In the interview with Scroll magazine, she explained, 'I was able to see an underlying connection between the politics of droughts in Marathwada, the uncertain lives of migrant sugarcane labourers who are bereft of rights, the aftermath to the suicides of farmers in Vidarbha, and the march undertaken by tribal peasants.'[55] If we agree that climate justice must inform mitigative (and adaptive) strategies and fair sharing of costs and burdens, based on the principle of 'common but differentiated responsibilities', then we can say that this novel is aligned towards achievement of Goal 13 of the SDGs in tandem with Goal 16, which is about broader justice issues and strong institutions.

The SDGs also recognize these interlinkages and intersections, and many of the goals find an echo in the telling of Agnihotri's tale. Among these, we can see that the novel engages with Goal 1 (poverty), Goal 5 (Gender equality), Goal 6 (Clean water and sanitation), Goal 8 (Decent work and economic growth) and Goal 10 (Reduced inequalities). It is obvious that as a text of climate justice this novel is engaged by a large number of goals of sustainable development and can be a useful text for an activist's library.

We have now read this climate novel with all the three prongs (Figure 2.2) of the approach to climate fiction we developed in the first part of the book. There and elsewhere we noted how postcolonial concerns can mould the climate novel in certain ways, something we already noted in the case of Amitav Ghosh's fiction. In the final section of this chapter, we attempt a brief survey of Agnihotri's novel using some tools of postcolonial ecocriticism.

## Postcolonial concerns in an intersectional work on climate change

Intuitively, we can expect a climate novel set in a postcolonial nation, and focusing on justice issues, to be engaged with postcolonial concerns. Agnihotri is an Indian writer writing in Bangla, with an oeuvre that often addresses issues of justice, environment and deprivation. So a postcolonial ecocritical reading of her work will help to further illuminate issues of climate justice that she tackles in this novel.

The story unfolds in affected communities eking out their living in precarious circumstances where poverty, droughts, unpredictable weather, economic exploitation, corruption, patriarchy and social evils have equal roles to play. These precarious settings and social systems echo what Scott Slovic describes as 'threatened environments'[56] and their complex relationship with literature from developing regions, many of which are postcolonial nations.

We have earlier noted how postcolonial ecocriticism centres a justice approach by drawing attention to the intersection of social and environmental issues in literature. We will also recall from our discussion of environmental justice how the concept, 'yokes concern for the environment, including all life on the planet, to commitment to social justice'.[57] In this context, social justice encompasses 'human equity in terms of race, gender, religion, nationality, and class'.[58] The importance of activism as the political manifestation of environmental justice was also highlighted in our discussion. All this applies equally for climate justice and Agnihotri's novel by situating poverty, gender and ethnicity (Adivasis) issues within a climate-affected tortured setting of scarcities and exploitation, which demonstrates its strong commitment to environmental justice thereby revealing clear concerns of a postcolonial ecocritical text. Besides this, our detailed examination of the novel with the lens of justice has already established the author's justice concerns, which is the beating heart of a postcolonial ecocritical work.

One of the exemplars of environmental justice movements is what Ramachandra Guha calls the 'environmentalism of the poor'. In a well-represented depiction of environmentalism of the poor, the novel tells us how Adivasis like Rukma Bai in fact protect the forest, using it sustainably while they fear that their land will be taken away 'under the pretext of creating land banks for industrial houses'.[59] Later with the continuing trampling upon of their rights, all the affected communities of farmers, Adivasis and climate migrants among others come together in a groundswell of protest, in a movement that shares their *raison d'etre* and dynamics with environmental justice movements like Chipko[60] or Narmada Bachao Andolan.

Following Tiffin and Huggan's argument to look for the underpinnings of colonialism in the text, we can see how colonial attitudes of ecological imperialism persist in the storyworld of *The Sickle*. This is evinced in the attitudes of corrupt politicians, corporate land-grabbing and the workings of the water mafia. And it doesn't stop at colonizing the non-human; it extends further into the domain of the less-privileged humans, inflicting a slow but definite violence, as we see in the exploitation of sugarcane labourers, indebted cotton farmers, and through patriarchy and violence upon the bodies and minds of women.

Being a novel of climate justice, the examination of the insidious workings of power in the story also exposes the underlying realities of climate change and unpredictable weather, and how it intersects with and aggravates these power dynamics. While the novel does not talk of emissions directly and prefers a regional rather than planetary setting, it does mention global warming and engages with the skewed distribution and consumption of resources like water. Because of colonial pasts and neocolonial presents, it is germane that the postcolonial novel of climate change will often be more exercised by the task of exposing power and the new avatars of colonialism while telling the story of suffering through the lens of justice, but nevertheless remaining conscious of larger forces like climate change working in the background.

True to its postcolonial ecological concerns which examine neocolonial power and hegemony refracted through economics, politics, environmental degradation and patriarchy, Agnihotri's novel casts a searching gaze at the workings of power and corruption in a postcolonial context and how it initiates and perpetuates deprivation and suffering. Her postcolonial attitude, unlike Amitav Ghosh's, is, however, not imbued with postmodern engagements with cosmopolitanism or in the digging out of lost stories and parallel narratives.

The novel is not cosmopolitan and transnational in a postcolonial sense. Once in a while, the book digs out marginalized pasts, as in the mentions of the Adivasis farming the land in the hills and forests for generations, a right which is now increasingly under threat despite a law being passed. There are also descriptions of rituals like bull worship or the myth of Lavanasura connected to the crater lake. However, these myths or forgotten pasts do not flow parallel to the main narrative or drive the plot in the way they do in *Gun Island*, whose postmodern elements we have noted earlier. Still, these marginalized and ignored pasts and practices do provide the impetus for the Adivasis finally rising in protest.

However, in its close engagement with economic hardship and the struggle for rights and entitlements and the involvement of members of a real farmers' organization (All India Kisan Sabha) of the communist party in the plot, some of whom bear the red sickle and hammer flags of the party, the novel presents ample scope for a Marxist reading. Such a Marxist reading, because of the settings and themes of the book, can be further nuanced by employing Marx's ecological perspectives,[61] captured in the concept of 'metabolic rift'[62] which analyses how capitalism affects 'social metabolism' by aggravating the relationship between human beings and nature.[63]

Beyond the surface markers of a postcolonial text and its continuing critique of power and exploitation, the novel also demonstrates interests and engagements which demonstrate its postcolonial engagement. We will remember, following Rob Nixon,[64] that displacement as against primacy of 'place' is a postcolonial concern, and *The Sickle* being largely a story of migrant labour (internal migration), is very much a work in that mould. Also, the nature that Agnihotri engages is seldom 'pure' or 'virgin wilderness'[65] but already corrupted and denuded by human action which, as we mentioned in the beginning, speaks to Slovic's assertion about threatened environments. In all of this, Agnihotri's novel, while being a postcolonial text, goes further along the road, bringing the sphere of the human and that of nature together in its stories of exploitation, suffering and collective protest.

## The long road to justice

It is obvious by now that climate fiction set in a postcolonial developing nation can have its own set of concerns and methods for engaging with the causes, manifestations and systemic interconnections of climate change. In our reading of Anita Agnihotri's novel, we have seen how the important issue of justice gets foregrounded in climate writing set among vulnerable communities of a postcolonial nation. Here we have also noted how and why climate change cannot be properly engaged without addressing justice and how fictional representations of the climate crisis will remain politically incomplete if the bedrock of justice is not addressed.

Depending on the author, her subject and style, the strategies for addressing justice in climate fiction could be many. In Agnihotri's case, we noted a focus on the lives of drought-stricken and indebted farmers and farm labourers of Maharashtra who are forced to migrate for work or even kill themselves, in the face of rising debts. We also noted how climate, farm labour and poverty are implicated in a situation where the girl child is better not born and where women's rights barely exist. We also read the story of Indigenous people and how they have to fight for their rights to land and forest produce. In almost all of these, climate change, drought, corruption and policy paralysis have overlapping and aggravating impacts.

In our reading of the novel with a justice lens, we found how the story and the authorial asides addressed issues that we find in the Bali Principles of Climate Justice and in other theoretical and activist framings, dealing with distributional, procedural, representational and other interlinked issues of justice and climate change. Moreover, our analysis also revealed how distinctive features of cli-fi like nature-culture and non-human agency are embedded in the plot, while planetarity is not addressed at scale. Also, aesthetics is not a prime concern of this work which shows a clear preference for the politics. As a novel, which often presents facts connected to the climate crisis and other intersectional issues, which, entwined with the suffering of characters, create a strong political impetus for the plot, *The Sickle* stands out as a powerful document of social realism. It is yet another experiment in climate writing, where the disadvantaged, whom the author knows well, try to tell their stories of suffering and injustice.

Through its representation of movements and collective action, and because of addressing issues pertaining to a number of Sustainable Development Goals, *The Sickle* comes out strong in its politics while being well aware of the contours of the problems at hand. Thus, it is a significant addition to the library of postcolonial climate fiction, as a new kind of narrative that tells the story of suffering and injustice while issuing a clarion call for change.

# Part Three

# Discoveries

8

# The cortege and the suncatcher

## *The abiding possibilities of climate stories*

As we arrive at the end of this journey, where we tried to map literature's encounter with climate change using critical insights and the work of novelists, I am somehow reminded once again of a day as an activist on the streets of Kolkata. By then, my old pair of sneakers was gone, hopefully to some recycling facility, and I had become attached to the merits of a multinational brand of reasonably priced footwear which looked like it would last forever. Later, a bad fall on the banks of the Hooghly would help to dispel this illusion.

While writing climate novels or trying to analyse these stories, I am often reminded of experiences gathered as an environment activist. I suppose the work of imagining, writing, reading or reviewing climate fiction leads me through a secret portal at the other end of which are the gritty streets and battlefields of activism, where action is sacred just as in my trade, the word is.

It was the morning rush hour, and we had assembled near a major intersection close to the busy Camac Street crossing of Kolkata. There were about thirty of us, maybe a few more, and we stood patiently in the sweltering summer heat waiting for the others. In a few minutes, we started walking in a disciplined double line.

Those at the head of the procession were bearing an elaborately decorated cortege with a wooden bed, dressed with sticks of *rajanigandha* and jasmine. On the bed lay an old refrigerator with three large funeral wreaths of carnations placed on top. Following funeral custom, one of us went on scattering popped rice from a paper packet as we went.

Those of us following the cortege bore placards and posters with messages about obsolete and environmentally harmful technologies, like fridge and air-conditioning coolants, which were damaging the ozone layer and were also aggravating climate change. Others chanted '*Bolo Hori, Hori bol*' to mark the journey of the deceased.

As we stepped out on the main street, walking against a sea of automobiles, all traffic came to a halt. The curious got out of their cars to watch, passengers poked their heads out of broken windows to read the placards, babies bawled, motorcyclists honked and honked and then seeing the cortege, fell quiet.

Just as we were nearing the next crossing, a traffic police sergeant speaking animatedly on his wireless set came roaring in on his red Bullet motorbike, determined to stop us and charge us for traffic obstruction. I could see him clenching his jaw, glaring in our direction. But as soon as he swung into the main street, he saw the cortege decked with flowers and slowed down. He braked and stopped. Joining both hands, he slowly raised them to touch his forehead in a *pranam* as a mark of respect to the dead before speeding off in the other direction.

We breathed a sigh of relief. Some of us broke into titters, before continuing on our way towards the office of a refrigerator manufacturer, where we submitted memoranda urging them to switch to climate- and ozone-friendly technologies. Obviously, the message of climate-damaging technologies was lost on the police officer but later, thinking about this incident, I realized how deeply this scene was imbued with satire.

If we look deeper, we cannot miss the fact that the carefully decorated cortege with the wreaths was, in fact, a triple signifier of activism, planetary crises, as well as a representational effort melding the aesthetic with the satirical. Of course, I had not thought through all of this when I had planned the mock funeral of environment-damaging technology. It would have perhaps helped if I could have used satire alongside activist arguments when I had met the official at the multinational refrigeration company, long back on that day of end-of-the-world weather in Stockholm, trying to convince him about quickly phasing out harmful technologies.

But ideas always elude you when you need them the most. That's the problem with *l'esprit de l'escalier*. But today, in hindsight, and as this journey recording literature's encounter with climate change is about to be completed, I realize that activism, a capacious planetary sense and aesthetics are some of the distinctive features we noticed in the novels we read. Added to that, like in our mock funeral of environment-damaging technologies, a sprinkling of satire always helps.

This is, however, no accident. Writers and artists negotiating the crossroads of the climate crisis will tend to build their work on a scaffolding where one or more among the planetary, the activist and the aesthetic will be present.

## Planet, art and justice

As we have seen throughout this book, each author has certain representational goals, and this has led to a visible focus on one of the three features above. In the case of Amitav Ghosh, it is the sense of planet which shines through his climate story; for Emmi Itäranta, the aesthetic is significant; while for Anita Agnihotri it is justice, captured in the politics and activism, that defined her work.

For Ghosh, we have also seen how the planetarity of his novel connects distant geographies and people, both in the present and the past, in a network of interconnections through which the realities of the climate crisis are represented and engaged. There is also in his work, and especially in the scenes of migrating sea creatures and birds flocking around the refugees' boat, or in the story of the orcaellas, an inclusive eco-cosmopolitan imagination which connects humans and other beings. In Itäranta's novel, which we labelled climate literary, we found how literariness and literary writing can bring a dystopian climate story alive while conjuring up the climate uncanny. Finally, Agnihotri's novel, through the story of droughts, exploitation and the workings of power, demonstrated how a postcolonial climate novel can foray into issues of justice and equity which form the bedrock of the climate crisis. While the elements of planetarity, aesthetics and justice have been the focus of the novels of Ghosh, Itäranta and Agnihotri, respectively, these authors have sometimes demonstrated an engagement with the issues not their prime focus.

So we have seen how politics and its representation through climate justice issues assume significance in Ghosh's story, especially in the plotline dealing with the refugees on the Blue Boat, their exploitation and their final rescue which weaves in with Tipu and Rafi's tales. While aesthetics and poetic prose are not significant in this Ghosh novel, nevertheless, we have come across that rare passage of striking beauty. Also in the depth of Deen and Cinta's character, and especially Deen's interiority, when he is alone, we have noticed features of literary fiction.

In the case of *Memory of Water*, we have similarly noticed how a sense of planet sometimes surfaces in the story and how it breaks down in the dystopian world where technologies have been lost and connections have been broken. Justice and politics, though not a significant plot driver for this novel, are nevertheless perceived in the distant rumbles of protest and revolution and the stark difference in conditions and entitlements between the city and the rural area where Noria lives. Here, the rural population is not only worse off because of water scarcity and rationing, but their hardships are further worsened by the oppression of the occupying forces.

*The Sickle*, while primarily being a novel about climate justice, sometimes uses literary language and descriptions, as in the scenes around the crater lake, or even in the descriptions of the drought-affected terrain, where the story unfolds. The author of the novel is also a published poet, and on a few occasions she employs language which is memorable. Agnihotri's novel, however, does not demonstrate a sense of planet as such, though it does connect the hardships and human costs of droughts, policy paralysis and patriarchy, weaving together different regions and peoples of Maharashtra into a searing account of crisis.

Finally, it will also be interesting to examine how and if one of the three salient features (politics, planetarity and aesthetics) has a bearing on some of the other creative-thematic features of each novel that are specific or relevant to climate change. Besides, we can also try to uncover if these salient features influence the transformative possibilities of the novel as a potential tool for awareness and action. In other words, we can try to examine if planetarity in case of Ghosh, aesthetics in case of Itäranta and justice in case of Agnihotri have a bearing on their engagement with nature-culture entanglements, the climate uncanny, non-human agency, the role of collectives, long time horizons and scale effects, their transformative potential and, in case of two books, their specificities as a postcolonial climate text. This might afford us a deeper understanding of how certain major thematic or technical priorities of a climate novel may influence the handling of the material and the politics of climate change.

In the case of Ghosh's novel, where the planetary aspects and the cosmopolitan imagination come out strong, we have found nature-culture entanglements, non-human agency, the role of collectives and the shifts in time scales are all significant in the plot. The potential role of this novel as an activist tool and the consciousness of the text about production and consumption flows are also strong, and it has obvious and underlying characteristics of an engaged postcolonial-ecocritical text which, moreover, makes clear connections with anthropogenic emissions as the source of the climate crisis. Climate uncanny is also occasionally represented in that story.

As we have seen earlier, the sense of planet and the eco-cosmopolitan imagination are about networks and connections between humans, non-humans and the planet in general. This thematic focus creates a strong grounding for the observed engagement with nature-culture connections, non-human agency and the role of collectives that we find in Ghosh. Non-human agency and nature-culture entanglements in turn can create the possibility for evoking the climate uncanny which surfaces a number of times in the text. Besides this, a planetary focus by revealing global connections and the interconnected dynamics through which climate change is manifest and affects the living also provides the basis for the novel to demonstrate a consciousness of production and consumption flows and sustainability goals which strengthens its potential as a tool for awareness that can leave a clear impression and possibly influence readers of cli-fi. We also noted how Ghosh places his novel in the present and that its focus on the climate uncanny surfaces only a few times in the text.

We have noticed how the literariness of Itäranta's novel and especially the technique of clustering used by her have a strong connection with how successfully the book evokes the uncanny. Beyond that, literariness does in certain scenes help to portray the non-human agency of water as it also, though not consistently, has a bearing on the depiction of natureculture. For addressing these, the author however also takes recourse to speculative techniques of future history, catachronism, systemic connections and scientific understanding of climate change. This becomes necessary because literariness is a technical as against a thematic choice, and its connections to the handling of material presented by climate change and the representational possibilities therein will not be automatically established without the conscious effort of the author. So, in Itäranta's case, literariness is consciously employed to foreground the non-human agency of water, while it's not employed consistently in depicting how the ice melted, the sea levels rose and humans had to migrate. Such (but not all) nature-culture connections are instead depicted through straightforward narration supported by speculation and climate science.

Itäranta's story, which we dubbed 'climate literary', engages deeply with temporal scales as it unveils past climate change, forgotten expeditions and the impact of humans on the planet. Here too the literariness of the novel, being a technical aspect, does not have much to do about these choices and depictions. Similarly, the role of collectives in the story does not demonstrate much of a dependence on its literary techniques, except for the impression left by the overall beauty of the prose that is encountered throughout the book. Finally, the novel's definite awareness of the causes and effects of climate change is not guaranteed by the literariness of the text. However, because of the poetic beauty of its prose style, which flows from its literariness, as well as deft characterization and other features, *Memory of Water* can have a definite advantage in creating awareness and influencing readers, particularly those already leaning towards literary fiction.

Climate justice being the thematic focus of Agnihotri's novel lays the groundwork for the text to deeply examine nature-culture connections, non-human agency and the role of collectives in the story. Like Ghosh's novel, Agnihotri too sets her story in the present, avoiding dystopian or utopian depictions. Descriptions of the non-human natural world, stressed by disrupted weather patterns, overlapping socio-political factors and their ultimate impact on lives, create the context and the dynamics for her human narratives of exploitation and finally a collective quest for justice. The novel does have a scene where temporal scales are strongly invoked, but the book's thematic choice of justice has only indirect bearing on that particular scene around the crater lake. Similarly, its evocation of the climate uncanny, in any case minimal, does not reveal any dependency on its thematic choice.

The thematic focus on justice and the awareness of the text about climate impacts (not the origins), aggravated by other socio-political causes, and the final activist groundswell for rights in the closing pages imbues this novel with the possibilities of its adoption as a tool for awareness and climate action. However, the anthropogenic origin of emissions being not discussed in the text makes it less suitable for engaging the production and consumption flows that drive the climate crisis. Being a postcolonial climate novel of justice, this work is more focused on injustice and exploitation, arising from a concatenation of forces and systemic fault lines aggravated by climate impacts which in itself imparts it with political agency and value in the context of climate action without any obvious reference to emissions.

From the above discussion, we can broadly conclude that literariness or aesthetics of the text doesn't automatically afford any special advantage in handling some of the complex material presented by climate change, nor does it guarantee that all the possible representational goals of a climate novel will be met. The analysis of Itäranta's novel makes it clear that literariness, which resides in the text, has to be often supported or combined with other techniques and choices on the part of the author, as well as a grounding in science and politics, to enable fiction's handling of the complexities of the material and creative challenges presented by climate change.

On the other hand, planetary, in its wider sense,[1] and justice themes can serve as useful maps for literature as it navigates the representational challenges and political complexities of the climate crisis, thereby charting a course for a deeper engagement with a number of climate-connected issues and goals. Fiction's meaningful encounter with climate change then is in representing these distinctive thematic features of planetarity and justice, among others, which, helped by literary technique, can present the reader with illuminating and enjoyable reads.

All the three novels we discussed do this to different extents. The final choice, of course, resides with the author as to what issues and material she will use and how she will tell her story. Whether they would adopt a stance of thematic engagement which allows them to deal with the resistance offered by climate change to fictional representation, or they would let flights of literariness leave a moody and sensory impression about her material is a choice best left to them. We have examined the inherent efficacies of the first course while also noting how an aesthetic approach can still be guided by the author's choices to meet certain representational goals of climate fiction.

The two postcolonial climate novels also presented us with a unique perspective on creative choices. Agnihotri's story stayed more with the trouble, focusing on exploitation and injustice aggravated by climate change and other factors, while Ghosh's novel, while not shying away from justice issues, because of its planetary theme and historical-scientific consciousness, could present a more complete picture about anthropogenic emissions and how this is implicated in the climate crisis.

## Catching the light

All of this goes to show that climate fiction is a dynamic genre which is continuously working out newer strategies for depicting climate change as well as imagining the future. While the novels we analysed were either set in the present or dealt with dystopian future imaginaries, there are whole new subgenres of cli-fi today, imagining better worlds. Anchored in the belief of a better tomorrow, and buttressed by studies, which show hopeful futures can influence more people to work towards a better, more sustainable and equitable world, these new genres of solarpunk, lunarpunk, hopepunk and others are beginning to imagine better, more sustainable worlds where small-scale decentralized action makes a difference.

In our discussion about utopian fiction, I had mentioned two such volumes[2] of solarpunk stories written by authors from around the world. In these stories and in the general creative churn around solarpunk and allied sub-genres, we find values like mutuality, cooperation, ingenuity, conviviality, the commons, degrowth, community, kinship and multispecies justice creating contexts for storyworlds where hope and action for a better future for all beings take centre stage. These transformative imaginaries, powered by low-tech, regenerative agriculture, wind, water and the sun, strive to chart out maps through the darkness of a planetary crisis towards a world of light. Like the suncatchers we put up to catch and refract sunlight into a palette of brilliant colours, these stories provide us with a spectrum of imaginative possibilities on the pathway to a better future.

In these stories too, the problems of depiction and representation we discussed throughout this book are equally important and carefully addressed. There too we find storytellers who focus on the aesthetic value of the text while others are more allied to frameworks of planetarity, science, justice and other issues that have a direct connection with climate change. What matters finally is the impact of these stories and the enjoyment they provide the reader.

In a time of commodified advice, we often tend to forget the long legacy of stories in changing the world. Sticky, troubling, joyous, mysterious and glowing with the light of better worlds, stories will be with us for as long as humanity survives, and they will definitely continue to be one of our greatest allies in imagining a better tomorrow.

# Notes

## Chapter 1

1 Michael Crichton, *State of Fear* (UK: HarperCollins, 2005).

2 Oliver Milman, '"Smoking Gun Proof": Fossil Fuel Industry Knew of Climate Danger as Early as 1954, Documents Show', *The Guardian*, 30 January 2024, https://www.theguardian.com/us-news/2024/jan/30/fossil-fuel-industry-air-pollution-fund-research-caltech-climate-change-denial. For a wider perspective about how capitalism and neoliberal markets are implicated in climate change, see Naomi Klein, *This Changes Everything: Capitalism vs. The Climate* (India: Simon & Schuster, 2014).

3 Geoffrey Supran, Stefan Rahmstorf and Naomi Oreskes, 'Assessing ExxonMobil's Global Warming Projections'. *Science, 379*(6628) (12 January 2023), 153, eabk0063, https://doi.org/10.1126/science.abk0063

4 The Montreal Protocol is an international agreement to facilitate the phasing-out of the production and consumption of ozone-depleting substances and thereby protect and mend the stratospheric ozone layer. The Montreal Protocol has been signed by 197 countries.

5 Climate fiction and climate change fiction are used interchangeably throughout this book.

6 Depending on the context, the terms distinctive features (or just features) and creative-thematic challenges, features or strategies are used interchangeably as these map into each other. Also, for the sake of brevity, creative-thematic challenges, features or strategies are on certain occasions replaced with creative challenges, features or strategies. See Figures 2.2 and 2.3.

7 Throughout this book, the words 'planetarity', 'planetariness' and 'planetary sense' are used as shorthand for the 'sense of planet', as evinced in works of fiction, a concept extensively discussed (see Chapter 5) by Ursula Heise. By employing the word 'planetarity', we are not conflating Heise's 'sense of planet' with Gayatri Chakravorty Spivak's idea of planetarity which was first presented by her in

'Imperatives to Re-imagine the Planet' at Stiftung-Dialogik in Zurich in 1997. Spivak's 'planetarity', stands in contrast to the homogenizing dynamics of globalization, and her 'planet-thought', is a means to embrace various forms of 'alterity' that happens through othering. It is possible to weave certain conceptual connections between Spivak's planetarity and the way we use the concept, but this lies beyond the scope of the current work. See Gayatri Chakravorty Spivak, 'Planetarity'(Box 4, WELT). *Paragraph*, *38*(2), Edinburgh University Press, https://doi.org/10.3366/para.2015.01; Gayatri Chakravorty Spivak, *An Aesthetic Education in the Era of Globalization* (Cambridge, MA, and London: Harvard University Press, 2012), 335–50, https://doi.org/10.2307/j.ctv1n1bsfh

8 In a later chapter, we draw on the work of Russian formalists to elucidate the meaning of literariness, a concept they used to capture the artistic (aesthetic) or poetic quality of a work. While Russian formalists thereon argued that art (literary work) stands separate from life, we will see how, in practice, a work of climate fiction can demonstrate literariness while not eschewing an engagement with life and politics. 'Formalists called "literariness" – the qualities that make a work artistic', see Carol Any, 'Russian Literary Formalism', *Routledge Encyclopedia of Philosophy*, Taylor and Francis (1998), doi: 10.4324/9780415249126-E060-1.

9 See Ursula K. Heise, *Sense of Place and Sense of Planet: The Environmental Imagination of the Global* (United Kingdom: Oxford University Press, 2008).

## Chapter 2

1 Siying Chen et al., 'Climate Records in Ancient Chinese Diaries and Their Application in Historical Climate Reconstruction – a Case Study of Yunshan Diary'. *Climate of the Past, 16*(5) (2020): 1873–87, https://doi.org/10.5194/cp-16-1873-2020

2 Ibid. These quotes and descriptions of Bi Guo's journey are from the excellent analysis of the Yunshan diary by Siying Chen et al. Parts of the Yunshan diary with many references to weather are available here:

Guo Bi, 'Yunshan Diary', 13th–14th century CE, https://ctext.org/wiki.pl?if=gb&res=908804&remap=gb

3 Ibid.

4 James Kai-sing Kung and Chicheng Ma, 'Can Cultural Norms Reduce Conflicts? Confucianism and Peasant Rebellions in Qing China'. *Journal of Development Economics, 111* (2014): 132–49, https://doi.org/10.1016/j.jdeveco.2014.08.006

5 Ka-wai Fan, 'The Little Ice Age and the Fall of the Ming Dynasty: A Review'. *Climate, 11*(3) (2023): 5, https://doi.org/10.3390/cli11030071

6 See Alfred W. Crosby, *Ecological Imperialism: The Biological Expansion of Europe, 900–1900* (United Kingdom: Cambridge University Press, 2015) and *The Columbian Exchange* (United Kingdom: Greenwood Publishing, 1972).

7 See Val Plumwood, *Environmental Culture: The Ecological Crisis of Reason* (United Kingdom: Taylor & Francis, 2002), 3–5.

8 'Andrew Marvell's To His Coy Mistress: Love in the Little Ice Age' Produced by Rising Tide of Humber team, University of Hull, 2023, https://risingtide.hull.ac.uk/wp-content/uploads/2023/06/Andrew-Marvell%E2%80%B2s-To-his-Coy-Mistress_-Love-in-the-Little-Ice-Age_Final-version.pdf. Also see, Stewart Mottram, 'Deluge and Disease: Plague, the Poetry of Flooding, and the History of Health Inequalities in Andrew Marvell's Hull'. *The Seventeenth Century, 38*(2) (5 December 2022): 263–90, https://doi.org/10.1080/0268117x.2022.2142656

9 Historian Geoffrey Parker quoted in Amitav Ghosh, *The Great Derangement: Climate Change and the Unthinkable* (India: Penguin, 2016), 91.

10 Julia Pongratz et al., 'Coupled Climate–Carbon Simulations Indicate Minor Global Effects of Wars and Epidemics on Atmospheric CO2 between AD 800 and 1850'. *The Holocene, 21*(5) (2011): 843–51, https://doi.org/10.1177/0959683610386981

11 Chen Qide was a school teacher whose essays provide valuable insights into the disaster that befell Ming China. See Timothy Brook, *The Price of Collapse: The Little Ice Age and the Fall of Ming China* (Princeton, NJ: Princeton University Press, 2023), 137.

12 Philipp Blom, *Nature's Mutiny: How the Little Ice Age of the Long Seventeenth Century Transformed the West and Shaped the Present* (United Kingdom: Pan Macmillan, 2019).

13 Peter M. J. Douglas et al., 'Drought, Agricultural Adaptation, and Sociopolitical Collapse in the Maya Lowlands'. *Proceedings of the National Academy of Sciences, 112*(18) (20 April 2015): 5607–12, https://doi.org/10.1073/pnas.1419133112

14 Ulf Büntgen et al., 'Cooling and Societal Change during the Late Antique Little Ice Age from 536 to Around 660 AD', *Nature Geoscience, 9*(3) (8 February 2016): 231–36, https://doi.org/10.1038/ngeo2652

15 Andrey Korotayev, 'Sixth Century Global Climatic Disaster, the Origins of Islam, and Its World-System Consequences'. *Journal of World-Systems Research, 31*(1) (17 April 2025): 8–18, https://doi.org/10.5195/jwsr.2025.1325

16 Qiang Chen, 'Climate Shocks, Dynastic Cycles and Nomadic Conquests: Evidence from Historical China'. *Oxford Economic Papers, 67*(2) (2014): 185–204, https://doi.org/10.1093/oep/gpu032

17 The Intergovernmental Panel on Climate Change which deals with the science of climate change and publishes the authoritative Assessment Reports.

18 The main decision-making body of the United Nations Framework Convention on Climate Change (UNFCCC).

19 'WMO Confirms 2024 as Warmest Year on Record at about 1.55 °C above Pre-industrial Level', *World Meteorological Organization*, 10 January 2025, https://wmo.int/news/media-centre/wmo-confirms-2024-warmest-year-record-about-155degc-above-pre-industrial-level

20 'Global Surface Temperature', NASA Global Climate Change, Climate Change: Vital Signs of the Planet, n.d., accessed 28 June 2025, https://climate.nasa.gov/vital-signs/global-temperature/?intent=121

21 'Scientific Consensus', NASA Science, accessed 6 July 2025, science.nasa.gov/climate-change/scientific-consensus.

22 Ibid.

23 'WGII Summary for Policymakers Headline Statements', IPCC, 28 February 2022, www.ipcc.ch/report/ar6/wg2/resources/spm-headline-statements

24 'Paris Agreement', United Nations, 2015, https://unfccc.int/sites/default/files/english_paris_agreement.pdf

25 Mark Poynting, 'World's First Year-long Breach of Key 1.5C Warming Limit', 8 February 2024, www.bbc.com/news/science-environment-68110310

26 See Sadie J. Ryan et al., 'Global Expansion and Redistribution of Aedes-borne Virus Transmission Risk with Climate Change', *PLOS*, 28 March 2019, https://journals.plos.org/plosntds/article?id=10.1371/journal.pntd.0007213

27 William J. Ripple et al., 'Many Risky Feedback Loops Amplify the Need for Climate Action'. *One Earth*, *6*(2) (2023): 86–91, https://doi.org/10.1016/j.oneear.2023.01.004

28 Somnath Baidya Roy and Justin J. Traiteur, 'Impacts of Wind Farms on Surface Air Temperatures'. *Proceedings of the National Academy of Sciences*, *107*(42) (October 2010): 17899–904, https://doi.org/10.1073/pnas.1000493107

29 A coinage attributed to journalist and teacher Dan Bloom.

30 See Ghosh, *The Great Derangement*, 78–82.

31 A term attributed to Jim Clarke. See Axel Goodbody and Adeline Johns-Putra, 'The Rise of the Climate Change Novel', in *Climate and Literature*, ed. Adeline Johns-Putra (Cambridge: Cambridge University Press eBooks, 2019), 231, https://doi.org/10.1017/9781108505321.015

32 Jeffrey Barber, 'Imagining Sustainable Futures in Popular Culture: Moving Beyond Dystopia and Techno-Fantasy Narratives'. Paper presented at IAMCR, Oregon, (2018): 16.

33 Stef Craps and Rick Crownshaw, 'Introduction: The Rising Tide of Climate Change Fiction'. *Studies in the Novel*, *50*(1) (2018): 4, 6, https://doi.org/10.1353/sdn.2018.0000

34 Adam Trexler, *Anthropocene Fictions: The Novel in a Time of Climate Change* (Charlottesville and London: University of Virginia Press, 2015), 14–15.

35 Sophia David, *Eco-Fiction: Bringing Climate Change into the Imagination* (United Kingdom: University of Exeter, 2016), 27, https://ore.exeter.ac.uk/repository/handle/10871/24331

36 Gregers Andersen, *Climate Fiction and Cultural Analysis: A New Perspective on Life in the Anthropocene* (United Kingdom: Routledge, Taylor & Francis Group, 2021), 10.

37 Ibid., 1–3.

38 Stephanie LeMenager, '12. Climate Change and the Struggle for Genre', in *Anthropocene Reading: Literary History in Geologic Times*, ed. Tobias Menely and Jesse Oak Taylor (University Park, USA: Penn State University Press, 2017), 222, https://doi.org/10.1515/9780271080390-013

39 Ibid.

40 Ibid.

41 Nick Admussen, 'Six Proposals for the Reform of Literature in the Age of Climate Change'. *The Critical Flame* (42) (May–June 2016), accessed 6 September 2019, criticalflame.org/six-proposals-for-the-reform-of-literature-in-the-age-of-climate-change/

42 See Hu Shi, '9. Some Modest Proposals for the Reform of Literature', in *Modern Chinese Literary Thought: Writings on Literature, 1893–1945*, ed. Kirk A. Denton (Redwood City, CA: Stanford University Press, 1996), 123–39, https://doi.org/10.1515/9781503615830-013

43 Admussen, 'Six Proposals'.

44 Ibid.

45 Rob Nixon, *Slow Violence and the Environmentalism of the Poor* (Cambridge, MA: Harvard University Press, 2013).

46 Admussen, 'Six Proposals'.

47 Here, Andersen, acknowledging a lack of availability of climate fiction from the global South, expresses his inability to attempt a cultural comparison between Northern and Southern cli-fi. See Andersen, *Climate Fiction and Cultural Analysis*, 5.

48 Axel Goodbody and Adeline Johns-Putra, *Cli-Fi: A Companion* (Oxford, United Kingdom: Peter Lang Verlag, 2019), 2.

49 Trexler, *Anthropocene Fictions*, 35.

50 Schneider-Mayerson et al., 'The Climate Reality Check – A Bechdel Wallace Test for a World on Fire', *Good Energy and Buck Lab for Climate and Environment Colby College* (2024): 2, https://www.colby.edu/wp-content/uploads/2024/06/The-Climate-Reality-Check-A-Bechdel-Wallace-Test-for-a-World-on-Fire-1.pdf

51 August 2025.

52 Andersen, *Climate Fiction and Cultural Analysis.*

53 For the rise of the Linnaean system and the role of the powerful Spanish empire in imposing it on scientific institutions, see Antonio

Lafuente and Nuria Valverde, 'Linnaean Botany and Spanish Imperial Biopolitics', in *Colonial Botany: Science, Commerce, and Politics in the Early Modern World*, ed. Londa Schiebinger and Claudia Swan (United States: University of Pennsylvania Press, Incorporated, 2007), 134–47.

54 Matthew Schneider-Mayerson, 'The Influence of Climate Fiction: An Empirical Survey of Readers'. *Environmental Humanities, 10*(2) (November 2018): 481, https://doi.org/10.1215/22011919-7156848

55 Trexler, *Anthropocene Fictions*, 14.

56 Richard Kerridge, 'Ecocritical Approaches to Literary Form and Genre: Urgency, Depth, Provisionality, Temporality', in *The Oxford Handbook of Ecocriticism*, ed. Greg Garrard (Oxford: Oxford University Press, 2013), 369–70.

57 Andersen, *Climate Fiction and Cultural Analysis, 31–63, 131–8.*

58 Jean-Paul Sartre, *The Imaginary* (United Kingdom: Routledge, 2004).

59 Cornelius Castoriadis, *The Imaginary Institution of Society* (Cambridge, MA: MIT Press, 1987).

60 Gregers Andersen defines imaginaries as 'a set of dominant narrative templates that underlie the imagination of anthropogenic global warming'. See Andersen, *Climate Fiction and Cultural Analysis,* 3.

61 Ibid. Also this essay by Gregers Andersen, 'Cli-fi: A Short Essay on its Worlds and Its Importance', Dragonfly.eco, 2014, accessed 1 July 2025, https://dragonfly.eco/cli-fi-short-essay-worlds-importance/

62 Ibid.

63 Robert Costanza, 'Four Visions of the Century Ahead: Will It Be *Star Trek, Ecotopia, Big Government* or *Mad Max*?' *Futurist,* 33(2) (1999): 23–8.

64 Zeke Hausfather, 'Explainer: How "Shared Socioeconomic Pathways" Explore Future Climate Change', *Carbon Brief*, 2018, accessed 29 June 2025, https://www.carbonbrief.org/explainer-how-shared-socioeconomic-pathways-explore-future-climate-change/

65 This study is a case in point. See Alexandra Nikoleris, Johannes Stripple and Paul Tenngart, 'Narrating Climate Futures: Shared Socioeconomic Pathways and Literary Fiction'. *Climatic Change, 143*(3–4) (8 July 2017): 307–19, https://doi.org/10.1007/s10584-017-2020-2

66 Working with an international team of authors, scientists and game designers, we had written stories for a branching-narrative video

game which used a model similar to the SSPs framework to predict and creatively imagine the various futures that are possible, depending on a variety of choices that humanity makes. This video game, now also published as a book and teaching aid, presents various kinds of alternative cli-fi narratives that visualize possible climate and socio-economic scenarios and choices that humanity makes. See *Survive the Century* (Sam Beckbessinger, Christopher Trisos and Simon Nicholson, Three Kids in a Trenchcoat, 2021) Internet game, Fiction contributors: Lauren Beukes, Maria Turtschaninoff, Rajat Chaudhuri and Sophia Al-Maria, https://survivethecentury.net

67 Matthew Schneider-Mayerson, 'Climate Change Fiction', in *American Literature in Transition, 2000–2010*, ed. Rachel Greenwald Smith (Cambridge: Cambridge University Press, 2017), 309–21.

68 Abel Gustafson et al., 'Personal Stories Can Shift Climate Change Beliefs and Risk Perceptions: The Mediating Role of Emotion'. *Communication Reports*, *33*(3) (2020): 121–35, https://doi.org/10.1080/08934215.2020.1799049

69 Caren Irr, 'Climate Fiction in English', *Oxford Research Encyclopedia of Literature,* 27 February 2017, accessed 29 June 2025, https://oxfordre.com/literature/view/10.1093/acrefore/9780190201098.001.0001/acrefore-9780190201098-e-4

70 Used in the context of climate fiction, catachronism refers to a reconfiguration of the past and the present in terms of an unrealized future. See, Srinivas Aravamudan, 'The Catachronism of Climate Change'. *Diacritics, 41*(3) (2013): 6–30, https://dx.doi.org/10.1353/dia.2013.0019

71 Trexler, *Anthropocene Fictions,* 34.

72 Ibid., 236.

73 Darko Suvin describes science fiction as 'the literature of cognitive estrangement'. See Darko Suvin, 'On the Poetics of the Science Fiction Genre', in *Science Fiction Criticism*, ed. Rob Latham (UK: Bloomsbury Academic eBooks, 2017), 116–27, https://doi.org/10.5040/9781474248655.0018

74 For a detailed discussion of 'novums' as found in sci-fi including climate fiction (from India), see Sami Ahmad Khan, *Star Warriors of the Modern Raj – Materiality, Mythology and Technology of Indian Science Fiction* (UK: University of Wales Press, 2021).

75 Robinson says, 'People sometimes think that science fiction is about predicting the future, but that isn't true. Since predicting the future is impossible, that would be a high bar for science fiction to have to get over. It would always be failing. And in that sense it always is failing. But science fiction is more of a modeling exercise, or a way of thinking. Another thing I've been saying for a long time is something slightly different: "We're in a science fiction novel now, which we are all cowriting together."' See Kim Stanley Robinson, 'The Realism of Our Times: Kim Stanley Robinson on How Science Fiction Works' Interview by John Plotz, Public Books, 23 September 2020, https://www.publicbooks.org/the-realism-of-our-times-kim-stanley-robinson-on-how-science-fiction-works/

76 Mark McGurl, 'The Posthuman Comedy', *Critical Inquiry, 38*(3) (March 2012): 533–53, https://doi.org/10.1086/664550

77 Craps and Crownshaw, 'Introduction: The Rising Tide of Climate Change Fiction', 2–3.

78 Irr, 'Climate Fiction in English'.

79 Schneider-Mayerson, 'The Influence', 474, 481.

80 A word with religious signification which, following The Book of Revelation, denotes the end times, which is a period of suffering followed by the victory of good over evil.

81 Michael Svoboda, 'Ice-fi: The Legacy of *Day after Tomorrow*', *Yale Climate Connections*, 22 May 2024, yaleclimateconnections.org/2014/10/ice-fi-the-motion-pictur-ice-sque-legacy-of-the-day-after-tomorrow.

82 See Denise Baden, 'Solution-Focused Stories Are More Effective Than Catastrophic Stories in Motivating Proenvironmental Intentions'. *Ecopsychology, 11*(4) (13 September 2019): 254–63, https://doi.org/10.1089/eco.2019.0023

83 For example, see Kathryn Stevenson and Nils Peterson, 'Motivating Action through Fostering Climate Change Hope and Concern and Avoiding Despair among Adolescents'. *Sustainability, 8*(1) (2016): 6, 1, https://doi.org/10.3390/su8010006

84 Jem Bendell and Institute of Leadership and Sustainability (IFLAS), 'Deep Adaptation: A Map for Navigating Climate Tragedy'. Report, *IFLAS Occasional Paper 2* (27 July 2018): 13, https://mahb.stanford.edu/wp-content/uploads/2018/08/deepadaptation.pdf

85 Schneider-Mayerson, 'The Influence', 476, 483.

86 David, *Eco-Fiction*, 33.

87 Barnita Bagchi, 'Must There Be an Apocalypse? An Analysis of South Asian Speculative Fiction', *Frame Journal of Literary Studies*, 26 June 2015, http://www.tijdschriftframe.nl/wp-content/uploads/2015/06/Frame-26_1-Barnita-Bagchi.pdf

88 Amitav Ghosh, 'Amitav Ghosh on *Gun Island* and How to Make Sense of the World'. Interview by Karthik Shankar, Huffington Post Online, 22 June 2019, accessed 19 August 2019, www.huffingtonpost.in/entry/amitav-ghosh-gun-island-and-how-to-make-sense-of-the-world_in_5d0cdb4fe4b07ae90d9bec1c

89 My friend, the Italian solarpunk author and publisher Francesco Verso has been critical of the term 'hope'. He argues it is a 'heteronomous force', depending on external conditions. See Rajat Chaudhuri, 'Solarpunk: A Brilliant Subculture, Its Solutions and Visions', The Telegraph, 27 November 2022, https://www.telegraphindia.com/science-tech/solarpunk-a-brilliant-subculture-its-solutions-and-visions/cid/1900585

90 Irr, 'Climate Fiction in English'.

91 For example, see Baden, 'Solution-Focused Stories', 254–63.

92 Mustapha Mond and the savage John represent opposing philosophies and ideas of utopia. See Aldous Huxley, *Brave New World* (Garden City, NY: Doubleday, Doran, Incorporated, 1932).

93 Staying with the trouble, an idea of multispecies feminist theorist Donna Haraway, acknowledging the messy realities of the present, calls for building alliances across different beings and people while avoiding simple binaries and clear-cut solutions to complex problems like climate change. See Donna Haraway, *Staying with the Trouble: Making Kin in the Chthulucene* (Durham, NC: Duke University Press, 2016).

94 Fredric Jameson, *Archaeologies of the Future: The Desire Called Utopia and Other Science Fictions* (London: Verso Publication, 2007), xv.

95 Books, not necessarily cli-fi, that immediately come to mind include Aldous Huxley's *Island* and Ernest Callenbach's *Ecotopia*.

96 For a detailed discussion of critical dystopias, see Raffaella Baccolini, 'Ursula K. LeGuin's Critical Dystopia', in *Critical Insights: Dystopia*, ed. M. Keith Booker (Ipswich, MA: Salem Press, 2013), 37–53. Also

Raffaella Baccolini and Tom Moylan, eds, *Dark Horizons: Science Fiction and the Dystopian Imagination* (New York: Routledge, 2003). Also see Bagchi, 'Must There Be an Apocalypse?'

97 Barber also includes a third category of transformative books. See Jeffrey Barber, 'The Challenge of Imagining Sustainable Futures: Climate Fiction in Sustainability Communication', in *The Sustainability Communication Reader*, ed. Franzisca Weder, Larissa Krainer and Matthias Karmasin (Wiesbaden: Springer VS, 2021), 149–53, https://doi.org/10.1007/978-3-658-31883-3_9

98 Schneider-Mayerson, 'Climate Change Fiction', 309–21.

99 Irr, 'Climate Fiction in English'.

100 Bioderegulation refers to the impact of the global neoliberal order, and its allied imperative to work and consume more, on human bodies, minds and ecologies as free time diminishes continuously. It implies deregulation of bodies and environments because of the imperatives of the market. The term was coined by Australian feminist philosopher and psychoanalyst Teresa Brennan. Also see David Graber's critic of meaningless jobs and how they cause harm in David Graeber, *Bullshit Jobs: A Theory* (United Kingdom: Penguin Books, 2018).

101 LeMenager, 'Climate Change and the Struggle for Genre', 220–38.

102 Kyle P. Whyte, 'Indigenous Science (Fiction) for the Anthropocene: Ancestral Dystopias and Fantasies of Climate Change Crises'. *Environment and Planning E Nature and Space, 1*(1–2) (March 2018): 224–42. https://doi.org/10.1177/2514848618777621.

103 Ibid.

104 Malwika, 'Ecological Concerns in the Works of Hansda Sowvendra Shekhar: An Ecocritical Study'. *Creative Flight, 3*(2) (October 2022): 137–46, accessed 30 June 2025, https://www.creativeflight.in/ecological-concerns-in-works-of-hansdahttps://drive.google.com/file/d/1nF_j79dCsfvkhiVrb_TRE9DJqfTCiCxN/view

## Chapter 3

1 Despite this tension, the political and the aesthetic can be entangled in a work, for example, when a particular form represents political

turmoil and social divisions in the story. The French philosopher Jacques Rancière has argued that while art has no politics, aesthetics does have a politics. However, the politics and its effects may not be foreseen by the artist or the writer. See Jacques Rancière, *The Politics of Aesthetics* (United Kingdom: Bloomsbury Publishing, 2013).

2 Théophile Gautier, *Mademoiselle de Maupin*, Volume 1 (of 2), trans. I. G. Burham (1835; Philadelphia, PA: George Barrie and Sons, 1897) eBook#48893, htm. https://www.gutenberg.org/files/48893/48893-h/48893-h.htm

3 Terry Eagleton, *Literary Theory – An Introduction* (UK: Blackwell Publishing, 1996), 18.

4 Especially in the works of Immanuel Kant, Friedrich Schiller and Hegel.

5 Edmund Burke distinguished between the beautiful, embodied in the object, and the powerful sublime, connecting the later to a feeling of awe and thereby stressing on subjective experience and response. See Edmund Burke, *A Philosophical Enquiry into the Origin of Our Ideas of the Sublime and Beautiful* (United Kingdom: J. Dodsley, 1767).

6 The expression 'serious literature' or 'serious fiction' follows the sense in which it is used by Ghosh in *The Great Derangement* (32). The characterization has divided critics and its meaning has often conflated 'mainstream', 'highbrow', 'critical acclaim', 'literariness' and so on. For our purpose, we assume reviews in distinguished literary journals, the literariness (aesthetic quality) of the text among the markers for 'seriousness'. In framing his arguments, Ghosh often focuses on the 'modern realist novel' as a baseline lacking in certain features necessary for representing climate change. This modern realist novel arguably has some similarities with 'literary fiction' in the importance granted to character, slower pacing and emotional depth, among other features. For example, Gustave Flaubert's *Madame Bovary* (1856), which Ghosh mentions, or Balzac's *Père Goriot* (1835) can be counted in either category. See Ghosh, *The Great Derangement*, 22–4, 30–2. Also see the discussion on 'literariness' in a later chapter. Joyce G. Saricks and his category of 'intellect genres' is worth exploring. See Joyce G. Saricks, *The Readers' Advisory Guide to Genre Fiction* (Chicago, IL: American Library Association, 2009), 177–96. Cf. James Bradley, 'The Best Climate

Change Novels', Five Books, accessed 1 July 2025, https://fivebooks.com/best-books/climate-change-novels/

7 Translated as 'literature of commitment', it was also a critique of the art-for-art's sake movement. *La littérature engagée* was a post-war French existentialist position, with Sartre at its centre, where the author's social responsibility, as evinced through his work, is of utmost importance. Climate fiction writers, it can be argued, practise a literature of commitment. Contrast this with *littérature de l'engagement* or literature of engagement which suggests broader thematic engagement with socio-political issues seen in various genres.

8 David, *Eco-Fiction*, 44–6.

9 In this context, also see Rancière's arguments. Rancière, *The Politics of Aesthetics, 12–20.*

10 Following from Matthew Arnold and the British critic F. R. Leavis. The Leavisite tradition has drawn the charge of cultural elitism. For example, see F. R. Leavis, *The Great Tradition: George Eliot, Henry James, Joseph Conrad* (New York: George W. Stewart, 1950).

11 Kerridge, 'Ecocritical Approaches', 371.

12 Kerridge articulates the idea of 'care' to bridge the gap between our knowledge of planetary crises and the apparent absence of action on our part, a phenomena he explains with the psychological concept of 'splitting'. 'If the fundamental aim of literary ecocriticism is that environmental care should become stronger and more pervasive throughout literary culture, ecocritics will not be looking for a single form of literature that meets all the criteria at once.' Care in his formulation, 'preserves the range of possibilities, from incremental and gradually spreading change to abrupt social revolution. The word encompasses feeling ("care about") and action ("take care of"). It can be interpreted in a way that gives us both active, vigilant policy and the range of phenomena indicated by the word "affect," including personal emotion, bodily reaction and collective, communicated mood.' See Kerridge, 'Ecocritical Approaches', 369–70.

13 Axel Goodbody, 'Cli-Fi beyond the American Thriller: Cultural and Aesthetic Alternatives in Climate Change Fiction since 2010', in *Nuevos horizontes de la literatura comparada*, Vol. 2, *Ecocrítica*, ed. Bruno Echauri Galván and Julia Ori (Sociedad Española de Literatura General y Comparada (SELGYC), 2021), 22, accessed 30 June 2025, https://www.selgyc.com/mat/ecocritica_01_goodbody.pdf

14 Barbara Kingsolver, *Flight Behavior* (United Kingdom: HarperCollins, 2012).

15 Johan Rockström et al., 'A Safe Operating Space for Humanity'. *Nature, 461*(7263) (1 September 2009): 472–75, https://doi.org/10.1038/461472a

16 Konstantin Ash and Nick Obradovich, 'Climatic Stress, Internal Migration, and Syrian Civil War Onset'. *Journal of Conflict Resolution, 64*(1) (25 July 2019): 3–31, https://doi.org/10.1177/0022002719864140

17 Heise, *Sense of Place and Sense of Planet.*

18 For the landslide event in 2010 in the Monarch Butterfly Biosphere Reserve, Angangueo, see Irasema Alcántara-Ayala, José López-García and Ricardo J. Garnica, 'On The Landslide Event in 2010 in the Monarch Butterfly Biosphere Reserve, Angangueo, Michoacán, Mexico'. *Landslides, 9*(2) (26 August 2011): 263–73, https://doi.org/10.1007/s10346-011-0291-7

19 Hyperobjects like climate change, black hole or the Amazon rainforest are 'massively distributed in time and space relative to humans'. See Ian Buchanan, *A Dictionary of Critical Theory* (Oxford: Oxford University Press, 2018), https://www.oxfordreference.com/display/10.1093/acref/9780198794790.001.0001/acref-9780198794790-e-771. The expression was coined by Timothy Morton. Morton has theorized hyperobjects in his book: Timothy Morton, *Hyperobjects: Philosophy and Ecology after the End of the World* (Minneapolis: University of Minnesota Press, 2013).

20 Francis of Assisi, 'The Canticle of the Creatures' (1225), in *Francis of Assisi: Early Documents. Volume I: The Saint*, ed. Regis J. Armstrong, O.F.M. Cap., J. A. Wayne Hellman, O.F.M. Conv. and William J. Short, O.F.M. (New York: New City Press, 1999), 113.

21 Science fiction, unlike the modern realist novel, affords this advantage of using time leaps. See the section on Ockham's razor later in this book.

22 This is not a shopping list, but the story I was writing and the depiction of climate and environmental disaster therein called for attention to these creative-thematic features. See Figure 2.2.

23 Ibid.

24 Franco Moretti, *The Bourgeois: Between History and Literature* (United Kingdom: Verso, 2013), 15–16.
25 C. P. Snow, 'The Two Cultures', *New Statesman*, 27 September 2015, www.newstatesman.com/culture/2013/01/c-p-snow-two-cultures
26 Donna J. Haraway, *The Companion Species Manifesto* (United States: Prickly Paradigm Press, 2003).
27 See Bruno Latour, *We Have Never Been Modern*, trans. Catherine Porter (Cambridge, MA: Harvard University Press, 1993).
28 Dipesh Chakrabarty, 'The Climate of History: Four Theses'. *Critical Inquiry, 35*(2) (Winter 2009): 201, https://doi.org/10.1086/596640
29 Ghosh, *The Great Derangement*, 95–7.
30 For examples, see Jeremy Rosen, 'Literary Fiction and the Genres of Genre Fiction', *Post45 – American Literature and Culture since 1945*, 16 July 2019, https://post45.org/2018/08/literary-fiction-and-the-genres-of-genre-fiction/
31 For a detailed discussion with examples of works that bring together fields of science (nature) and the human (culture), see Ghosh, *The Great Derangement*, 92–8.
32 Timothy Clark, 'Scale: Derangements of Scale', in *Telemorphosis: Theory in the Era of Climate Change*, Vol. 1, ed. Tom Cohen (Ann Arbor, MI: Open Humanities Press eBooks, 2012), 9–15, http://dx.doi.org/10.3998/ohp.10539563.0001.001
33 See Rajat Chaudhuri, 'How Did the Oceans Vanish', in *Wonder Tales for a Warming Planet* (Delhi: Niyogi, 2025), 85–104.
34 Actants occur in the narrative theory of A. J. Greimas. An actant performs a certain fictional role and they occur in pairs like Subject/Object, Helper/Opponent, Sender/Receiver among others. The actants can also exchange positions; for example, the object can become the subject. See Algirdas Julien Greimas, *Structural Semantic: An Attempt at a Method*, trans. Daniele McDowell, Ronald Schleifer and Alan R. Velie (Lincoln: University of Nebraska Press, 1983).
35 Michel de Montaigne, *The Essays of Montaigne,* ed. William Carew Hazlitt, trans. Charles Cotton (1877), ebook #3600, html, 28 May 2001, https://gutenberg.org/files/3600/3600-h/3600-h.htm#link2HCH0001

36 'How the Trees Stopped Talking', The Earth Stories Collection, accessed 30 June 2025, theearthstoriescollection.org/en/how-the-trees-stopped-talking.

37 Philippe Descola, *Beyond Nature and Culture* (Chicago, IL: University of Chicago Press, 2013), 72.

38 Parts of this discussion on nature-culture and non-human agency are developed from a keynote address delivered on 21 September 2023 at the Centre for Post Humanities, Bankura University, India. The interactions with Dr Subhadeep Paul, who is the joint Chair of the Centre and research scholars who attended, allowed me to further refine my thoughts about nature-culture and non-human agency which I have presented here.

39 See Bruno Latour, *Reassembling the Social: An Introduction to Actor–Network Theory* (Oxford, UK: Oxford University Press, 2005) and his *Science in Action: How to Follow Scientists and Engineers through Society* (Cambridge, MA: Harvard University Press, 1987).

40 The élan vital (vital impulse) persists across living beings and animates the process of 'creative evolution'. See Henri Bergson, *Creative Evolution* (United States, University Press of America, 1984).

41 See Alfred North Whitehead, *Process and Reality* (United Kingdom: Free Press, 2010).

42 Nicolas Bencherki, 'Actor–Network Theory', in *The International Encyclopedia of Organizational Communication* (Malden, MA, and Oxford: Wiley eBooks, 2016), https://doi.org/10.1002/9781118955567.wbieoc002

43 A concept we owe to Bruno Latour, a hybrid is something difficult to categorize as it entails a mixing up of subject and object or the social world and the natural. See Latour, *We Have Never Been Modern*, 1–12.

44 Rajat Chaudhuri, 'Rethinking Literature: The Wicked Problem of Climate Change and Our Entanglement with It', *Scroll.in*, 23 April 2023, https://scroll.in/article/1047822/rethinking-literature-the-wicked-problem-of-climate-change-and-our-entanglement-with-it

45 Gregers Andersen, 'Cli-Fi and the Uncanny'. *ISLE Interdisciplinary Studies in Literature and Environment*, *23*(4) (2016): 855–66, https://doi.org/10.1093/isle/isw068

46 Sigmund Freud, *The Uncanny*, trans. David MacLintock (1919; London: Penguin, 2003).

47 Ibid., 148.

48 Latour, *We Have Never Been Modern*, 51–5. Also see Bruno Latour, *Facing Gaia: Eight Lectures on the New Climatic Regime*, trans. Catherine Porter (Cambridge: Polity Press, 2017), 62.

49 Ibid., 144. Here Latour mentions the ozone hole, the Monsanto chemical industry among such quasi-objects.

50 Ibid., 55.

51 Andersen, 'Cli-Fi and the Uncanny', quoting Hermann Schmitz the founder of neo-phenomenology, 859.

52 Ghosh, *The Great Derangement*, 42–3.

53 Throughout this book, by 'uncanny', unless the context suggests otherwise, we will mean the climate uncanny or environmental uncanny as a creative-thematic feature of cli-fi. This can be either Freudian or Heideggerian or both.

54 There is a rich tradition exploring linkages between mind and ecology. In this context, Félix Guattari's work, which establishes connections between psychology, ecology and the social spheres, is worth examining. Félix Guattari, *The Three Ecologies* (United Kingdom: Athlone Press, 2000).

55 Literally meaning the earth, the name comes from a primordial earth goddess of Greek mythology. The Gaia hypothesis suggests a self-regulating and interconnected planet. The hypothesis was formulated by the British scientist and environmentalist James Lovelock and the name was suggested to him by novelist William Golding, who was well versed in the classics.

56 Liz Jensen, *The Rapture* (United States: Doubleday, 2009).

57 Kerridge, 'Ecocritical Approaches', 368.

58 David, *Eco-Fiction*, 68. Also see, Andrew Key for the possibility of an avant-garde imaginary in the face of disaster which focuses on the 'everyday' and reconfigures it, allowing for slowing down, contemplation, care and reflections on the past. 'Writing, Aesthetics, Climate (a Bricolage)', *New Socialist*, 16 October 2021, accessed 20 November 2019, www.newsocialist.org.uk/approaching-avant-garde-eco-socialist-political-imaginary-writing-aesthetics-climate-bricolage. For the argument about how the avant-garde in literature allowed the

partitioning project to continue consigning our kinship with the non-human to oblivion, see Ghosh, *The Great Derangement*, 93–4, 106–8.

59 Ghosh, *The Great Derangement*, 108–13.

60 Paul Vincent Spade and Claude Panaccio, 'William of Ockham', *The Stanford Encyclopedia of Philosophy*, ed. Edward N. Zalta (Stanford University: Spring 2019 Edition), https://plato.stanford.edu/archives/spr2019/entries/ockham/

61 Heise, *Sense of Place and Sense of Planet* (61). Also see the explanation of 'eco-cosmopolitanism' in the fifth chapter of this book.

62 Anthony Burke, 'Interspecies Cosmopolitanism: Non-Human Power and the Grounds of World Order in the Anthropocene'. *Review of International Studies, 49*(2) (2023): 201–22, doi:10.1017/S0260210522000171

63 Heise's main focus is to 'establish conceptual connections between environmentalism and ecocriticism, on one hand, and theories of globalization, transnationalism, and cosmopolitanism, on the other. It proposes the concept of "eco-cosmopolitanism" as a shorthand for envisioning these connections and the cultural and aesthetic forms into which they translate. Part II [of her book] focuses on conceptualizations of environmental danger and connects environmentalist and ecocritical thought with the interdisciplinary field of risk theory in the social sciences, arguing that environmental justice theory and ecocriticism stand to benefit from closer consideration of the theories of cosmopolitanism that have arisen in this field from the analysis of transnational communities at risk.' See Ursula K. Heise, 'Abstract', in *Sense of Place and Sense of Planet* (New York: Oxford University Press eBooks, 2008), https://doi.org/10.1093/acprof:oso/9780195335637.001.0001; https://www.researchgate.net/publication/289471709_Sense_of_Place_and_Sense_of_Planet_The_Environmental_Imagination_of_the_Global

64 Admussen, 'Six Proposals'.

65 Ursula K. Heise, 'Science Fiction and the Time Scales of the Anthropocene'. *ELH, Project MUSE, 86*(2) (2019): 275–304, https://dx.doi.org/10.1353/elh.2019.0015

66 Alongside Heise's specific 'sense of planet' and 'eco-cosmopolitanism', it is possible to think of the 'planetary' to encompass geological time and space besides ecologies and the interconnected networks of human and nonhuman. However, in this book, we use more granular analysis.

67 In this simplified triangulation method, the political approach which is captured through climate justice will go alongside postcolonial ecocritical readings and signals from the elements listed under transformative potential (Figure 2.2) of cli-fi. Part Two of this book provides a more intensive and granular reading of the text using both major and minor lenses but it provides fair indication of the simplified method developed here.

## Chapter 4

1 This has a rather long title. See Harriet Beecher Stowe, *A Reply to 'the Affectionate and Christian Address of Many Thousands of Women of Great Britain and Ireland, to Their Sisters, the Women of the United States of America', on Behalf of Many Thousands of American Women* (London: Sampson Low, Son, 1863), ebook#70613, txt, 21 April 2023, https://www.gutenberg.org/cache/epub/70613/pg70613.txt
2 Noel Bertram Gerson, *Harriet Beecher Stowe: A Biography* (United States: Praeger Publishers, 1976), 64–165.
3 Charles Edward Stowe, *The Life of Harriet Beecher Stowe Compiled from Her Letters and Journals by Her Son Charles Edward Stowe* (Boston, MA, and New York: Houghton, Mifflin, 1890), 371, ebook#6702, txt, 1 October 2004, https://www.gutenberg.org/ebooks/6702
4 For more examples covering the environment and larger political contexts, see Maddie Stone, 'Can Climate Fiction Deliver Climate Justice?' *Fix*, 16 August 2022, https://grist.org/fix/climate-fiction/can-climate-fiction-deliver-climate-justice/
5 Nikoleris et al., 'Narrating Climate Futures', 307–19.
6 Jeffrey Barber et al., 'Examining Sustainability Challenges Using Science-Fiction Film Scenarios', in *Storytelling for Sustainability in Higher Education: An Educator's Handbook*, ed. Petra Molthan-Hill et al. (United Kingdom: Taylor & Francis, 2020), 117–30.
7 'The Sustainable Development Goals are a call for action by all countries – poor, rich and middle-income – to promote prosperity while protecting the planet. They recognize that ending poverty must go hand-in-hand with strategies that build economic growth and

address a range of social needs including education, health, social protection, and job opportunities, while tackling climate change and environmental protection.' 'The 17 Goals', United Nations, https://sdgs.un.org/goals These goals were adopted by United Nations members in 2015. Each goal includes a number of targets.

8 Ken Wilber's ideas integrating Western and Eastern thought into an integral theory are popular among various subcultures, as well as among some scholars. However, it has also received its share of criticism. For more on integral theory and the four quadrant framework, see Ken Wilber, *The Spectrum of Consciousness* (Wheaton, Illinois: Theosophical Publishing House, 1977) and Ken Wilber, *Sex, Ecology, Spirituality: The Spirit of Evolution* (Boston, MA, & London: Shambhala Publications, 1995).

9 Barber et al., 'Examining Sustainability Challenges', 117–30.

10 See Sean Esbjörn-Hargens and Michael E. Zimmerman, *Integral Ecology: Uniting Multiple Perspectives on the Natural World* (Boston, MA: Integral Books, 2011); Part 4 of this book demonstrates various applications of the integral ecology approach.

11 Chris Riedy, 'Futures of the Climate Action Movement: Insights from an Integral Futures Approach'. *Journal of Futures Studies, 15*(3) (March 2011): 33–52, https://jfsdigital.org/wp-content/uploads/2014/01/153-A03.pdf

12 Nikoleris et al., 'Narrating Climate Futures', 307–19.

13 A video game we worked on uses some of these strategies. See Beckbessinger Sam, Christopher Trisos and Simon Nicholson, *Survive the Century.*

14 For this approach, see Joost M. Vervoort et al., 'Not Just Playing: The Politics of Designing Games for Impact on Anticipatory Climate Governance'. *Geoforum, 137* (2022), 213–21, https://doi.org/10.1016/j.geoforum.2022.03.009; The Anticiplay channel on Medium discusses many game designing approaches for climate governance, https://anticiplay.medium.com/

15 Reader-response criticism focuses on the reader and the 'interpretive community's' response to a text which is in contrast to formalist and New Criticism schools which consider meaning to be embedded in the text. Stanley Fish, considered to be one of the major proponents of

reader-response writes, 'For the formalist, reading poetry is equivalent to noticing and sharing in the craft and labor that produced it', and that formalist analysis 'always point in as many directions as there are interpreters; that is, not only will it prove something, it will prove anything'. See Stanley Fish, *Is There a Text in This Class? The Authority of Interpretive Communities* (United Kingdom: Harvard University Press, 1980), 132, 150, especially the essay, 'Literature in the Reader: Affective Stylistics'.

16 Schneider-Mayerson, 'The Influence', 474.

17 Mathew Schneider-Mayerson et al., 'Environmental Literature as Persuasion: An Experimental Test of the Effects of Reading Climate Fiction'. *Environmental Communication, 17*(1) (2020): 35–50, https://doi.org/10.1080/17524032.2020.1814377

18 Baden, 'Solution-Focused Stories', 254–63.

19 The results are noteworthy. Ninety-eight per cent changed attitudes and sixty per cent adopted at least one green alternative. See Denise Baden, 'Readers' Emulation of Green Behaviours in Fiction: A Case Study of Habitat Man', *Sustainable Innovation 2023: Accelerating Sustainability in the Creative Economy and Creative Industries, Online. 20 Mar – 26 April 2023*, https://eprints.soton.ac.uk/476059/

20 Gustafson et al., 'Personal Stories Can Shift Climate Change Beliefs', 121–35.

21 Robin L. Nabi, Abel Gustafson and Risa Jensen, 'Framing Climate Change: Exploring the Role of Emotion in Generating Advocacy Behavior'. *Science Communication, 40*(4) (2018): 442–68, https://doi.org/10.1177/1075547018776019

22 Scott Slovic, Swarnalatha Rangarajan and Vidya Sarveswaran, eds, *Ecocriticism of the Global South* (United Kingdom: Bloomsbury-Lexington Books, 2015), 3.

23 The impact of colonialism differed between countries as a result of the political and economic systems introduced by the colonizing power. Daron Acemoğlu, Simon Johnson and James A Robinson have demonstrated that settler colonialism which often introduced inclusive institutions resulted in better economic outcomes for the nations in the long run. Contrary to this, extractive colonial policies in non-settler colonies, which introduced authoritarian systems, have resulted in far

worse economic outcomes for these colonized countries in the long run. This work won the three professors the Nobel Prize for Economics in 2024. See Daron Acemoğlu and James A Robinson, *Why Nations Fail: The Origins of Power, Prosperity, and Poverty* (United Kingdom: Crown, 2012).

24 Willibald of Mainz, *The Life of Saint Boniface*, trans. George W. Robinson (760; Cambridge, MA: Harvard University Press, 1916), 63–4. Willibald's original biography in Latin was written around 760 CE.

25 See Emil Doepler junior and Dr. W. Ranisch, *Walhall: Die Götterwelt der Germanen* (Berlin: Martin Oldenbourg, 1905), 16.

26 I am grateful to historian Prof Amanda Power, who was my co-lecturer for a climate course, for mentioning this incident among others in an illuminating talk on History and Climate Change at the University of Oxford in October 2021.

27 Gen. 1:28 (New International Version).

28 Also, the Biblical idea that God created man in his own image can be read as support for anthropocentrism. For an alternative argument, see Stephen Grosse, 'Building a Relationship with the Earth: Humans and Ecology in Genesis 1–3'. *Denison Journal of Religion, 5*(4) (2005): 1–35.

29 Graham Huggan and Helen Tiffin, *Postcolonial Ecocriticism: Literature, Animals, Environment* (UK Routledge, 2015), 5. The quotes are from Val Plumwood, 'Decolonizing Relationships with Nature', in *Decolonizing Nature: Strategies for Conservation in a Post-Colonial Era*, ed. William H. Adams and Martin Mulligan (London: Earthscan, 2003), 53.

30 Cheryll Glotfelty and Harold Fromm, *The Ecocriticism Reader: Landmarks in Literary Ecology* (Athens: University of Georgia Press, 1996), xviii.

31 Ibid., xxv.

32 Huggan and Tiffin, *Postcolonial Ecocriticism*, 2–3.

33 T. V. Reed, 'Toward an Environmental Justice Ecocriticism', in *The Environmental Justice Reader: Politics, Poetics, and Pedagogy*, ed. Joni Adamson, Mei Mei Evans and Rachel Stein (United States: University of Arizona Press, 2002), 148–9.

34 Generally, 'environmental writing' (or ecocriticism) addresses a North American context, but some of the analysis (as in Ramachandra Guha

and Martinez-Allier, 1997) applies as well to the differences between the global North and global South.

35 Ramachandra Guha and J. Martínez-Alier, *Varieties of Environmentalism: Essays North and South* (London: Earthscan, 1997), 12.

36 For a detailed study of the Chipko movement, see Ramachandra Guha, *The Unquiet Woods* (Berkeley: University of California Press, 2000).

37 Nixon, *Slow Violence*, 2.

38 Ibid., 236.

39 Huggan and Tiffin, *Postcolonial Ecocriticism*, 3.

40 Ibid.

41 Ibid.

42 In her essay on climate fiction in English, Caren Irr, distinguishes three waves of ecocriticism which all have a bearing on how cli-fi could be studied and interpreted. She starts with the ecocritics whose work focuses on nature as a figure in Romantic poetry and the nineteenth-century novel and their stress on the need to look for the 'role of the sacred' in the secular. The second wave of ecocriticism looks at more 'contemporary crisis', and here she mentions Dipesh Chakrabarty, who asserts the necessity to rethink the foundations of political and social history from the 'vantage point of ecocriticism'. Finally, a third wave of ecocriticism focuses on object-oriented ontologies and 'attempt to imagine the earth without reference to its human subjects', which connects with the derangements of scale (and temporality aspects) discussed by Timothy Clark. See Irr, 'Climate Fiction in English'.

43 Lawrence Buell, *The Future of Environmental Criticism: Environmental Crisis and Literary Imagination* (Germany: Wiley, 2009), 22. The first two quotes in Buell's argument are from Michael Bennett, 'From Wide Open Spaces to Metropolitan Places the Urban Challenge to Ecocriticism'. *ISLE: Interdisciplinary Studies in Literature and Environment*, 8(1) (Winter 2001): 32, https://doi.org/10.1093/isle/8.1.31. In framing the argument on environmental justice, Buell refers to Joni Adamson, Mei Mei Evans and Rachel Stein, eds, *The Environmental Justice Reader: Politics, Poetics, and Pedagogy* (Tucson: University of Arizona Press, 2002), and he also refers to J. Martínez-Alier (2002) while mentioning 'environmentalism of the poor'.

44 See Alfred W. Crosby, *The Columbian Exchange* (United Kingdom: Greenwood Publishing, 1972).

45 Huggan and Tiffin, *Postcolonial Ecocriticism*, 13.

46 Anne Maxwell, 'Postcolonial Criticism, Ecocriticism and Climate Change: A Tale of Melbourne under Water in 2035'. *Journal of Postcolonial Writing, 45*(1) (2009): 15–26, doi: https://doi.org/10.1080/17449850802636499

47 Adeline Johns-Putra, 'The Rest Is Silence: Postmodern and Postcolonial Possibilities in Climate Change Fiction'. *Studies in the Novel, 50*(1), Johns Hopkins University Press (2018): 26–42, https://doi.org/10.1353/sdn.2018.0002

48 Dipesh Chakrabarty has discussed Gayatri Chakravarti Spivak's intervention in subaltern studies and her challenge to the idea of 'subject' whose apparent autonomy is actually mediated by the forces of colonialism. See Dipesh Chakrabarty, 'Postcolonial Studies and the Challenge of Climate Change'. *New Literary History, 43*(1) (2012): 4, https://dx.doi.org/10.1353/nlh.2012.0007 and Gayatri-Chakravorty Spivak, 'Can the Subaltern Speak?' in *Marxism and the Interpretation of Culture*, ed. Cary Nelson and Lawrence Grossberg (USA: University of Illinois Press, 1988), 271–313.

49 Chakrabarty, 'Postcolonial Studies and the Challenge of Climate Change', 14–15.

50 Ibid.

## Chapter 5

1 Calotropis or crown flower (*akondo* in Bangla) is known to have medicinal properties and is used as a traditional antidote for snakebite.

2 A few passages of the story summary that follows are from my review of *Gun Island* which first appeared in Scroll magazine. See Rajat Chaudhuri, 'Can Literature Save the Planet? Reading *Gun Island* during an Impending Climate Crisis', review of *Gun Island,* by Amitav Ghosh, *Scroll.in*, 18 August 2019, https://scroll.in/article/934150/can-literature-

save-the-planet-reading-gun-island-during-an-impending-climate-crisis

3 Any book printed in the early days of printing, before the year 1501.

4 Nike used to pump the greenhouse gas sulphur hexafluoride in some of its shoes to give them a powerful cushion. See Ben Elgin, 'How Vintage Nike Airs Exposed a Flaw in a $700 Million Carbon Market', *Bloomberg*, 29 October 2024, https://www.bloomberg.com/news/features/2024-10-29/vintage-nike-air-shoes-expose-flaw-in-700-million-carbon-market

5 For a detailed analysis and the history of ideas, philosophies and practices leading up to her argument about the importance of a 'sense of planet', see Heise, *Sense of Place and Sense of Planet.*

6 Heise mentions Leopold's concept of the 'land ethic' alongside Martin Heidegger and Norwegian philosopher Arne Naess's writings as some of the foundational ideas behind 'contemporary environmentalist approaches to place'. Heise, *Sense of Place and Sense of Planet*, 28–49. Also see Aldo Leopold, *A Sand Country Almanac and Sketches Here and There* (London: Oxford University Press, 1949) which has left its stamp on ecological movements centred on place.

7 Zygmunt Bauman, *Postmodern Ethics* (Oxford: Blackwell, 1993).

8 Mitchell Thomashow, *Bringing the Biosphere Home: Learning to Perceive Global Environmental Change* (Cambridge, MA: MIT Press, 2002).

9 Tomlinson's deep engagement with 'deterritorialization' provides a useful conceptual basis for this part of Heise's arguments. See John Tomlinson, *Globalization and Culture* (Chicago, IL: University of Chicago Press, 1999).

10 Edwin Gilson, 'Planetary Los Angeles: Climate Realism and Transnational Narrative in Amitav Ghosh's *Gun Island (2019)*'. *Comparative American Studies an International Journal, 19*(2–3) (2022): 269–88, doi:10.1080/14775700.2022.2114286

11 Ibid., 5. The idea of 'imagined communities' is articulated by Benedict Anderson's in his influential work on nationalism. Heise draws on this vein of Anderson's critique of the imagined community of the nation to argue about 'cosmopolitanism' and thereon about eco-cosmopolitanism. See Benedict Anderson, *Imagined Communities:*

*Reflections on the Origin and Spread of Nationalism* (United Kingdom: Verso, 2006).

12 Nidhi Angurala, 'Postcolonial Eco-Discourse in Amitav Ghosh's *Gun Island* and *The Great Derangement*', *The Criterion, 11*(II) (April 2020): 27, accessed 2 July 2025, https://www.the-criterion.com/V11/n2/IN03.pdf

13 See this introduction to our book, Christoph Rupprecht et al., 'Introduction', in *Multispecies Cities: Solarpunk Urban Futures*, ed. Christoph Rupprecht, Deborah Cleland, Norie Tamura, Rajat Chaudhuri and Sarena Ulibarri (USA: World Weaver Press, 2021), 1–10, https://www.researchgate.net/publication/349027086_Multispecies_Cities_Solarpunk_Urban_Futures

14 The judgement however, as we have said before, is unevenly spread and not always meted out on the perpetrators that is Global North who are more responsible for emissions.

15 Irr, 'Climate Fiction in English', 13.

16 Amitav Ghosh, 'My Book Is Not an Apocalyptic Book at All. I Guess I'm Leaving Hope as a Possibility'. Interview by Harsimran Gill, *Scroll.in*, 17 June 2019, accessed 2 July 2025, https://scroll.in/article/927202/my-book-is-not-an-apocalyptic-book-at-all-i-guess-im-leaving-hope-as-a-possibility-amitav-ghosh

17 LeMenager, 'Climate Change and the Struggle for Genre', 225.

18 It is interesting to note how Heidegger's uncanny, being an affective state, speaks to how affects intervene and shape our perceptions. Asis De has employed affect theory to explore human/non-human relationships and its representation through the uncanny in *Gun Island*. See Asis De, 'Human/Non-human Interface and the Affective Uncanny in Amitav Ghosh's *Gun Island*'. *Revista Interdisciplinar de Literatura e Ecocrítica, 7*(1) (2021): 64–80, accessed 2 July 2025, https://asle-brasil.com/journal/index.php/aslebr/article/view/165

19 Amitav Ghosh engages with John Updike's idea about the importance of 'individual moral adventure'. See Ghosh, *The Great Derangement*, 102–6.

20 For examples: Ibid., 102–6. Also see Admussen, 'Six Proposals'.

21 It is possible to probe the novel with some other features of literary fiction (developed in the chapter discussing *Memory of Water*) but even

on a first reading one can say that Ghosh has travelled some distance away from that genre in this book.

22 We are focusing on the lens of planetarity for Amitav Ghosh's book. Justice issues, though important, are not as consistently engaged throughout the book as in *The Sickle* which we will read using a justice lens.

23 Alex Clark, 'Climate and Culture in Crisis', review of *Gun Island*, by Amitav Ghosh, *The Guardian*, 5 June 2019, accessed 3 November 2023, www.theguardian.com/books/2019/jun/05/gun-island-amitav-ghosh-review

24 The SSPs-based approach has been worked out in detail by others and can easily be adapted to test transformative possibilities of cli-fi. We are not repeating it here. See Nikoleris et al., 'Narrating Climate Futures', 307–19.

25 Barber et al., 'Examining Sustainability Challenges', 117–30.

26 Angurala, 'Postcolonial Ecodiscourse' follows a different approach. Angurala applies Susie O'Brien's characterization of the postcolonial approach in contrast to the ecocritical in her reading of *Gun Island*.

27 Slovic, Rangarajan and Sarveswaran, *Ecocriticism of the Global South*, 3.

28 The author has spoken about the novel's engagement with 'slow violence'. See Amitav Ghosh, '*Gun Island* Deals with the Slow Violence That Our World Is Experiencing Right Now', *The Economic Times*, 14 June 2019, accessed 23 September 2023, https://economictimes.indiatimes.com/magazines/panache/amitav-ghosh-gun-island-deals-slow-violence-that-the-world-is-experiencing-at-the-moment/articleshow/69786725.cms

## Chapter 6

1 Andreas Prater, *Venus at Her Mirror: Velázquez and the Art of Nude Painting*, trans. Ishbel Flett (Germany: Prestel, 2002), 7.

2 The video of the incident is available on X, see Just Stop Oil (@JustStop_Oil), 'SUFFRAGETTE PAINTING SMASHED: Our Government Have Revealed Plans for MORE Oil Licenses, Knowing

It Will Kill Millions. In Response, Two Supporters of Just Stop Oil …', X (Formerly Twitter), 6 November 2023, accessed 2 July 2025, x.com/JustStop_Oil/status/1721493745781113173?s=20

3 In fact, as we have discussed earlier, employing the arguments of Val Plumwood, Tiffin and Huggan, Crosby and others, colonial attitudes towards the 'natural' world, which subsumes less privileged humans (including women), led to the unleashing of forces whose continuance in our times precipitated anthropogenic climate and other planetary crises.

4 Yessenia Funes, 'Throwing Soup at a Van Gogh? Why Climate Activists are Targeting Art', *National Geographic*, 19 July 2023, accessed 1 July 2025, https://www.nationalgeographic.com/environment/article/famous-art-museums-climate-change-activists

5 Rajat Chaudhuri, 'Literary Fiction Meets a Clear-Eyed Appreciation of the Planetary Crises in "*Memory of Water*"', *Scroll.in*, 29 October 2022, accessed 1 July 2025, https://scroll.in/article/1035673/literary-fiction-meets-a-clear-eyed-appreciation-of-the-planetary-crises-in-memory-of-water

6 Goodbody, 'Cli-Fi beyond the American Thriller', 22.

7 Rajat Chaudhuri with Ajit Singh, *Water – What Are Our Rights to It?* (India: CUTS, 1998).

8 See Figure 2.2.

9 Russian Formalism as an approach to literary analysis is again echoed in the field of New Criticism. Both these schools emphasize the importance of the text through methods of close reading while generally discounting authorial intention as extraneous and not a primary focus of analysis.

10 Nasrullah Mambrol, 'Roman Jakobson's Contribution to Russian Formalism', *Literariness.org*, 16 March 2016, accessed 2 July 2025, https://literariness.org/2016/03/17/roman-jakobsons-contribution-to-russian-formalism/

11 This is from the entry on 'literariness', in Chris Baldick, *The Oxford Dictionary of Literary Terms* (United Kingdom: Oxford University Press, 2008).

12 In the famous essay 'Art as Technique'.

13 Alternatively 'estrangement'. See Victor Shklovsky, *Theory of Prose*, trans. Benjamin Sher (Elmwood Park, IL: Dalkey Archive Press, 1991).

14 Ibid., 6.

15 David S. Miall and Don Kuiken, 'What Is Literariness? Three Components of Literary Reading'. *Discourse Processes, 28*(2) (1999): 121–38, https://doi.org/10.1080/01638539909545076

16 Nancy Easterlin has argued for a fresh approach combining humanities and cognitive sciences in the reading and interpretation of texts. See Nancy Easterlin, *A Biocultural Approach to Literary Theory and Interpretation* (United States: Johns Hopkins University Press, 2012), 66.

17 Nancy Easterlin elsewhere discusses how aesthetics and ideology are bound up by different strands. Ibid., 41. In our case we complement our lens of aesthetics with tools that address politics. See Figures 2.2 and 3.4 and the accompanying discussion.

18 See this Britannica article about 'popular literature' for varied meanings and perspectives about literary fiction. John M. Cunningham, 'Popular Literature: History, Definition, Examples, Books, and Facts', *Encyclopedia Britannica*, accessed 2 July 2025, https://www.britannica.com/art/popular-literature

19 See his excellent essay, Rosen, 'Literary Fiction and the Genres of Genre Fiction'.

20 The meaning of genre is pithily explained by Frederic Jameson: 'Genres are essentially contracts between a writer and his readers; or rather, to use the term which Claudio Guillén has so usefully revived, they are literary institutions, which like the other institutions of social life are based on tacit agreements or contracts.' See Fredric Jameson, 'Magical Narratives: Romance as Genre'. *New Literary History, 7*(1) (1975): 135–63, https://doi.org/10.2307/468283

21 Some of these points are discussed by Joyce G. Saricks who places 'literary fiction', alongside psychological suspense, mysteries and science fiction in his sub-category of 'Intellect Genres'. See Saricks, *The Readers' Advisory*, 177–96.

22 Czech literary critic Jan Mukařovský's paper articulates how the formalist technique of foregrounding explains the difference between poetic language and standard language. See Jan Mukařovský, 'Standard

Language and Poetic Language', in *Chapters from the History of Czech Functional Linguistics*, ed. Jan Chovanec. 1. vyd (Brno: Masarykova Univerzita, 2014), 41–53, accessed 30 June 2025, https://digilib.phil.muni.cz/sites/default/files/pdf/131565.pdf

23 The reader will remember that the word 'genre' or 'genre fiction' can be used to create a separation between 'serious fiction' and other forms. Here we have used genre in a more general sense.

24 Ibid., 178.

25 For another view, it is important to note Amitav Ghosh's critic of modernity championed by an avant-garde, which led to the suppression of that kind of realist writing where collectives were important. The role of collectives, as we have also noted earlier, is important in climate fiction. *Cf.* Ghosh, *The Great Derangement*, 106.

26 Ghosh, *The Great Derangement*, 104–8.

27 Katarina Leppänen, 'Memory of Water: Boundaries of Political Geography and World Literature'. *European Review, 28*(1) (2020): 5, https://doi.org/10.1017/S1062798719000541

28 Ibid.

29 For such an argument about climate stories, see Khan, *Star Warriors of the Modern Raj*, 191–5.

30 Leppänen, '*Memory of Water:* Boundaries', 1.

31 Fatma Aykanat, 'Mnemonic Agency of Water in the Anthropocene: Material and Discursive Entanglements in Emmi Itäranta's Dystopian Cli-fi Novel *Memory of Water*', *Journal of Social Sciences: Environment and Literature*, Special Issue 16, (1/2), MCBÜ [Manisa Celal Bayar Üniversitesi] (May 2018): 3, doi:10.18026/cbayarsos.423287

32 Admussen, 'Six Proposals'.

33 Goodbody, 'Cli-Fi beyond the American Thriller', 23.

34 Leppänen, '*Memory of Water:* Boundaries', 6.

35 Of course, as Jacques Rancière has argued, the aesthetic act can be political. For example, the young Noria's silent rebellion reconfigures the role expected from her by the existing order and is therefore political. See Rancière, *The Politics of Aesthetics*, 60–7.

## Chapter 7

1 Close to 15,000 mature trees were uprooted in the city of Kolkata by cyclone Amphan.

2 Woland is actually the Devil himself in this novel. Mikhail Bulgakov, *The Master and Margarita* (United Kingdom: Grove Atlantic, 2016).

3 Overlapping crises and entwined disasters have become more common over the years and is an important area of study. For example, see: Alessandra Jerolleman, Shirley Laska and Julie Torres, 'Lessons from Concurrent Disasters: COVID-19 and Eight Hurricanes', Natural Hazards Center Quick Response Research Report Series, Report 327. Natural Hazards Center, University of Colorado Boulder (2021), accessed 2 July 2025, https://hazards.colorado.edu/quick-response-report/lessons-from-co-occurring-disasters

4 Rajat Chaudhuri, '*The Sickle* Book Review: Heart of Darkness', *The New Indian Express*, 19 June 2021, https://www.newindianexpress.com/lifestyle/books/2021/Jun/20/the-sickle-book-review-heart-of-darkness-2317788.html

5 Bhasker Tripathi, 'In Rural India, Climate Migrants Have Hysterectomies to Survive', *Context-Thomson Reuters Foundation Newsroom,* 7 March 2024, https://www.context.news/climate-risks/in-rural-india-climate-migrants-have-hysterectomies-to-survive

6 The Chinese mandarin thought experiment appears in Balzac's *Le Père Goriot*, where the ambitious Eugène de Rastignac asks the medical student Bianchon a similar question. Honoré de Balzac, *Pere Goriot* (1835; Paris: Gallimard, 1971), 186–7.

7 See 'categorical imperative' and the idea that our actions should be based on universal principles in Immanuel Kant, *Groundwork of the Metaphysics of Morals*, trans. Mary Gregor (1785; United Kingdom: Cambridge University Press, 1997), x–xi.

8 John Rawls, *A Theory of Justice* (United States: Harvard University Press, 1999), 101–5.

9 Klaudijo Klaser, Lorenzo Sacconi and Marco Faillo, 'John Rawls and Compliance to Climate Change Agreements: Insights from a Laboratory Experiment'. *International Environmental Agreements*

*Politics Law and Economics*, *21*(3) (2021): 531–51, https://doi.org/10.1007/s10784-021-09533-8

10 Joni Adamson, Mei Mei Evans and Rachel Stein, eds, *The Environmental Justice Reader: Politics, Poetics, and Pedagogy* (United States: University of Arizona Press, 2002), 3.

11 Elisabeth Ammons and Madhumita Roy, eds, *Sharing the Earth: An International Environmental Justice Reader* (United States: University of Georgia Press, 2015), 1.

12 Greta Gaard, 'What's the Story? Competing Narratives of Climate Change and Climate Justice'. *Forum for World Literature Studies*, *6*(6) (2014), 272, accessed 2 July 2025, https://fwls.org/uploads/soft/210603/10479-2106031IH3.pdf

13 Ibid., 273.

14 Wulf Wilde, 'Fact Check: How Bad Is Eating Meat for the Planet?' *Deutsche Welle*, 30 October 2022, accessed 2 July 2025, https://www.dw.com/en/fact-check-is-eating-meat-bad-for-the-environment/a-63595148

15 Rupprecht et al., 'Introduction', in *Multispecies Cities: Solarpunk Urban Futures*, 3.

16 'Bali Principles of Climate Justice' (2002), International Climate Justice Network, 28 August 2002, accessed 5 March 2024, https://www.corpwatch.org/article/bali-principles-climate-justice

17 Bhargabi Bharadwaj, 'A New European Court of Human Rights Ruling Has Established a Vital New Precedent', Chatham House, 18 April 2024, accessed 11 March 2024, https://www.chathamhouse.org/2024/04/new-european-court-human-rights-ruling-has-established-vital-new-precedent

18 This was a complicated case where protection of an endangered species and climate change mitigation through solar power, in this case transmission lines, stood in opposition to each other. See Shrestha Mathur, 'M K Ranjitsinh v. Union of India: The Supreme Court's Very Own Sophie's Choice Moment', *Bar and Bench*, 27 April 2024, accessed 23 June 2024, https://www.barandbench.com/columns/mk-ranjitsinh-v-union-of-india-the-supreme-courts-very-own-sophies-choice-moment

19 Francis, '*Laudato Si*' (Vatican City: 2015), https://www.vatican.va/content/francesco/en/encyclicals/documents/papa-francesco_20150524_enciclica-laudato-si.html

20 Paul Cairney, Irina Timonina and Hannes Stephan, 'How Can Policy and Policymaking Foster Climate Justice? A Qualitative Systematic Review', *Open Research Europe* (31 March 2023): 5, https://doi.org/10.12688/openreseurope.15719.2. Besides the three constituents, two additional aspects – restitution and reparation – have also entered climate justice debates. For example, see Prakash Kashwan, *Climate Justice in India*, Vol. 1 (New York: Cambridge University Press, 2024), 11.

21 Multispecies justice expands the scope of the justice approach to other beings.

22 Neo-liberal approaches addressing climate change depend on market-based instruments like emissions trading, put more reliance on technology and centre the role of 'experts'. Johnson (quoted in Cairney et al., 'How Can Policy') writes, 'Neoliberal environmentalism … relies on technical "experts" to function and legitimise apolitical interventions. Environmental neoliberal interventions are often depicted as common sense, objective or neutral through a process of depoliticization, or "to remove issues from political contention", as opposed to value-laden and normative, political, issues due to considerations of equity and justice. "Expert knowledge," then, becomes a way to empower market actors and others while marginalising locals and context-specific concerns.' See Shannon Johnson, 'Discourse and Practice of REDD+ in Ghana and the Expansion of State Power'. *Sustainability, 13*(20) (2021): 4, https://doi.org/10.3390/su132011358/ For a comparison of neo-liberal and social justice informed approaches, see Table 2 in Cairney et al., 15.

23 Vandana Shiva, 'Soil Not Oil: Environmental Justice in an Age of Climate Crisis'. *Alternatives Journal, 35*(3) (2009): 18+. *Gale Academic OneFile,* accessed 1 August 2025, https://link.gale.com/apps/doc/A200106391/AONE?u=anon~8e1f625&sid=googleScholar&xid=d903ac87

24 Ibid.

25 Rajat Chaudhuri, 'Estranged Times and the Decades Ahead', *New Indian Express*, 27 December 2020, https://www.newindianexpress.

com/magazine/voices/2020/Dec/27/estranged-times-andthe-decades-ahead-2240793.html

26 This was at our lecture series on climate change at the University of Oxford which I have referred to earlier.

27 'Explainer: How Gender Inequality and Climate Change Are Interconnected', UN Women, 21 April 2025, https://www.unwomen.org/en/news-stories/explainer/2022/02/explainer-how-gender-inequality-and-climate-change-are-interconnected

28 Chukwumerije Okereke, 'Climate Justice and the International Regime'. *WIREs Climate Change, 1*(3) (2010): 462–74, https://doi.org/10.1002/wcc.52

29 Internal displacement refers to 'each new forced movement of person within the borders of their country recorded during the year'. Climate change often has a bearing on the frequency, intensity or occurrence of such disasters. See 'Country Profile, India' Internal Displacement Monitoring Centre, https://www.internal-displacement.org/countries/india/

30 Pooja Adhikari and Vani Shree, 'Human Cost of Sugar – Living and Working Conditions of Migrant Cane-Cutters in Maharashtra'. *Oxfam India Discussion Paper* (2020): 3, accessed 3 July 2025, https://www.oxfamindia.org/sites/default/files/2020-02/%23Human%20Cost%20of%20Sugar_Maharashtra%20Case.pdf

31 Ibid., 12.

32 'India Emerges as the World's Largest Producer and Consumer of Sugar and World's 2nd Largest Exporter of Sugar', Ministry of Consumer Affairs, Food & Public Distribution, Government of India, 5 October 2022, https://pib.gov.in/PressReleaseIframePage.aspx?PRID=1865320

33 The Indian government has been 'implementing Ethanol Blended Petrol (EBP) Programme throughout the country except Union Territories of Andaman Nicobar and Lakshadweep islands, wherein OMCs (public sector oil-marketing companies) sell petrol blended with 10% ethanol', 'Ethanol Blended Petrol (EBP) Programme', Ministry of Petroleum and Natural Gas, accessed 21 May 2024, https://mopng.gov.in/en/refining/ethanol-blended-petrol

34 Etienne Piguet, Antoine Pecoud and P. De Guchteneire, 'Migration and Climate Change: An Overview'. *Refugee Survey Quarterly, 30*(3) (8 June 2011): 23, http://dx.doi.org/10.1093/rsq/hdr006

35 Ritu Bharadwaj, N. Karthikeyan and Ira Deulgaonkar, 'Urgent Preventative Action for Climate-Related Suicides in Rural India'. *IIED Briefing Paper*, IIED (May 2023): 1–4, accessed 3 July 2025, https://www.iied.org/21436iied

36 Shagun, 'Research Establishes Link between Farmer Suicides and Climate Change', *Down to Earth*, 19 May 2023, https://www.downtoearth.org.in/news/climate-change/research-establishes-link-between-farmer-suicides-and-climate-change-89452

37 Chaiti Bhagawat and Divya Nazareth, *Climate Change Impacts on Maharashtra Agriculture*, Institute for Sustainable Communities (2021): 44, https://sustain.org/wp-content/uploads/2021/06/ISC-Report_Impact-of-Climate-Change-on-Maharashtra-Agriculture.pdf

38 Trexler, *Anthropocene Fictions*, 31.

39 It will be interesting to compare him with Piya of *Gun Island* and Noria's mother in *Memory of Water*.

40 'Retire the portrait of the single soul', writes Nick Admussen in the second of his six proposals. See Admussen, 'Six Proposals'.

41 Cairney et al., 'How Can Policy', 5.

42 Actants, either individual, collective or abstract, perform certain functions within a narrative. See Greimas, *Structural Semantics – An Attempt at a Method*, 197–221.

43 Swati Bhattacharya, '*Ki Bhayanok Sei Bancha, Shei Kaj*' ['How Terrible That Life, That Living'], review of *The Sickle,* by Anita Agnihotri, *Anandabazar Patrika*, 25 May 2024, accessed 25 May 2024, https://www.anandabazar.com/culture/book-reviews/book-review-of-anita-agnihotri-1.1079404

44 'The warmth of human existence, being in the vicinity of people, is crucial to my writing process. But this is not fieldwork or research. The attempt to weave myself into a country that lies beyond the urban experience is an integral part of my writing', see Anita Agnihotri, 'How a Farmers' March in 2018 Entered Anita Agnihotri's Newly Translated Novel in Real Time', *Scroll.in*, 9 March 2021, accessed 25 May 2024,

scroll.in/article/988966/how-a-farmers-march-in-2018-entered-anita-agnihotris-newly-translated-novel-in-real-time

45 Rabin Pal, '*Kaste: Chakravyuha o Pratirodher Akhyan*' ['The Sickle: A Narrative of Entrapment and Resistance'], review of *The Sickle,* by Anita Agnihotri, *Parabaas*, no. 76, (September 2019): 30, accessed 25 May 2024, https://www.parabaas.com/PB76/LEKHA/brRobin76.shtml

46 See Joseph Campbell, *The Hero's Journey* (New World Library, 2014).

47 Sudipta Dutta, 'By the Sweat of Their Brows', review of *The Sickle*, by Anita Agnihotri, *The Hindu*, 1 May 2021, accessed 25 May 2024, https://www.thehindu.com/books/by-the-sweat-of-their-brows-sudipta-datta-reviews-the-sickle-by-anita-agnihotri-trs-arunava-sinha/article34447032.ece

48 Somak Ghosal, 'Marathwada Chronicles: Notes from the Land of Thirst'. Dutta, 'By the Sweat of Their Brows'. *MintLounge*, accessed 25 May 2024, https://lifestyle.livemint.com/news/big-story/marathwada-chronicles-notes-from-the-land-of-thirst-111615719911435.html

49 Pal, *Kaste: Chakravyuha o Pratirodher Akhyan.*

50 For a discussion of the impact of setting on plot and character, see Trexler and Johns-Putra, 'Climate Change in Literature' and Trexler, *Anthropocene Fictions*, 234–5.

51 It would be interesting to compare how Anita Agnihotri and Emmi Itäranta represent water scarcity in their novels.

52 For detailed elucidations about the environmentalism of the poor, as well as post-materialist, conservationist, preservationist and other forms of environmentalism through global and local lenses, see Guha and Martínez-Alier, *Varieties of Environmentalism;* Ramachandra Guha, *Environmentalism: A Global History* (Oxford: Oxford University Press, 2000); and Joan Martínez-Alier, *The Environmentalism of the Poor: A Study of Ecological Conflicts and Valuation* (Cheltenham: Edward Elgar, 2002).

53 Agnihotri, 'How a Farmers' March'.

54 Anita Agnihotri has served in the Indian Administrative Service for thirty-seven years. See https://www.anitaagnihotri.com/about-anita-agnihotri.html

55 Agnihotri, 'How a Farmers' March'.

56 Slovic, Rangarajan and Sarveswaran, *Ecocriticism of the Global South*, 3.
57 Ammons and Roy, *Sharing the Earth*, 1.
58 Ibid.
59 Agnihotri, 'How a Farmers' March'.
60 The Chipko movement, spearheaded by women like Gaura Devi, and propagated by environment leaders like Sunderlal Bahuguna and Chandi Prasad Bhatt, originated in protests against commercial logging of trees in Chamoli district of Uttarakhand in India.
61 New research, based on Marx's recently published notebooks, have noticed his extensive ecological interests, and have characterized his final vision of post-capitalism as 'degrowth communism' in a non-productivist setting. See Kohei Saito, *Marx in the Anthropocene: Towards the Idea of Degrowth Communism* (United Kingdom: Cambridge University Press, 2023).
62 Developed from Marx's discussion about metabolism in Capital, the expression was coined by John Bellamy Foster. See John Bellamy Foster, *Marx's Ecology: Materialism and Nature* (United Kingdom: Monthly Review Press, 2000).
63 Social metabolism is a concept found in Marx. It focuses on the movement or interchange of material (Stoffwechsel) in a social system and how labour affects and mediates the relationship between humans and nature. Marx writes in Volume 1 of Capital, 'Capitalist production collects the population together in great centres, and causes the urban population to achieve an ever-growing preponderance … it disturbs the metabolic interaction between man and the earth, i.e. it prevents the return to the soil of its constituent elements consumed by man in the form of food and clothing; hence it hinders the operation of the eternal natural condition for the lasting fertility of the soil.' See Karl Marx, *Capital: A Critique of Political Economy*, Vol. 1, trans. Ben Fowkes (England: Penguin with New Left Review, 1976), 637.
64 Nixon, *Slow Violence*, 236.
65 Ibid.

## Chapter 8

1 See the discussion about Ockham's razor in Chapter 3.

2 Rupprecht et al., eds, *Multispecies Cities: Solarpunk Urban Futures;* and Christoph Rupprecht, Deborah Cleland, Rajat Chaudhuri, Sarena Ulibarri, Melissa Ingaruca Moreno and Norie Tamura, *Solarpunk Creatures* (USA: World Weaver Press, 2021).

# Bibliography


Acemoğlu Daron and James A. Robinson. *Why Nations Fail: The Origins of Power, Prosperity, and Poverty*. United Kingdom: Crown, 2012.

Adamson, Joni, Mei Mei Evans and Rachel Stein, eds, *The Environmental Justice Reader: Politics, Poetics, and Pedagogy*. United States: University of Arizona Press, 2002.

Adhikari, Pooja and Vani Shree. 'Human Cost of Sugar – Living and Working Conditions of Migrant Cane-Cutters in Maharashtra'. *Oxfam India Discussion Paper* (2020): 1–24. https://www.oxfamindia.org/sites/default/files/2020-02/%23Human%20Cost%20of%20Sugar_Maharashtra%20Case.pdf.

Admussen, Nick. 'Six Proposals for the Reform of Literature in the Age of Climate Change'. *The Critical Flame* (42), May–June 2016. criticalflame.org/six-proposals-for-the-reform-of-literature-in-the-age-of-climate-change/.

Adorno, Theodor. *The Culture Industry*. London: Routledge, 1973.

Agnihotri, Anita. *Kaste*. Kolkata: Dey's Publishing, 2019.

Agnihotri, Anita. 'Interview: Anita Agnihotri'. Interview by Rajat Chaudhuri. 5 August 2020. *Niyogi Books on Instagram*. https://www.instagram.com/tv/CDgpfwVgGqt/?utm_source=ig_embed&utm_campaign=loading.

Agnihotri, Anita. *Kaste* [The Sickle]. Translated by Arunava Sinha. New Delhi: Juggernaut Books, 2021.

Agnihotri, Anita. 'How a Farmers' March in 2018 Entered Anita Agnihotri's Newly Translated Novel in Real Time'. *Scroll.in*, 9 March 2021. Accessed 25 May 2024. scroll.in/article/988966/how-a-farmers-march-in-2018-entered-anita-agnihotris-newly-translated-novel-in-real-time.

Akbar, Prayaag. *Leila: A Novel*. India: Simon & Schuster, 2017.

Alcántara-Ayala, Irasema, José López-García and Ricardo J. Garnica. 'On the Landslide Event in 2010 in the Monarch Butterfly Biosphere Reserve, Angangueo, Michoacán, Mexico'. *Landslides* 9, no. 2 (26 August 2011): 263–73. https://doi.org/10.1007/s10346-011-0291-7.

Ammons, Elisabeth and Madhumita Roy, eds, *Sharing the Earth: An International Environmental Justice Reader*. Athens: University of Georgia Press, 2015.

Andersen, Gregers. 'Cli-Fi: A Short Essay on Its Worlds and Its Importance'. Dragonfly.eco, 2014. Accessed 1 July 2025. https://dragonfly.eco/cli-fi-short-essay-worlds-importance/.

Andersen, Gregers. 'Cli-Fi and the Uncanny'. *ISLE Interdisciplinary Studies in Literature and Environment* 23, no. 4 (2016): 855–66. https://doi.org/10.1093/isle/isw068.

Andersen, Gregers and University of Copenhagen. 'Fiction Prepares Us for a World Changed by Global Warming'. 23 April 2014. https://www.sciencedaily.com/releases/2014/04/140423102758.htm.

Anderson, Benedict. *Imagined Communities: Reflections on the Origin and Spread of Nationalism*. United Kingdom: Verso, 2006.

Angurala, Nidhi. 'Postcolonial Eco-Discourse in Amitav Ghosh's *Gun Island* and the Great Derangement'. *The Criterion* 11, no. II (April 2020): 23–33. https://www.the-criterion.com/V11/n2/IN03.pdf.

Anticiplay Channel. Medium. https://anticiplay.medium.com/.

Aravamudan, Srinivas. 'The Catachronism of Climate Change'. *Diacritics* 41, no. 3 (2013): 6–30. https://dx.doi.org/10.1353/dia.2013.0019.

Ash, Konstantin and Nick Obradovich. 'Climatic Stress, Internal Migration, and Syrian Civil War Onset'. *Journal of Conflict Resolution* 64, no. 1 (25 July 2019): 3–31. https://doi.org/10.1177/0022002719864140.

Atwood, Margaret. *Oryx and Crake*. United Kingdom: Little, Brown Book Group, 2009.

Aykanat, Fatma. 'Mnemonic Agency of Water in the Anthropocene: Material and Discursive Entanglements in Emmi Itäranta's Dystopian Cli-Fi Novel *Memory of Water*'. *Journal of Social Sciences: Environment and Literature* 16, no. 1/2. MCBÜ [Manisa Celal Bayar Üniversitesi] (May 2018): 1–26. doi:10.18026/cbayarsos.423287.

Baccolini, Raffaella. 'Ursula K. LeGuin's Critical Dystopia'. In *Critical Insights: Dystopia*. Edited by M. Keith Booker, 37–53. Ipswich, MA: Salem Press, 2013.

Baccolini, Raffaella and Tom Moylan, eds, *Dark Horizons: Science Fiction and the Dystopian Imagination*. New York: Routledge, 2003.

Bacigalupi, Paolo. *The Windup Girl*. India: Hachette India, 2012.

Baden, Denise. 'Solution-Focused Stories Are More Effective Than Catastrophic Stories in Motivating Proenvironmental Intentions'.

*Ecopsychology* 11, no. 4 (13 September 2019): 254–63. https://doi.org/10.1089/eco.2019.0023.

Baden, Denise. *Habitat Man*. Habitat Press, 2021.

Baden, Denise. 'Readers' Emulation of Green Behaviours in Fiction: A Case Study of Habitat Man'. *Sustainable Innovation 2023: Accelerating Sustainability in the Creative Economy and Creative Industries, Online. 20 Mar – 26 Apr 2023*. https://eprints.soton.ac.uk/476059/.

Baden, Denise and Jeremy Brown. 'Climate Fiction to Inspire Green Actions: A Tale of Two Authors'. *Springer eBooks* (2024): 203–24. https://doi.org/10.1007/978-3-031-54790-4_10.

Bagchi, Barnita. 'Must There Be an Apocalypse? An Analysis of South Asian Speculative Fiction'. *Frame Journal of Literary Studies* (26 June 2015). http://www.tijdschriftframe.nl/wp-content/uploads/2015/06/Frame-26_1-Barnita-Bagchi.pdf.

Baldick, Chris. *The Oxford Dictionary of Literary Terms*. United Kingdom: Oxford University Press, 2008.

Ballard, J. G. *The Drowned World*. United Kingdom: HarperCollins Publishers, 2010.

Balzac, Honoré de. *Pere Goriot*. 1835. Paris: Gallimard, 1971.

Banerjee, Sarnath. *All Quiet in Vikaspuri*. India: HarperCollins Publishers India, 2015.

Barber, Jeffrey. 'Imagining Sustainable Futures in Popular Culture: Moving Beyond Dystopia and Techno-Fantasy Narratives'. 16, Paper presented at IAMCR 2018, Oregon.

Barber, Jeffrey. 'The Challenge of Imagining Sustainable Futures: Climate Fiction in Sustainability Communication'. In *The Sustainability Communication Reader*. Edited by Franzisca Weder, Larissa Krainer and Matthias Karmasin, 143–60. Wiesbaden: Springer VS, 2021.

Barber, Jeffrey, Karen Onthank, Tony Wall, Nerise Johnson and Anna Mackenzie. 'Examining Sustainability Challenges Using Science-Fiction Film Scenarios'. In *Storytelling for Sustainability in Higher Education: An Educator's Handbook*. Edited by Petra Molthan-Hill, Heather Luna, Tony Wall, Helen Puntha and Denise Baden, 271–82. United Kingdom: Taylor & Francis, 2020.

Bauman, Zygmunt. *Postmodern Ethics*. Oxford: Blackwell, 1993.

Beckbessinger Sam, Christopher Trisos and Simon Nicholson. *Survive the Century*, Three Kids in a Trenchcoat (2021) Internet game, Fiction contributors: Lauren Beukes, Maria Turtschaninoff, Rajat Chaudhuri and Sophia Al-Maria. https://survivethecentury.net.

Bencherki, Nicolas. 'Actor-Network Theory'. In *The International Encyclopedia of Organizational Communication*. Wiley eBooks, 2016. https://doi.org/10.1002/9781118955567.wbieoc002.

Bendell, Jem. 'Deep Adaptation: A Map for Navigating Climate Tragedy'. *IFLAS Occasional Paper* 2 (27 July 2018): 13. https://mahb.stanford.edu/wpcontent/uploads/2018/08/deepadaptation.pdf.

Bergson, Henri. *Creative Evolution*. United States: University Press of America, 1984.

Bhagawat, Chaiti and Divya Nazareth. *Climate Change Impacts on Maharashtra Agriculture*. Institute for Sustainable Communities (2021): 1–78. https://sustain.org/wp-content/uploads/2021/06/ISC-Report_Impact-of-Climate-Change-on-Maharashtra-Agriculture.pdf.

Bharadwaj, Bhargabi. 'A New European Court of Human Rights Ruling Has Established a Vital New Precedent'. Chatham House, 18 April 2024. https://www.chathamhouse.org/2024/04/new-european-court-human-rights-ruling-has-established-vital-new-precedent.

Bharadwaj, Ritu, N. Karthikeyan and Ira Deulgaonkar. 'Urgent Preventative Action for Climate-Related Suicides in Rural India'. *IIED Briefing Paper*. IIED, May 2023. Accessed 3 July 2025. https://www.iied.org/21436iied.

Bhattacharya, Swati. 'Ki Bhayanok Sei Bancha, Shei Kaj' ['How Dreadful That Life, That Living'], Review of *The Sickle*, by Anita Agnihotri, *Anandabazar Patrika*, 25 May 2024. Accessed 25 May 2024. https://www.anandabazar.com/culture/book-reviews/book-review-of-anita-agnihotri-1.1079404.

Blom, Philipp. *Nature's Mutiny: How the Little Ice Age of the Long Seventeenth Century Transformed the West and Shaped the Present*. United Kingdom: Pan Macmillan, 2019.

Bradley, James. 'The Best Climate Change Novels'. Five Books. Accessed 1 July 2025. https://fivebooks.com/best-books/climate-change-novels/.

Brin, David. *Earth*. United Kingdom: Little, Brown Book Group, 2011.

Brook, Timothy. *The Price of Collapse: The Little Ice Age and the Fall of Ming*. China: Princeton University Press, 2023.

Buchanan, Ian. *A Dictionary of Critical Theory*. London: Oxford University Press, 2018. https://www.oxfordreference.com/display/10.1093/acref/9780198794790.001.0001/acref-9780198794790-e-771.

Buell, Lawrence. *The Environmental Imagination: Thoreau, Nature Writing, and the Formation of American Culture*. Cambridge, MA: Harvard University Press, 1995.

Buell, Lawrence. *Writing for an Endangered World: Literature, Culture, and Environment in the United States and Beyond*. Cambridge, MA: Harvard University Press, 2001.

Buell, Lawrence. *The Future of Environmental Criticism: Environmental Crisis and Literary Imagination*. Germany: Wiley, 2009.

Bulgakov, Mikhail. *The Master and Margarita*. United Kingdom: Grove Atlantic, 2016.

Büntgen, Ulf, Vladimir S. Myglan, Fredrik Charpentier Ljungqvist, Michael McCormick, Nicola Di Cosmo, Michael Sigl and Johann Jungclaus. 'Cooling and Societal Change during the Late Antique Little Ice Age from 536 to Around 660 AD'. *Nature Geoscience* 9, no. 3 (8 February 2016): 231–6. https://doi.org/10.1038/ngeo2652.

Burke, Anthony. 'Interspecies Cosmopolitanism: Non-human Power and the Grounds of World Order in the Anthropocene'. *Review of International Studies* 49, no. 2 (2023): 201–22. doi:10.1017/S0260210522000171.

Burke, Edmund. *A Philosophical Enquiry into the Origin of Our Ideas of the Sublime and Beautiful*. United Kingdom: J. Dodsley, 1767.

Butler, Octavia E. *Parable of the Sower*. United Kingdom: Headline, 2014.

Cairney, Paul, Irina Timonina and Hannes Stephan. 'How Can Policy and Policymaking Foster Climate Justice? A Qualitative Systematic Review'. *Open Research Europe* 3:51 (31 March 2023): 1–42. https://doi.org/10.12688/openreseurope.15719.2.

Callenbach, Ernest. *Ecotopia*. United Kingdom: Random House Publishing Group, 1990.

Campbell, Joseph. *The Hero's Journey*. United States: New World Library, 2014.

Canavan, Gerry and Kim Stanley Robinson, eds, *Green Planets – Ecology and Science Fiction*. Middletown, CT: Wesleyan University Press, 2014.

Carson, Rachel. *Silent Spring*. Boston, MA: Houghton Mifflin, 1962.

Castoriadis, Cornelius. *The Imaginary Institution of Society*. Cambridge, MA: MIT Press, 1987.

Chabria, Priya Sarukkai. *Earthrise Stories: Pasts Potentials Prophecies*. India: Red River, 2025.

Chakrabarty, Dipesh. 'The Climate of History: Four Theses'. *Critical Inquiry* 35, no. 2 (Winter 2009): 197–222. https://doi.org/10.1086/596640.

Chakrabarty, Dipesh. 'Postcolonial Studies and the Challenge of Climate Change'. *New Literary History* 43, no. 1 (2012): 1–18. https://dx.doi.org/10.1353/nlh.2012.0007.

Chatterjee, Rimi B. *Ashquabad: City of Stories*. India: Rimi B. Chatterjee, 2024. Kindle.

Chaudhuri, Rajat with Singh, Ajit. *Water – What Are Our Rights to It?* India: CUTS, 1998.

Chaudhuri, Rajat. *The Butterfly Effect*. India: Niyogi Books, 2018.

Chaudhuri, Rajat. 'Cormac McCarthy's *The Road*: A Bleakly Beautiful Journey across a Devastated American Wasteland'. *Scroll.in*, 7 January 2018. Accessed 1 July 2025. https://scroll.in/article/864065/cormac-mccarthys-the-road-a-bleakly-beautiful-journey-across-a-devastated-american-wasteland.

Chaudhuri, Rajat. 'Can Literature Save the Planet? Reading during an Impending Climate Crisis'. Review of *Gun Island*, by Amitav Ghosh, *Scroll.in*, 18 August 2019. Accessed 1 July 2025. https://scroll.in/article/934150/can-literature-save-the-planet-reading-gun-island-during-an-impending-climate-crisis.

Chaudhuri, Rajat. 'Estranged Times and the Decades Ahead'. *New Indian Express*, 27 December 2020. https://www.newindianexpress.com/magazine/voices/2020/Dec/27/estranged-times-andthe-decades-ahead-2240793.html.

Chaudhuri, Rajat. 'Heart of Darkness'. Review of *The Sickle*, by Anita Agnihotri. *The New Indian Express*, 19 June 2021. https://www.newindianexpress.com/lifestyle/books/2021/Jun/20/the-sickle-book-review-heart-of-darkness-2317788.html.

Chaudhuri, Rajat. 'Literary Fiction Meets a Clear-Eyed Appreciation of the Planetary Crises in *Memory of Water*'. *Scroll.in*, 29 October 2022. Accessed 1 July 2025. https://scroll.in/article/1035673/literary-fiction-meets-a-clear-eyed-appreciation-of-the-planetary-crises-in-memory-of-water.

Chaudhuri, Rajat. 'Solarpunk: A Brilliant Subculture, Its Solutions and Visions'. The Telegraph, 27 November 2022. Accessed 1 July 2025. https://www.telegraphindia.com/science-tech/solarpunk-a-brilliant-subculture-its-solutions-and-visions/cid/1900585.

Chaudhuri, Rajat. 'Rethinking Literature: The Wicked Problem of Climate Change and Our Entanglement with It'. *Scroll.in*, 23 April 2023. Accessed

1 July 2025. https://scroll.in/article/1047822/rethinking-literature-the-wicked-problem-of-climate-change-and-our-entanglement-with-it.

Chaudhuri, Rajat. *Spellcasters*. India: Niyogi Books, 2023.

Chaudhuri, Rajat. *Wonder Tales for a Warming Planet*. New Delhi: Niyogi, 2025.

Chen, Qiang. 'Climate Shocks, Dynastic Cycles and Nomadic Conquests: Evidence from Historical China'. *Oxford Economic Papers* 67, no. 2 (2014): 185–204. https://doi.org/10.1093/oep/gpu032.

Chen, Siying, Yun Su, Xiuqi Fang and Jia He. 'Climate Records in Ancient Chinese Diaries and Their Application in Historical Climate Reconstruction – a Case Study of Yunshan Diary'. *Climate of the Past* 16, no. 5 (2020): 1873–87. https://doi.org/10.5194/cp-16-1873-2020.

Childs, Peter. *Modernism*. London: Routledge, 2000.

Clark, Alex. '*Gun Island* by Amitav Ghosh Review – Climate and Culture in Crisis'. Review of *Gun Island*, by Amitav Ghosh. *The Guardian*, 5 June 2019. www.theguardian.com/books/2019/jun/05/gun-island-amitav-ghosh-review.

Clark, Timothy. 'Scale: Derangements of Scale'. In *Telemorphosis: Theory in the Era of Climate Change*, Volume 1. Edited by Tom Cohen, 9–15. London: Open Humanities Press eBooks, 2012. http://dx.doi.org/10.3998/ohp.10539563.0001.001.

Costanza, Robert. 'Four Visions of the Century Ahead: Will It Be *Star Trek, Ecotopia, Big Government* or *Mad Max*?' *Futurist* 33, no. 2 (1999): 23–8.

Craps, Stef and Richard Crownshaw. 'Introduction: The Rising Tide of Climate Change Fiction'. *Studies in the Novel* 50, no. 1 (2018): 4. https://doi.org/10.1353/sdn.2018.0000.

Crichton, Michael. *State of Fear*. UK: HarperCollins, 2005.

Crosby, Alfred W. *The Columbian Exchange*. United Kingdom: Greenwood Publishing, 1972.

Crosby, Alfred W. *Ecological Imperialism: The Biological Expansion of Europe, 900–1900*. United Kingdom: Cambridge University Press, 2015.

Cunningham, John M. 'Popular Literature: History, Definition, Examples, Books, and Facts'. *Encyclopedia Britannica*. https://www.britannica.com/art/popular-literature.

David, Sophia. *Eco-Fiction: Bringing Climate Change into the Imagination*. United Kingdom: University of Exeter, 2016. Accessed 28 June 2025. https://ore.exeter.ac.uk/repository/handle/10871/24331.

De, Asis. 'Human/Non-human Interface and the Affective Uncanny in Amitav Ghosh's *Gun Island*'. *Revista Interdisciplinar de Literatura e*

*Ecocrítica*. 7, no. 1 (2021): 64–80. Accessed 2 July 2025. https://asle-brasil.com/journal/index.php/aslebr/article/view/165.

Descola, Philippe. *Beyond Nature and Culture*. Chicago: University of Chicago Press, 2013.

Doepler, Emil junior and Dr. W. Ranisch. *Walhall: die Götterwelt der Germanen*. Berlin: Martin Oldenbourg, 1905.

Douglas, Peter M. J., Mark Pagani, Marcello A. Canuto, Mark Brenner, David A. Hodell, Timothy I. Eglinton and Jason H. Curtis. 'Drought, Agricultural Adaptation, and Sociopolitical Collapse in the Maya Lowlands'. *Proceedings of the National Academy of Sciences* 112, no. 18 (20 April 2015): 5607–12. https://doi.org/10.1073/pnas.1419133112.

Dutta, Sudipta. 'By the Sweat of their Brows'. Review of *The Sickle*, by Anita Agnihotri. *The Hindu*, 1 May 2021. Accessed 25 May 2024. https://www.thehindu.com/books/by-the-sweat-of-their-brows-sudipta-datta-reviews-the-sickle-by-anita-agnihotri-trs-arunava-sinha/article34447032.ece.

Eagleton, Terry. *Literary Theory – An Introduction*. UK: Blackwell, 1996.

Earth Stories Collection. 'How the Trees Stopped Talking'. Accessed 30 June 2025. theearthstoriescollection.org/en/how-the-trees-stopped-talking.

Easterlin, Nancy. *A Biocultural Approach to Literary Theory and Interpretation*. United Kingdom: Johns Hopkins University Press, 2012.

Elgin, Ben. 'How Vintage Nike Airs Exposed a Flaw in a $700 Million Carbon Market'. *Bloomberg*, 29 October 2024. https://www.bloomberg.com/news/features/2024-10-29/vintage-nike-air-shoes-expose-flaw-in-700-million-carbon-market.

Esbjörn-Hargens, Sean and Michael E. Zimmerman. *Integral Ecology: Uniting Multiple Perspectives on the Natural World*. Boston, MA: Integral Books, 2011.

Fan, Ka-Wai. 'The Little Ice Age and the Fall of the Ming Dynasty: A Review'. *Climate* 11, no. 3 (17 March 2023): 1–8. https://doi.org/10.3390/cli11030071.

Farmar, Katherine. '*Memory of Water* by Emmi Itäranta'. *Strange Horizons*, 15 August 2014. https://web.archive.org/web/20150305132249/http://www.strangehorizons.com/reviews/2014/08/memory_of_water.shtml.

Fish, Stanley. *Is There a Text in This Class? The Authority of Interpretive Communities*. United Kingdom: Harvard University Press, 1980.

Foster, John Bellamy. *Marx's Ecology: Materialism and Nature*. United Kingdom: Monthly Review Press, 2000.

Francis, Laudato Si. (Vatican City: 2015). https://www.vatican.va/content/francesco/en/encyclicals/documents/papa-francesco_20150524_enciclica-laudato-si.html.

Francis, of Assisi, Saint. 'The Canticle of the Creatures' (1225). In *Francis of Assisi: Early Documents. Volume I: The Saint*. Edited by Regis J. Armstrong, O.F.M. Cap., J. A. Wayne Hellman, O.F.M. Conv. and William J. Short, O.F.M., 113. New York: New City Press, 1999.

Freud, Sigmund. *The Uncanny*. Translated by David MacLintock. London: Penguin, 2003.

Funes, Yessenia. 'Throwing Soup at a Van Gogh? Why Climate Activists Are Targeting Art'. *National Geographic*, 19 July 2023. https://www.nationalgeographic.com/environment/article/famous-art-museums-climate-change-activists.

Gaard, Greta. 'What's the Story? Competing Narratives of Climate Change and Climate Justice'. *Forum for World Literature Studies*, no. 6 (2014): 272–91. https://fwls.org/uploads/soft/210603/10479-2106031IH3.pdf.

Garrard, Greg, ed, *The Oxford Handbook of Ecocriticism*. United States: Oxford University Press, 2014.

Gautier, Théophile. *Mademoiselle de Maupin*. 1835. Volume 1 of 2. Translated by I. G. Burham. Philadelphia, PA: George Barrie and Sons, 1897. eBook#48893, htm. https://www.gutenberg.org/files/48893/48893-h/48893-h.htm.

Germanwatch. 'Global Climate Risk Index'. 2025. https://www.germanwatch.org/en/cri.

Gerson, Noel Bertram. *Harriet Beecher Stowe: A Biography*. United States: Praeger Publishers, 1976.

Ghosal, Somak. 'Marathwada Chronicles: Notes from the Land of Thirst'. Mint Lounge. Accessed 25 May 2024. https://lifestyle.livemint.com/news/big-story/marathwada-chronicles-notes-from-the-land-of-thirst-111615719911435.html.

Ghosh, Amitav. *The Hungry Tide: A Novel.* United States: Houghton Mifflin Harcourt, 2014.

Ghosh, Amitav. *The Great Derangement: Climate Change and the Unthinkable.* India: Penguin, 2018.

Ghosh, Amitav. *Gun Island.* India: Penguin Random House, 2019.

Ghosh, Amitav. '"*Gun Island*" Deals with the Slow Violence That Our World Is Experiencing Right Now'. *The Economic Times*, 14 June 2019. Accessed 23 September 2023. https://economictimes.indiatimes.com/magazines/panache/amitav-ghosh-gun-island-deals-slow-violence-that-the-world-is-experiencing-at-the-moment/articleshow/69786725.cms.

Ghosh, Amitav. 'My Book Is Not an Apocalyptic Book at All. I Guess I'm Leaving Hope as a Possibility'. Interview by Harsimran Gill. *Scroll.in*, 17 June 2019. Accessed 2 July 2025. https://scroll.in/article/927202/my-book-is-not-an-apocalyptic-book-at-all-i-guess-im-leaving-hope-as-a-possibility-amitav-ghosh.

Ghosh, Amitav. 'Amitav Ghosh on *Gun Island* and How to Make Sense of the World'. Huffington Post Online, Interview by Karthik Shankar. *HuffPost*, 22 June 2019. Accessed 19 August 2019. www.huffingtonpost.in/entry/amitav-ghosh-gun-island-and-how-to-make-sense-of-the-world_in_5d0cdb4fe4b07ae90d9bec1c.

Ghosh, Amitav. *The Nutmeg's Curse: Parables for a Planet in Crisis.* The Chicago, IL: University of Chicago Press, 2021.

Ghosh, Amitav. '*Sakkhatkar: Amitav Ghosh*' ('Interview: Amitav Ghosh'). Interview by Rajat Chaudhuri. *Daakbangla*, 19 August 2023. Accessed 5 May 2025. https://daakbangla.com/2023/08/sakkhatkar-amitabha-ghosh/.

Giggs, Rebecca. 'The Green Afterword: Cormac McCarthy's *The Road* and the Ecological Uncanny'. In *Criticism, Crisis, and Contemporary Narrative: Textual Horizons in an Age of Global Risk.* Edited by P. Crosthwaite, 201–17. Routledge Studies in Contemporary Literature; Volume. 4. London: Routledge, Taylor and Francis Group, 2011.

Gilson, Edwin. 'Planetary Los Angeles: Climate Realism and Transnational Narrative in Amitav Ghosh's *Gun Island* (2019)'. *Comparative American Studies an International Journal* 19, nos. 2–3 (2022): 269–88. https://doi.org/10.1080/14775700.2022.2114286.

Glotfelty, Cheryll and Harold Fromm. *The Ecocriticism Reader: Landmarks in Literary Ecology*. Athens: University of Georgia Press, 1996.

Goodbody, Axel. 'Cli-Fi beyond the American Thriller: Cultural and Aesthetic Alternatives in Climate Change Fiction since 2010'. In *Nuevos horizontes de la literatura comparada* (Vol. 2) *Ecocrítica*. Edited by Bruno Echauri Galván and Julia Ori, 19–30. Sociedad Española de Literatura General y Comparada (SELGYC), 2021. https://www.selgyc.com/mat/ecocritica_01_goodbody.pdf.

Goodbody, Axel and Adeline Johns-Putra. *Cli-Fi: A Companion*. Oxford, United Kingdom: Peter Lang Verlag, 2019.

Goodbody, Axel and Adeline Johns-Putra. 'The Rise of the Climate Change Novel'. In *Climate and Literature*. Edited by Adeline Johns-Putra, 229–45. Cambridge: Cambridge University Press eBooks, 2019. https://doi.org/10.1017/9781108505321.015.

Graeber, David. *Bullshit Jobs: A Theory*. United Kingdom: Penguin Books, 2018.

Greimas, Algirdas Julien. *Structural Semantics: An Attempt at a Method*. Translated by Daniele McDowell, Ronald Schleifer and Alan R. Velie. Lincoln: University of Nebraska Press, 1983.

Grosse, Stephen. 'Building a Relationship with the Earth: Humans and Ecology in Genesis 1–3'. *Denison Journal of Religion* 5, no. 4 (2005): 1–35.

Grove, Richard. *Green Imperialism: Colonial Expansion, Tropical Island Edens and the Origins of Environmentalism, 1600–1860*. Cambridge: Cambridge University Press, 1995.

Gu, H. and W. Li, eds, *A Series of Diaries in the Jin and Yuan Dynasty*. Shanghai: Shanghai Bookstore Publishing House, 2013 (in Chinese).

Guattari, Félix. *The Three Ecologies*. United Kingdom: Athlone Press, 2000.

Guha, Ramachandra. *Environmentalism: A Global History*. Oxford: Oxford University Press, 2000.

Guha, Ramachandra. *The Unquiet Woods*. Berkeley: University of California Press, 2000.

Guha, Ramachandra and J. Martínez-Alier. *Varieties of Environmentalism: Essays North and South*. London: Earthscan, 1997.

Guo, Bi. *Snowy Bamboo*. 14th century CE. Handscroll; ink on silk, National Palace Museum, Taipei. http://www.chinaonlinemuseum.com/painting-bamboo-guo-bi.php.

Guo, Bi. *Withered Tree*. 14th century CE, Handscroll; ink on silk, Kyoto National Museum. https://www.kyohaku.go.jp/eng/collection/meihin/chuugoku/item06/.

Guo, Bi. 'Yunshan Diary'. 13th–14th century CE. https://ctext.org/wiki.pl?if=gb&res=908804&remap=gb.

Gustafson, Abel, Matthew T. Ballew, Matthew H. Goldberg, Matthew J. Cutler, Seth A. Rosenthal and Anthony Leiserowitz. 'Personal Stories Can Shift Climate Change Beliefs and Risk Perceptions: The Mediating Role of Emotion'. *Communication Reports* 33, no. 3, (2020): 121–35. https://doi.org/10.1080/08934215.2020.1799049.

Hambrick, Keira. 'Destroying Imagination to Save Reality: Environmental Apocalypse in Science Fiction'. In *Environmentalism in the Realm of Science Fiction and Fantasy Literature*. Edited by Chris Baratta, 129–42. UK: Cambridge Scholars Publishing, 2012.

Haraway, Donna J. *The Companion Species Manifesto*. United States: Prickly Paradigm Press, 2003.

Haraway, Donna J. *Staying with the Trouble: Making Kin in the Chthulucene*. USA: Duke University Press, 2016.

Hausfather, Zeke. 'Explainer: How "Shared Socioeconomic Pathways" Explore Future Climate Change'. *Carbon Brief*, 2018. https://www.carbonbrief.org/explainer-how-shared-socioeconomic-pathways-explore-future-climate-change/.

Hayden, Gabriel and Greg Garrard. 'Reading and Writing Climate Change'. In *Teaching Ecocriticism and Green Cultural Studies*. Edited by Greg Garrard, 117–29. London: Palgrave Macmillan, 2012. https://doi.org/10.1057/9780230358393_10.

Heise, Ursula K. 'Abstract'. In *Sense of Place and Sense of Planet: The Environmental Imagination of the Global*. New York, 2008; online edn, Oxford Academic, 1 September 2008. Accessed 24 June 2025. https://doi.org/10.1093/acprof:oso/9780195335637.001.0001.

Heise, Ursula K. *Sense of Place and Sense of Planet: The Environmental Imagination of the Global*. Oxford: Oxford University Press, 2008.

Heise, Ursula K. 'Science Fiction and the Time Scales of the Anthropocene'. *ELH* 86, no. 2 (2019): 275–304. https://dx.doi.org/10.1353/elh.2019.0015.

Hiltner, Ken, ed, *Ecocriticism: The Essential Reader*. Oxon: Routledge, 2014.

Ho, Bong Joon, director. *Snowpiercer*. CJ Entertainment, 2013. 2 hr., 6 min. https://www.imdb.com/title/tt1706620/.

Hobbes, Thomas. *Leviathan*. Edited by G. A. J. Rogers and Karl Schuhmann (A critical edition). 1635. London: Bloomsbury Publishing, 2006.

Huggan, Graham and Helen Tiffin. *Postcolonial Ecocriticism: Literature, Animals, Environment*. UK: Routledge, 2015.

Huxley, Aldous. *Brave New World*. Garden City, NY: Doubleday, Doran, Incorporated, 1932.

Huxley, Aldous. *Island*. United Kingdom: Random House, 2009.

Internal Displacement Monitoring Centre. 'Country Profile, India'. https://www.internal-displacement.org/countries/india/.

International Climate Justice Network. 'Bali Principles of Climate Justice'. 28 August 2002. Accessed 5 March 2024. https://www.corpwatch.org/article/bali-principles-climate-justice.

IPCC. 'WGII Summary for Policymakers Headline Statements'. 28 February 2022. Accessed 28 June 2025. www.ipcc.ch/report/ar6/wg2/resources/spm-headline-statements.

Irr, Caren. 'Climate Fiction in English'. *Oxford Research Encyclopedia of Literature*, February 2017. https://doi.org/10.1093/acrefore/9780190201098.013.4.

Itäranta, Emmi. *Memory of Water*. London: HarperVoyager, 2014 (Kindle Ebook) Version: 2014-03-18.

Jameson, Fredric. 'Magical Narratives: Romance as Genre'. *New Literary History* 7, no. 1 (1975): 135–63. https://doi.org/10.2307/468283.

Jameson, Fredric. *Archaeologies of the Future: The Desire Called Utopia and Other Science Fictions*. London: Verso Publication, 2007.

Jensen, Liz. *The Rapture*. United Kingdom: Bloomsbury Publishing, 2009.

Jensen, Liz. *Your Wild and Precious Life: On Grief, Hope and Rebellion*. United Kingdom: Canongate Books, 2024.

Jerolleman, Alessandra, Shirley Laska and Julie Torres. 'Lessons from Concurrent Disasters: *COVID-19 and Eight Hurricanes*'. Natural Hazards Center Quick Response Research Report Series, Report 327. Natural Hazards Center, University of Colorado Boulder. 2021. Accessed 2 July 2025. https://hazards.colorado.edu/quick-response-report/lessons-from-co-occurring-disasters.

Johnson, Shannon. 'Discourse and Practice of REDD+ in Ghana and the Expansion of State Power'. *Sustainability* 13, no. 20 (2021): 1–21. https://doi.org/10.3390/su132011358/.

Johns-Putra, Adeline. 'Climate Change in Literature and Literary Studies: From Cli-Fi, Climate Change Theater and Ecopoetry to

Ecocriticism and Climate Change Criticism'. *WIREs Climate Change* 7, no. 2 (2016): 266–82. https://doi.org/10.1002/wcc.385. Accessed 21 September 2019.

Johns-Putra, Adeline. 'The Rest Is Silence: Postmodern and Postcolonial Possibilities in Climate Change Fiction'. *Studies in the Novel* 50, no. 1. Johns Hopkins University Press (2018): 26–42. doi:doi.org/10.1353/sdn.2018.0002.

Just Stop Oil (@JustStop_Oil). 'SUFFRAGETTE PAINTING SMASHED: Our Government Have Revealed Plans for MORE Oil Licences, Knowing It Will Kill Millions. In Response, Two Supporters of Just Stop Oil ...'. X (Formerly Twitter), 6 November 2023, 5:14 PM. Accessed 2 July 2025. x.com/JustStop_Oil/status/1721493745781113173?s=20.

Kant, Immanuel. *Groundwork of the Metaphysics of Morals*. 1785. Translated by Mary Gregor. Cambridge: Cambridge University Press, 1997.

Kashwan, Prakash. *Climate Justice in India*. Volume 1. New York: Cambridge University Press, 2024.

Kerridge, Richard. 'Ecocritical Approaches to Literary Form and Genre: Urgency, Depth, Provisionality, Temporality'. In *The Oxford Handbook of Ecocriticism*. Edited by Greg Garrard, 361–76. Oxford: Oxford University Press, 2013.

Key, Andrew. 'Writing, Aesthetics, Climate (a Bricolage)'. *New Socialist*, 16 October 2021. Accessed 20 November 2019. www.newsocialist.org.uk/approaching-avant-garde-eco-socialist-political-imaginary-writing-aesthetics-climate-bricolage.

Khan, Sami Ahmad. *Star Warriors of the Modern Raj – Materiality, Mythology and Technology of Indian Science Fiction*. UK: University of Wales Press, 2021.

Kimmerer, Robin Wall. *Braiding Sweetgrass: Indigenous Wisdom, Scientific Knowledge and the Teachings of Plants*. United States: Milkweed Editions, 2013.

Kingsolver, Barbara. *Flight Behavior*. United Kingdom: HarperCollins, 2012.

Kirkus Reviews. '*Memory of Water*'. Review of *Memory of Water* by Emmi Itäranta. 15 May 2014. https://www.kirkusreviews.com/book-reviews/emmi-itaranta/memory-of-water/.

Klaser, Klaudijo, Lorenzo Sacconi and Marco Faillo. 'John Rawls and Compliance to Climate Change Agreements: Insights from a Laboratory Experiment'. *International Environmental Agreements Politics Law and*

*Economics* 21, no. 3 (2021): 531–51. https://doi.org/10.1007/s10784-021-09533-8.

Klein, Naomi. *This Changes Everything: Capitalism vs. The Climate*. India: Simon & Schuster, 2014.

Kohn, Eduardo. *How Forests Think: Toward an Anthropology beyond the Human*. University of California Press, 2013.

Korotayev, Andrey. 'Sixth Century Global Climatic Disaster, the Origins of Islam, and Its World-System Consequences'. *Journal of World-Systems Research* 31, no. 1 (17 April 2025): 8–18. https://doi.org/10.5195/jwsr.2025.1325.

Kung, James Kai-Sing and Chicheng Ma. 'Can Cultural Norms Reduce Conflicts? Confucianism and Peasant Rebellions in Qing China'. *Journal of Development Economics* 111(C) (6 September 2014): 132–49. Elsevier. https://doi.org/10.1016/j.jdeveco.2014.08.006.

Lafuente, Antonio and Nuria Valverde. 'Linnaean Botany and Spanish Imperial Biopolitics'. In *Colonial Botany: Science, Commerce, and Politics in the Early Modern World*. Edited by Londa Schiebinger and Claudia Swan, 134–48. United States: University of Pennsylvania Press, Incorporated, 2007.

Langer, Jessica. *Postcolonialism and Science Fiction*. New York: Palgrave Macmillan, 2011.

Latour, Bruno. *Science in Action: How to Follow Scientists and Engineers through Society*. Cambridge, MA: Harvard University Press, 1987.

Latour, Bruno. *We Have Never Been Modern*. Translated by Catherine Porter. Cambridge, MA: Harvard University Press, 1993.

Latour, Bruno. *Reassembling the Social: An Introduction to Actor–Network Theory*. Oxford, UK: Oxford University Press, 2005.

Latour, Bruno. *Facing Gaia: Eight Lectures on the New Climatic Regime*. Translated by Catherine Porter. Cambridge: Polity Press, 2017.

Leavis, F. R. *The Great Tradition: George Eliot, Henry James, Joseph Conrad*. New York: George W. Stewart, 1950.

LeMenager, Stephanie. '12. Climate Change and the Struggle for Genre'. In *Anthropocene Reading: Literary History in Geologic Times*. Edited by Tobias Menely and Jesse Oak Taylor, 220–38. University Park, USA: Penn State University Press, 2017. https://doi.org/10.1515/9780271080390-013.

Leopold, Aldo. *A Sand Country Almanac and Sketches Here and There*. London: Oxford University Press, 1949.

Leppänen, Katarina. '*Memory of Water*: Boundaries of Political Geography and World Literature'. *European Review* 28, no. 3 (2020): 425–34. https://doi.org/10.1017/S1062798719000541.

Lessing, Doris. *Mara and Dann*. United Kingdom: HarperCollins, 2009.

Li, Yali, Shelach-Lavi Gideon and Ronnie Ellenblum. 'Short-Term Climatic Catastrophes and the Collapse of the Liao Dynasty (907–1125): Textual Evidence'. *The Journal of Interdisciplinary History* 49, no. 4 (2019): 591–610. https://doi.org/10.1162/jinh_a_01339.

Lloyd, Saci. *The Carbon Diaries*. United Kingdom: Hachette Children's Group, 2011.

Lukács, György. *Studies in European Realism: A Sociological Survey of the Writings of Balzac, Stendhal, Zola, Tolstoy, Gorki and Others*. Translated by Edith Bone. London: Hilway, 1950.

Malwika. 'Ecological Concerns in the Works of Hansda Sowvendra Shekhar: An Ecocritical Study'. *Creative Flight* 3, no. 2 (October, 2022): 137–46. https://www.creativeflight.in/ecological-concerns-in-works-of-hansda,https://drive.google.com/file/d/1nF_j79dCsfvkhiVrb_TRE9DJqfTCiCxN/view.

Mambrol, Nasrullah. 'Roman Jakobson's Contribution to Russian Formalism'. *Literariness.org*., 16 March 2016. Accessed 2 July 2025. https://literariness.org/2016/03/17/roman-jakobsons-contribution-to-russian-formalism/.

Mansharamani, Vikram. 'A Major Contributor to the Syrian Conflict? Climate Change'. *PBS*, 17 March 2017. Accessed 15 November 2019. www.pbs.org/newshour/economy/a-major-contributor-to-the-syrian-conflict-climate-change.

Martínez-Alier, Joan. *The Environmentalism of the Poor: A Study of Ecological Conflicts and Valuation*. Cheltenham: Edward Elgar, 2002.

Marx, Karl. *Capital: A Critique of Political Economy*. Volume 1. Translated by Ben Fowkes, Penguin with New Left Review, 1976.

Mathur, Shrestha. 'M K Ranjitsinh v. Union of India: The Supreme Court's Very Own Sophie's Choice Moment'. *Bar and Bench*, 27 April 2024. https://www.barandbench.com/columns/mk-ranjitsinh-v-union-of-india-the-supreme-courts-very-own-sophies-choice-moment.

Maxwell, Anne. 'Postcolonial Criticism, Ecocriticism and Climate Change: A Tale of Melbourne under Water in 2035'. *Journal of Postcolonial Writing*. 45, no. 1 (2009): 15–26. https://doi.org/10.1080/17449850802636499.

McCarthy, Cormac. *The Road*. United Kingdom: Pan Macmillan, 2019.

McEwan, Ian. *Solar*. United Kingdom: Random House, 2010.

McGurl, Mark. 'The Posthuman Comedy'. *Critical Inquiry* 38, no. 3 (March 2012): 533–53. https://doi.org/10.1086/664550.

Miall David, S. and Don Kuiken. 'What Is Literariness? Three Components of Literary Reading'. *Discourse Processes* 28, no. 2 (1999): 121–38. https://doi.org/10.1080/01638539909545076.

Milman, Oliver. 'Smoking Gun Proof: Fossil Fuel Industry Knew of Climate Danger as Early as 1954, Documents Show'. *The Guardian*, 30 January 2024. Accessed 4 July 2025. https://www.theguardian.com/us-news/2024/jan/30/fossil-fuel-industry-air-pollution-fund-research-caltech-climate-change-denial.

Ministry of Consumer Affairs, Food & Public Distribution. 'India Emerges as the World's Largest Producer and Consumer of Sugar and World's 2nd Largest Exporter of Sugar'. Government of India, 5 October 2022. https://pib.gov.in/PressReleaseIframePage.aspx?PRID=1865320.

Ministry of Petroleum and Natural Gas. 'Ethanol Blended Petrol (EBP) Programme'. Accessed 21 May 2024. https://mopng.gov.in/en/refining/ethanol-blended-petrol.

Montaigne, Michel de. *The Essays of Montaigne*. Edited by William Carew Hazlitt, translated by Charles Cotton (1877), ebook #3600, html, 28 May 2001. https://gutenberg.org/files/3600/3600-h/3600-h.htm#link2HCH0001.

Moretti, Franco. *The Bourgeois: Between History and Literature*. New York: Verso, 2013.

Morton, Timothy. *Hyperobjects: Philosophy and Ecology after the End of the World*. Minneapolis: University of Minnesota Press, 2013.

Mottram, Stewart. 'Deluge and Disease: Plague, the Poetry of Flooding, and the History of Health Inequalities in Andrew Marvell's Hull'. *The Seventeenth Century* 38, no. 2 (5 December 2022): 263–90. https://doi.org/10.1080/0268117x.2022.2142656.

Mukařovský, Jan. 'Standard Language and Poetic Language'. In *Chapters from the History of Czech Functional Linguistics*. Edited by Jan Chovanec. 1. Vyd, 41–53. Brno: Masarykova Univerzita, 2014. Accessed 30 June 2025. https://digilib.phil.muni.cz/sites/default/files/pdf/131565.pdf.

Nabi, Robin L., Abel Gustafson and Risa Jensen. 'Framing Climate Change: Exploring the Role of Emotion in Generating Advocacy Behavior'. *Science Communication* 40, no. 4 (2018): 442–68. https://doi.org/10.1177/1075547018776019.

NASA. 'Global Surface Temperature'. NASA Global Climate Change, Climate Change: Vital Signs of the Planet. https://climate.nasa.gov/vital-signs/global-temperature/?intent=121.

NASA Science. 'Scientific Consensus'. Accessed 6 July 2025, science.nasa.gov/climate-change/scientific-consensus.

Nikoleris, Alexandra, Johannes Stripple and Paul Tenngart. 'Narrating Climate Futures: Shared Socioeconomic Pathways and Literary Fiction'. *Climatic Change* 143, no. 3–4 (8 July 2017): 307–19. https://doi.org/10.1007/s10584-017-2020-2.

Nixon, Rob. *Slow Violence and the Environmentalism of the Poor*. Cambridge, MA: Harvard University Press, 2013.

O'Brien, Susan. 'Articulating a World of Difference: Ecocriticism, Postcolonialism and Globalization'. *Canadian Literature* Special issue no. 170–1 (2001): 140–58. https://doi.org/10.14288/cl.v0i170-171.

Okereke, Chukwumerije. 'Climate Justice and the International Regime'. *WIREs Climate Change* 1, no. 3 (2010): 462–74. https://doi.org/10.1002/wcc.52.

Oreskes, Naomi and Erik M. Conway. *The Collapse of Western Civilization: A View from the Future*. United States: Columbia University Press, 2014.

Pal, Rabin. '*Kaste: Chakravyuha o Pratirodher Akhyan*' ['The Sickle: A Narrative of Entrapment and Resistance'] Review of *The Sickle*, by Anita Agnihotri. *Parabaas*, no. 76 (September 2019): 30. Accessed 25 May 2024. https://www.parabaas.com/PB76/LEKHA/brRobin76.shtml.

Panda, Nila Madhab, director. *Kadvi Hawa* (*Dark Wind*). Eros International and Drishyam Films, 2017. 1 hr., 39 min. https://www.imdb.com/title/tt6143422/.

Pariat, Janice. *Everything the Light Touches*. India: Fourth Estate, 2022.

Piguet, Etienne, Antoine Pecoud and P. De Guchteneire. 'Migration and Climate Change: An Overview'. *Refugee Survey Quarterly* 30, no. 3 (8 June 2011): 1–23. http://dx.doi.org/10.1093/rsq/hdr006.

Plumwood, Val. *Environmental Culture: The Ecological Crisis of Reason*. United Kingdom: Taylor & Francis, 2005.

Poe, Edgar Allan. 'The Fall of the House of Usher'. In *Tales of Mystery and Imagination*, 323–44. London: Milner and Sowerby, 1860.

Pongratz, Julia, Ken Caldeira, Christian H. Reick and Martin Claussen. 'Coupled Climate–Carbon Simulations Indicate Minor Global Effects of Wars and Epidemics on Atmospheric $CO_2$ between AD

800 and 1850'. *The Holocene* 21, no. 5 (2011): 843–51. https://doi.org/10.1177/0959683610386981.

Poynting, Mark. 'World's First Year-long Breach of Key 1.5C Warming Limit'. 8 February 2024. www.bbc.com/news/science-environment-68110310.

Prater, Andreas. *Venus at Her Mirror: Velázquez and the Art of Nude Painting*. Germany: Prestel, 2002.

Quale, Steven, director. *Into the Storm*. Warner Bros. Pictures, 2014. 1 hr., 29 min. https://www.imdb.com/title/tt2106361.

Rancière, Jacques. *The Politics of Aesthetics*. United Kingdom: Bloomsbury Publishing, 2013.

Rangarajan, Swarnalatha. *Eco Critcism: Big Ideas and Practical Strategies*. India: Orient BlackSwan, 2018.

Rawls, John. *A Theory of Justice*. Cambridge, MA: Harvard University Press, 1999.

Reed, T.V. 'Toward an Environmental Justice Ecocriticism'. In *The Environmental Justice Reader: Politics, Poetics, and Pedagogy*. Edited by Joni Adamson, Mei Mei Evans and Rachel Stein, 145–62. United States: University of Arizona Press, 2002.

Riedy, Chris. 'Futures of the Climate Action Movement: Insights from an Integral Futures Approach'. *Journal of Futures Studies* 15, no. 3 (March 2011): 33–52. Accessed 7 July 2025. https://jfsdigital.org/wp-content/uploads/2014/01/153-A03.pdf.

Ripple William, J., Christopher Wolf, Timothy M. Lenton, Jillian W. Gregg, Susan M. Natali, Philip B. Duffy, Johan Rockström, and Hans Joachim Schellnhuber. 'Many Risky Feedback Loops Amplify the Need for Climate Action'. *One Earth* 6, no. 2 (2023): 86–91. https://doi.org/10.1016/j.oneear.2023.01.004.

'Robert Boyle'. *Encyclopedia Britannica*. https://www.britannica.com/biography/Robert-Boyle.

Robinson, Kim Stanley. *Pacific Edge*. United States: Tor Publishing Group, 1995.

Robinson, Kim Stanley. *Fifty Degrees Below*. United Kingdom: HarperCollins Publishers, 2013.

Robinson, Kim Stanley. *New York 2140*. United Kingdom: Little, Brown Book Group, 2017.

Robinson, Kim Stanley. *The Ministry for the Future*. United Kingdom: Little, Brown Book Group, 2020.

Robinson, Kim Stanley. 'The Realism of Our Times: Kim Stanley Robinson on How Science Fiction Works' Interview by John Plotz'. *Public Books*,

23 September 2020. https://www.publicbooks.org/the-realism-of-our-times-kim-stanley-robinson-on-how-science-fiction-works/.

Rockström, Johan, Will Steffen, Kevin Noone Åsa Persson, F. Stuart Chapin III, Eric F. Lambin, Timothy M. Lenton, Marten Scheffer, Carl Folke, Hans Joachim Schellnhuber, Björn Nykvist, Cynthia A. de Wit, Terry Hughes, Sander van der Leeuw, Henning Rodhe, Sverker Sörlin, Peter K. Snyder, Robert Costanza, Uno Svedin, Malin Falkenmark, Louise Karlberg, Robert W. Corell, Victoria J. Fabry, James Hansen, Brian Walker, Diana Liverman, Katherine Richardson, Paul Crutzen, and Jonathan A. Foley. 'A Safe Operating Space for Humanity'. *Nature* 461, no. 7263 (1 September 2009): 472–5. https://doi.org/10.1038/461472a.

Rosen, Jeremy. 'Literary Fiction and the Genres of Genre Fiction'. *Post45 - American Literature and Culture since 1945*, July 16, 2019. https://post45.org/2018/08/literary-fiction-and-the-genres-of-genre-fiction/.

Roy, Nilanjana S. *Black River*. India: Context, 2022.

Roy, Somnath Baidya and Justin J. Traiteur. 'Impacts of Wind Farms on Surface Air Temperatures'. *Proceedings of the National Academy of Sciences* 107, no. 42 (October 2010): 17899–904. https://doi.org/10.1073/pnas.1000493107.

Rupprecht, Christoph, Deborah Cleland, Norie Tamura and Rajat Chaudhuri. 'Introduction'. In *Multispecies Cities: Solarpunk Urban Futures*. Edited by Christoph Rupprecht, Deborah Cleland, Norie Tamura, Rajat Chaudhuri and Sarena Ulibarri, 1–10. USA: World Weaver Press, 2021. https://www.researchgate.net/publication/349027086_Multispecies_Cities_Solarpunk_Urban_Futures.

Rupprecht, Christoph, Deborah Cleland, Norie Tamura, Rajat Chaudhuri and Sarena Ulibarri. *Multispecies Cities: Solarpunk Urban Futures*. USA: World Weaver Press, 2021.

Rupprecht, Christoph, Deborah Cleland, Rajat Chaudhuri, Sarena Ulibarri, Melissa Ingaruca Moreno and Norie Tamura. *Solarpunk Creatures*. USA: World Weaver Press, 2024.

Ryan, Sadie J., Colin J. Carlson, Erin A. Mordecai and Leah R. Johnson 'Global Expansion and Redistribution of Aedes-borne Virus Transmission Risk with Climate Change'. *PLOS*, 28 March 2019. https://journals.plos.org/plosntds/article?id=10.1371/journal.pntd.0007213.

Saito, Kohei. *Marx in the Anthropocene: Towards the Idea of Degrowth Communism*. United Kingdom: Cambridge University Press, 2023.

Saricks, Joyce G. *The Readers' Advisory Guide to Genre Fiction*. Chicago, IL: American Library Association, 2009.

Sartre, Jean-Paul. *The Imaginary*. United Kingdom: Routledge, 2004.

Schatzing, Frank. *The Swarm: A Novel*. United States: HarperCollins, 2009.

Schneider-Mayerson, Matthew. 'Climate Change Fiction'. In *American Literature in Transition, 2000–2010*. Edited by Rachel Greenwald Smith, 309–21. Cambridge: Cambridge University Press, 2017.

Schneider-Mayerson, Matthew. 'The Influence of Climate Fiction: An Empirical Survey of Readers'. *Environmental Humanities*, 10, no. 2 (November 2018): 481. https://doi.org/10.1215/22011919-7156848.

Schneider-Mayerson, Matthew, Carmiel Banasky, Bruno Olmedo Quiroga and Anna Jane Joyner. 'The Climate Reality Check – A Bechdel Wallace Test for a World on Fire'. In *Good Energy and Buck Lab for Climate and Environment*. USA: Colby College, 2024. https://www.colby.edu/wp-content/uploads/2024/06/The-Climate-Reality-Check-A-Bechdel-Wallace-Test-for-a-World-on-Fire-1.pdf.

Schneider-Mayerson, Mathew, Abel Gustafson, Anthony Leiserowitz, Matthew H. Goldberg, Seth A. Rosenthal and Matthew Ballew. 'Environmental Literature as Persuasion: An Experimental Test of the Effects of Reading Climate Fiction'. *Environmental Communication* 17, no. 1 (2020): 35–50. https://doi.org/10.1080/17524032.2020.1814377.

Shapin, Steven and Simon Schaffer. *Leviathan and the Air-Pump: Hobbes, Boyle, and the Experimental Life*. Princeton, NJ: Princeton University Press, 2018.

Shekhar, Hansda Sowvendra. *The Mysterious Ailment of Rupi Baskey: A Novel*. India: Aleph Book Company, 2014.

Shekhar, Hansda Sowvendra. *Jwala Kumar and the Gift of Fire: Adventures in Champakbagh*. India: Speaking Tiger Publishing, 2018.

Shelley, Mary Wollstonecraft and Susan J. Wolfson. *Frankenstein, or, The Modern Prometheus*. United Kingdom: Pearson Longman, 2007.

Shi, Hu. '9 Some Modest Proposals for the Reform of Literature'. In *Modern Chinese Literary Thought: Writings on Literature, 1893–1945*. Edited by Kirk A. Denton, 123–39. Redwood City, CA: Stanford University Press, 1996. https://doi.org/10.1515/9781503615830-013.

Shiva, Vandana. *Soil Not Oil-Environmental Justice in an Age of Climate Crisis*. Cambridge, MA: South End Press, 2008.

Shiva, Vandana. 'Soil Not Oil: Environmental Justice in an Age of Climate Crisis'. *Alternatives Journal* 35, no. 3 (2009): 18+. *Gale Academic OneFile*. https://link.gale.com/apps/doc/A200106391/AONE?u=anon~8e1f625&sid=googleScholar&xid=d903ac87.

Shklovsky, Victor. *Theory of Prose*. Translated by Benjamin Sher. Elmwood Park, IL: Dalkey Archive Press, 1991.

Shklovsky, Victor. 'Art as Technique'. In *Twentieth-Century Literary Theory*. Edited by K. M. Newton, 3–5. London: Palgrave Macmillan, 1997. https://doi.org/10.1007/978-1-349-25934-2_1.

Sinclair, Upton and Anna Maria Hong. *The Jungle*. United Kingdom: Simon & Schuster, 2004.

Slovic, Scott, Swarnalatha Rangarajan and Vidya Sarveswaran, eds, *Ecocriticism of the Global South*. United Kingdom: Bloomsbury (Lexington Books), 2015.

Snow, C. P. 'The Two Cultures'. *New Statesman*, 27 September 2015. www.newstatesman.com/culture/2013/01/c-p-snow-two-cultures.

Sorlin, Sverker. 'Environmental Humanities: Why Should Biologists Interested in the Environment Take the Humanities Seriously?' *BioScience* 62, no. 9 (September 2012): 789. doi:10.1525/bio.2012.62.9.2.

Spade, Paul Vincent and Claude Panaccio. 'William of Ockham'. In *The Stanford Encyclopedia of Philosophy*. Edited by Edward N. Zalta. Stanford University, Spring 2019 Edition. https://plato.stanford.edu/archives/spr2019/entries/ockham/.

Spivak, Gayatri-Chakravorty, 'Can the Subaltern Speak?' In *Marxism and the Interpretation of Culture*. Edited by Cary Nelson and Lawrence Grossberg, 271–313. Chicago: University of Illinois Press, 1988.

Spivak, Gayatri Chakravorty. *An Aesthetic Education in the Era of Globalization*. United Kingdom: Harvard University Press, 2012, 335–50. https://doi.org/10.2307/j.ctv1n1bsfh.

Spivak, Gayatri Chakravorty. 'Planetarity' (Box 4, WELT). *Paragraph* 38, no. 2, Edinburgh University Press, 2015. https://doi.org/10.3366/para.2015.01.

Steinbeck, John. *The Grapes of Wrath*. New York: The Viking Press, 1939.

Stevenson, Kathryn and Nils Peterson. 'Motivating Action through Fostering Climate Change Hope and Concern and Avoiding Despair among Adolescents'. *Sustainability* 8, no. 1 (2016): 6. https://doi.org/10.3390/su8010006.

Stone, Maddie. 'Can Climate Fiction Deliver Climate Justice?' *Fix*, 16 August 2022. https://grist.org/fix/climate-fiction/can-climate-fiction-deliver-climate-justice/.

Stowe, Charles Edward. *The Life of Harriet Beecher Stowe Compiled from Her Letters and Journals by Her Son Charles Edward Stowe*. Boston, MA, and New York: Houghton, Mifflin, 1890. Ebook#6702, txt, 1 October 2004. https://www.gutenberg.org/ebooks/6702.

Stowe, Harriet Beecher. *Uncle Tom's Cabin: Or, Life Among the Lowly.* United States: J. P. Jewett, 1852.

Stowe, Harriet Beecher. *A Reply to 'the Affectionate and Christian Address of Many Thousands of Women of Great Britain and Ireland, to Their Sisters, the Women of the United States of America', on Behalf of Many Thousands of American Women.* London: Sampson Low, Son, 1863. Ebook#70613, txt, 21 April 2023. https://www.gutenberg.org/cache/epub/70613/pg70613.txt.

Supran, Geoffrey, Stefan Rahmstorf and Naomi Oreskes. 'Assessing ExxonMobil's Global Warming Projections'. *Science* 379, no. 6628 (12 January 2023): 153, eabk0063. https://doi.org/10.1126/science.abk0063.

Suvin, Darko. *Metamorphosis of Science Fiction – On the Poetics and History of a Literary Genre.* New Haven, CT, and London: Yale University Press, 1979.

Suvin, Darko. 'On the Poetics of the Science Fiction Genre'. In *Science Fiction Criticism*. Edited by Rob Latham, 116–27. London: Bloomsbury Academic eBooks, 2017. https://doi.org/10.5040/9781474248655.0018.

Svoboda, Michael. 'A Review of Climate Fiction (cli-fi) Cinema … Past and Present'. *Yale Climate Connections*, 22 October 2014. Accessed 17 November 2019. https://www.yaleclimateconnections.org/2014/10/a-review-of-climate-fiction-cli-fi-cinema-past-and-present/.

Svoboda, Michael. 'Ice-fi: The Legacy of *Day after Tomorrow*'. *Yale Climate Connections*, 22 May 2024. yaleclimateconnections.org/2014/10/ice-fi-the-motion-pictur-ice-sque-legacy-of-the-day-after-tomorrow.

Swarup, Shubhangi. *Latitudes of Longing.* India: HarperCollins, 2019.

The Oxford Dictionary of Literary Terms (Oxford Reference). 'Literariness'. Accessed 2 July 2025. https://www.oxfordreference.com/display/10.1093/oi/authority.20110803100108912.

Thomashow, Mitchell. *Bringing the Biosphere Home: Learning to Perceive Global Environmental Change.* Cambridge, MA: MIT Press, 2002.

Tomlinson, John. *Globalization and Culture.* Chicago, IL: University of Chicago Press, 1999.

Tomy, Sheela. *Valli: A Novel.* Translated by Jayasree Kalathil. India: Harper Perennial, 2022.

Trexler, Adam. *Anthropocene Fictions: The Novel in a Time of Climate Change.* Charlottesville and London: University of Virginia Press, 2015.

Trexler, Adam and Adeline Johns-Putra. 'Climate Change in Literature and Literary Criticism'. *Wiley Interdisciplinary Reviews Climate Change* 2, no. 2 (24 February 2011): 185–200. https://doi.org/10.1002/wcc.105.

Tribune Web Desk. 'Book Reviews, *The Sickle*'. Review of *The Sickle*, by Anita Agnihotri, 28 February 2021. Accessed 25 May 2024. https://www.tribuneindia.com/news/reviews/story/the-sickle-218578.

Tripathi, Bhasker. 'In Rural India, Climate Migrants Have Hysterectomies to Survive'. *Context-Thomson Reuters Foundation Newsroom*, 7 March 2024. https://www.context.news/climate-risks/in-rural-india-climate-migrants-have-hysterectomies-to-survive.

UN Women. 'Explainer: How Gender Inequality and Climate Change are Interconnected'. 21 April 2025. https://www.unwomen.org/en/news-stories/explainer/2022/02/explainer-how-gender-inequality-and-climate-change-are-interconnected.

UNEP. *GEO-6 Regional Assessment for Asia and the Pacific*, 32, United Nations Environment Programme. Nairobi, Kenya, 2016.

United Nations. 'Paris Agreement'. 2015. https://unfccc.int/sites/default/files/english_paris_agreement.pdf.

United Nations. 'The 17 Goals'. https://sdgs.un.org/goals.

University of Hull. 'Andrew Marvell's to His Coy Mistress: Love in the Little Ice Age'. Rising Tide of Humber Team, 2023. https://risingtide.hull.ac.uk/wp-content/uploads/2023/06/Andrew-Marvell%E2%80%B2s-To-his-Coy-Mistress_-Love-in-the-Little-Ice-Age_Final-version.pdf.

Vervoort, Joost M., Manjana Milkoreit, Lisette van Beek, Astrid C. Mangnus, David Farrell, Steven R. McGreevy,Kazuhiko Ota, Christoph D.D. Rupprecht, Jason B. Reed, and Matthew Huber. 'Not Just Playing: The Politics of Designing Games for Impact on Anticipatory Climate Governance'. *Geoforum* 137 (2022): 213–21. https://doi.org/10.1016/j.geoforum.2022.03.009.

Wallace-Wells, David. 'The Uninhabitable Earth'. *New York Magazine*, 10 July 2017. Accessed 5 July 2025. https://nymag.com/intelligencer/2017/07/climate-change-earth-too-hot-for-humans.html.

Whitehead, Alfred North. *Process and Reality*. United Kingdom: Free Press, 2010.

Whyte, Kyle P. 'Indigenous Science (Fiction) for the Anthropocene: Ancestral Dystopias and Fantasies of Climate Change Crises'. *Environment and Planning E Nature and Space* 1, no. 1–2 (March 2018): 224–42. https://doi.org/10.1177/2514848618777621.

Wilber, Ken. *The Spectrum of Consciousness*. Wheaton, IL: Theosophical Publishing House, 1977.

Wilber, Ken. *Sex, Ecology, Spirituality: The Spirit of Evolution*. Boston, MA, & London: Shambhala Publications, 1995.

Wilde, Wulf. 'Fact Check: How Bad is Eating Meat for the Planet?' *Deutsche Welle*. 30 October 2022. Accessed 2 July 2025. https://www.dw.com/en/fact-check-is-eating-meat-bad-for-the-environment/a-63595148.

Willibald of Mainz. *The Life of Saint Boniface*. 760. Translated by George W. Robinson. Harvard University Press, 1916.

Wood, Gillen D'Arcy. 'The Volcano That Changed the Course of History'. Slate, 9 April 2014. https://slate.com/technology/2014/04/tambora-eruption-caused-the-year-without-a-summer-cholera-opium-famine-and-arctic-exploration.html.

World Meteorological Organization. 'Climate Change Indicators Reached Record Levels in 2023'. 18 March 2024. Accessed 28 June 2025. wmo.int/news/media-centre/climate-change-indicators-reached-record-levels-2023-wmo.

Wright, Alexis. *The Swan Book: A Novel*. United Kingdom: Atria Books, 2016.

# Index

Page numbers in *italics* refer to figures and page numbers followed by "n" refer to end notes

# About the Author

**Rajat Chaudhuri** is a fiction writer, climate communicator, interdisciplinary researcher and literary critic. He is the author of the Book Riot-listed and critically acclaimed climate novel The *Butterfly Effect* among several other full-length works. As a fiction editor he has been part of the international teams that introduced and published the groundbreaking solarpunk fiction anthologies *Multispecies Cities – Solarpunk Urban Futures and Solarpunk Creatures.* He was also one of four contributing writers for the popular climate change video game Survive the Century which recently appeared as a book. Besides translating fiction, poetry and memoirs from Bengali, he also published *Wonder Tales for a Warming Planet,* a book of climate stories for children.

Rajat is a British Council Charles Wallace Creative Writing Fellow, a Hawthornden Castle Fellow, and he has represented civil society groups from developing nations at the United Nations Commission on Sustainable Development. He speaks and writes about climate change and possible futures in a variety of local and global venues. Rajat is a co-author of a forthcoming book by the Club of Rome.